PENGUIN BOOKS

MAGIC AND MYSTERY IN TIBET

Alexandra David-Neel was born in Paris. Drawn to both travel and solitude, she spent her school holidays exploring the loneliest regions she could find. After studies at the Sorbonne under the Sanskrit and Tibetan scholar Foucaux, she went several times to Asia—one journey lasting no less than fourteen years. On her way from China to India, she crossed on foot vast tracts of Tibetan territory that no white traveler before her had ever seen. She felt immediately "at home" among the Tibetans, and went on to devote many years to the study of their customs and beliefs. She was awarded a gold medal by the Geographical Society of Paris and was a Knight of the French Legion of Honor. Her numerous books have been translated into English, German, Spanish, Czech, Swedish, and Annamite. Madame David-Neel died in 1969.

MAGIC AND MYSTERY
IN TIBET

ALEXANDRA DAVID-NEEL

PENGUIN BOOKS

Penguin Books Ltd, Harmondsworth,
Middlesex, England
Penguin Books, 625 Madison Avenue,
New York, New York 10022, U.S.A.
Penguin Books Australia Ltd, Ringwood,
Victoria, Australia
Penguin Books Canada Limited, 2801 John Street,
Markham, Ontario, Canada L3R 1B4
Pengiun Books (N.Z.) Ltd, 182–190 Wairau Road,
Auckland 10, New Zealand

Parmi les Mystiques et les Magiciens du Tibet first published
in France by Librairie Plon 1929
First published in Great Britain under the title
With Mystics and Magicians in Tibet by The Bodley Head 1931
Published in Penguin Books in Great Britain 1936
Published in the United States of America under the title
Magic and Mystery in Tibet by University Books, Inc., 1958
Published in Penguin Books in the United States of America 1971
Reprinted 1973, 1975, 1978

Printed in the United States of America by
Kingsport Press, Inc., Kingsport, Tennessee
Set in Monotype Baskerville

CONTENTS

AUTHOR'S PREFACE

IT WOULD BE a great mistake to believe that the spread of scientific knowledge in our time has withered, among our contemporaries, the attraction of the marvellous and of extraordinary facts. The belief in psychic phenomena, in miracles, and in magic is as alive in our days as it was in the Middle Ages. What we have gained is the freedom to speak of these things and to attempt the experience of them without having to fear the stakes of the Inquisition.

Because I have lived in Tibet, I am assailed with demands to cause or to produce extraordinary happenings for the benefit of those who come to me for reasons whose nature varies. It ranges from the simple desire to satisfy curiosity to the desire to pass an examination, to obtain success in a business transaction, to cure an illness, or to accomplish crimes. For example, an abandoned wife, impelled by the thirst for vengeance, asked me simply to "suppress" the unfaithful husband and his accomplice. Of course it was not a matter of my arming myself with a revolver and banally going to assassinate the guilty pair, but of causing them to perish from a distance by occult means which I would use without leaving my room.

All of these seekers after miracles would perhaps be most surprised to hear me say that the Tibetans do not believe in *miracles*, that is to say, in *supernatural* happenings. They consider the extraordinary facts which astonish us to be the work of *natural* energies which come into action in exceptional circumstances, or through the skill of someone who *knows* how to release them, or, sometimes, through the agency of an individual who unknowingly contains within himself the elements apt to move certain material or mental mechanisms which produce extraordinary phenomena.

The Tibetans also tend to believe that everything which one imagines can be realized. They claim that if the imagined facts corresponded to no external reality, one could not conceive of their images.

Again, with relation to this, the Tibetans believe that by a very strong and very continuous concentration of thought one can actually create the living and acting external reality of the form upon which the mental concentration is exercised. We will see examples of this.

In all cases, as I have said, it is always a matter of natural energies whose action is either spontaneous or controlled by individuals who have the capacity to do so.

It is possible for these individuals to obtain, in certain cases, the aid of beings whose nature is other than human; this belief, too, is very widespread in Tibet.

It is, moreover, current in our countries also. Prayers addressed to the saints, promises of offerings made to them in order to induce them to fulfill our desires or to use their influence upon superior Powers in order to obtain this fulfillment, as well as the tenebrous pacts mentioned in the stories of the Middle Ages, all proceed from an analogous belief.

I did not go to Tibet with the idea of seeing miracles there. I was doing research on the forms which Buddhism assumed in becoming Lamaism, that is to say in annexing and blending a number of doctrinal or ritualistic elements borrowed from Nepalese Tantrism, from Bön, the ancient religion which dominated Tibet before the introduction of Buddhism, and of other elements of an Altaic or even more northern origin, which came to Tibet by mysterious ways. I also wanted to visit this country of the high summits where the Indians have believed their Gods to dwell.

It happened that my "voyage" became a "sojourn," and that I lived for many years travelling all through the singular regions into which I had ventured. In the course of my travels I witnessed unusual events, met strange people and brushed the threshold of a particular spirituality.

Thus this book should serve only as a roadmap— a book of the ways which led me from the beaten paths.

ALEXANDRA DAVID-NEEL

At Digne, French Alps
April 1965

AUTHOR'S PREFACE TO THE FIRST EDITION

Immediately after the publication of my account of my journey to Lhasa, many persons expressed a wish, both in articles devoted to my book and in private conversation, to know how I came to live among the lamas, and also to learn more about the doctrines and practices of the mystics and magicians of Tibet.

In this book, I attempt to satisfy their friendly

curiosity. This task is however frought with certain difficulties, owing to the limited space at my disposal.

In order to answer these two questions in the order in which they have been put to me, I have started by describing the events which brought me into contact with the religious world of the lamas and of the various kinds of magicians who surround them.

Next I have tried to group together a certain number of salient points concerning the occult and mystical theories and the psychic training practices of the Tibetans. Whenever I have discovered in the rich store of my recollections a fact bearing on these subjects, I have related it as it came. Consequently this book is not a record of travel, for the subject does not lend itself to that treatment.

In the course of such investigations as I have pursued, the information obtained on one particular day is sometimes not completed till several months or several years later. It is only by presenting the final results of information gathered in various places that one can hope to give an adequate idea of the subject I am describing.

It is my intention, later on, to treat the question of Tibetan mysticism and philosophy in a more technical work.

As in my previous book *My Journey to Lhasa*, the Tibetan names are generally transcribed phonetically only. The few cases in which the Tibetan orthography has been indicated will show how the correct pronunciation deviates from the spelling.

ALEXANDRA DAVID-NEEL

Samten Dzong, Route de Nice,
Digne (B-Alpes), France, 1929

INTRODUCTION

For many Westerners Tibet is wrapped in an atmosphere of mystery. The "Land of Snows" is for them the country of the unknown, the fantastic and the impossible. What superhuman powers have not been ascribed to the various kinds of lamas, magicians, sorcerers, necromancers and practitioners of the occult who inhabit those high tablelands, and whom both nature and their own deliberate purpose have so splendidly isolated from the rest of the world? And how readily are the strangest legends about them accepted as indisputable truths! In that country plants, animals and human beings seem to divert to their own purposes the best established laws of physics, chemistry, physiology and even plain common sense.

It is therefore quite natural that scholars accustomed to the strict discipline of experimental method should have paid to these stories merely the condescending and amused attention that is usually given to fairy tales.

Such was my own state of mind up to the day when I had the good fortune to make the acquaintance of Madame Alexandra David-Neel.

This well-known and courageous explorer of Tibet unites in herself all the physical, moral and intellectual qualities that could be desired in one who is to observe and examine a subject of this kind. I must insist on saying this, however much her modesty may suffer.

Madame David-Neel understands, writes and speaks fluently all the dialects of Tibet. She has spent fourteen consecutive years in the country and the neighbouring regions. She is a professed Buddhist, and so has been able to gain the confidence of the most important Lamas. Her adopted son is an ordained lama; and she herself has undergone the psychic exercises of which she speaks. Madame David-Neel has in fact become, as she herself says, a complete Asiatic, and what is still more important for an explorer of a country hitherto inaccessible to foreign travellers, she is recognized as such by those among whom she has lived.

This Easterner, this complete Tibetan, has nevertheless remained a Westerner, a disciple of Descartes and of Claude Bernard, practising the philosophic scepticism of the former which, according to the latter, should be the constant ally of the scientific observer. Unencumbered by any preconceived theory, and unbiassed by any doctrine or dogma, Madame David-Neel has observed everything in Tibet in a free and impartial spirit.

In the lectures which, in my capacity as professor of the Collège de France, succeeding my master Claude Bernard, I asked her to deliver, Madame David-Neel sums up her conclusions in these words:

Everything that relates, whether closely or more distantly, to psychic phenomena and to the action of psychic forces in general, should be studied just like any other science There is nothing miraculous or supernatural in them, nothing that should engender or keep alive superstition. Psychic training, rationally and scientifically conducted, can lead to desirable results. That is why the information gained about such training—even though it is practised empirically and based on theories to which we cannot always give assent—constitutes useful documentary evidence worthy of our attention.

Here, it is clear, is a true scientific determinism, as far removed from scepticism as from blind credulity. The studies of Madame David-Neel will be of interest to Orientalists, psychologists and physiologists alike.

DOCTEUR A. D'ARSONVAL
Member of the Académie des Sciences
and of the Académie de Médecine.
Professor of the Collège de France.
President of the Institut General Psychologique.

CHAPTER I

TIBET AND THE LAMAS

"WELL, then, it is understood. I leave Dawasandup with you as interpreter. He will accompany you to Gangtok."

Is it a man who is speaking to me? This short yellow-skinned being clad in a robe of orange brocade, a diamond star sparkling on his hat, is he not, rather, a genie come down from the neighbouring mountains?

They say he is an "incarnated Lama" and heir prince of a Himalayan throne, but I doubt his reality. Probably he will vanish like a mirage, with his caparisoned little steed and his party of followers, dressed in all the colours of the rainbow. He is a part of the enchantment in which I have lived these last fifteen days. This new episode is of the stuff that dreams are made of. In a few minutes, I shall wake up in a real bed, in some country not haunted by genii nor by "incarnated Lamas" wrapped in shimmering silk. A country where men wear ugly dark coats and the horses do not carry silver inlaid saddles on golden-yellow cloths.

The sound of a kettledrum makes me start, two hautboys intone a melancholy minor tune. The youthful genie straddles his diminutive courser, knights and squires jump into their saddles.

"I shall expect you," the lama-prince says, smiling graciously at me.

I hear myself, as if I were listening to some other person, promising him that I will start the next day

1

for his capital, and the little troop, headed by the musicians, disappears.

As the last murmurs of the plaintive melody die away in the distance, the enchantment that has held me spellbound dissipates.

I have not been dreaming, all this is real. I am at Kalimpong, in the Himalayas, and the interpreter given me when I arrived stands at my side.

I have already related [1] the circumstances which had brought me to the Himalayas. Political reasons had, at that time, led the Dalai Lama to seek refuge in British territory. It had seemed to me a unique opportunity, while he was stopping at the Indian frontier, of obtaining an interview and getting information from him about the special type of Buddhism that prevails in Tibet.

Very few strangers have ever approached the monk-king hidden in his sacred city, in the Land of Snows. Even in exile, he saw no one. Up to the time of my visit, he had obstinately refused an audience to any woman except Tibetans and I believe, even to this day, that I am the only exception to this rule.

As I left Darjeeling, in the early rosy dawn of a cool spring morning, I little guessed the far-reaching consequences of my request.

I thought of a short excursion, of an interesting but brief interview ; while, actually, I became involved in wanderings that kept me in Asia for full fourteen years.

At the beginning of that long series of journeys, the Dalai Lama figures, in my diaries, as an obliging host who, seeing a stranger without the walls, invites him to see over his domain.

This, the Dalai Lama did in a few words : " Learn the Tibetan language," he told me.

---

[1] In a previous book, *My Journey to Lhasa.*

If one could believe his subjects who call him the " Omniscient," [1] the sovereign of Tibet, when giving me this advice, foresaw its consequences, and consciously directed me, not only towards Lhasa, his forbidden capital, but towards the mystic masters and unknown magicians, yet more closely hidden in his wonderland.

At Kalimpong, the lama-king lived in a large house belonging to the minister of the Rajah of Bhutan. To give the place a more majestic appearance, two rows of tall bamboo poles had been planted in the form of an avenue. Flags flew from every pole, with the inscription *Aum mani padme hum !*, or the " horse of the air," surrounded by magic formulas.

The suite of the exiled sovereign was numerous and included more than a hundred servants. They were for the most part engaged in interminable gossip, and quiet reigned round the habitation. But on fête days, or when visitors of rank were to be received, a crowd of busy officials and domestics poured out from all sides, peering at one from every window, crossing and recrossing the large plot of ground in front of the house, hurrying, screaming, agitated, and all so remarkably alike in their dirty, greasy robes, that a stranger could easily make awkward mistakes about their rank.

The splendour, decorum and etiquette of the Potala were absent in that land of exile. Those who saw this road-side camp, where the Head of the Tibetan theocracy waited for his subjects to reconquer his throne, could not imagine what the Court at Lhasa was like.

The British expedition penetrating into the forbidden territory and parading his capital, in spite of the sorcery of the most famous magicians, had probably led the Dalai Lama to understand that foreign barbarians were masters in a material sense, by right of force. The inventions that he noticed during his trip through

[1] *Thamstched mkyenpa.*

India must also have convinced him of their ability to enslave and mould the material elements of nature. But his conviction that the white race is mentally inferior remained unshaken. And, in this, he only shared the opinion of all Asiatics—from Ceylon to the northern confines of Mongolia.

A Western woman acquainted with Buddhist doctrines seemed to him an inconceivable phenomenon.

If I had vanished into space while talking to him, he would have been less astonished. My reality surprised him most ; but, when finally convinced, he politely inquired after my " Master," assuming that I could only have learned of Buddha from an Asiatic. It was not easy to convince him that the Tibetan text of one of the most esteemed Buddhist books [1] had been translated into French before I was born. " Ah well," he murmured at last, " if a few strangers have really learned our language and read our sacred books, they must have missed the meaning of them."

This was my chance. I hastened to seize it.

" It is precisely because I suspect that certain religious doctrines of Tibet have been misunderstood that I have come to you to be enlightened," I said.

My reply pleased the Dalai Lama. He readily answered any questions I put to him, and a little later gave me a long written explanation of the various subjects we had discussed.

The prince of Sikkim and his escort having disappeared, it only remained for me to keep my promise and make ready to start for Gangtok. But there was something to be seen before moving on.

The evening before, I had witnessed the benediction of the pilgrims by the Dalai Lama, a widely different scene from the Pontifical benediction at Rome. For the Pope in a single gesture blesses the multitude, while

[1] The *Gyacher rolpa*, translated by Ed. Foucaux, Professor at the Collège de France.

the Tibetans are far more exacting and each expect an individual blessing.

Among Lamaists again the manner of the blessing varies with the social rank of the blessed. The Lama places both hands on the heads of those he most respects. In other cases only one hand, two fingers or even only one finger. Lastly comes the blessing given by slightly touching the head with coloured ribbons, attached to a short stick.

In every case, however, there is contact, direct or indirect, between the lama and the devotee. This contact, according to Lamaists, is indispensable because the benediction, whether of people or of things, is not meant to call down upon them the benediction of God, but to infuse into them some beneficial power that emanates from the lama.

The large number of people who came to Kalimpong to be touched by the Dalai Lama gave me some idea of his widespread prestige.

The procession took several hours to pass before him, and I noticed that not only Lamaists but many people from Nepal and from Bengal, belonging to Hindu sects, had joined the crowd.

I saw some, who had come only to look on, suddenly seized by an occult fervour, hurrying to join the pious flock.

As I was watching this scene, my eyes fell on a man seated on the ground, a little to one side. His matted hair was wound around his head like a turban, in the style common to Hindu ascetics. Yet, his features were not those of an Indian and he was wearing dirty and much-torn lamaist monastic garments.

This tramp had placed a small bag beside him and seemed to observe the crowd with a cynical expression.

I pointed him out to Dawasandup, asking him if he had any idea who this Himalayan Diogenes might be.

" It must be a travelling *naljorpa*," [1] he answered ;
and, seeing my curiosity, my obliging interpreter went
to the man and entered into conversation with him.

He returned to me with a serious face and said :

" This lama is a peripatetic ascetic from Bhutan. He
lives here and there in caves, empty houses or under
the trees. He has been stopping for several days in a
small monastery near here."

My thoughts returned to the vagabond when the
prince and his escort had disappeared. I had no
definite plan for the afternoon, why should I not go
to the *gompa* (monastery) where he was staying, and
persuade him to talk ? Was he really mocking, as he
seemed to be, at the Dalai Lama and the faithful ?
And if so, why ? There might be interesting reasons.

I communicated my desire to Dawasandup, who
agreed to accompany me.

We went on horseback and soon reached the *gompa*,
which was only a large-sized country-house.

In the *lha khang* (the room containing the holy
images) we found the *naljorpa* seated upon a cushion in
front of a low table, finishing his meal. Cushions were
brought and we were offered tea.

It was difficult to begin a conversation with the
ascetic, as his mouth appeared to be full of rice ; he
had only answered our polite greetings by a kind of
grunt.

I was trying to find a phrase to break the ice, when
the strange fellow began to laugh and muttered a few
words. Dawasandup seemed embarrassed.

" What does he say ? " I asked.

" Excuse me," answered the interpreter, " these
naljorpas sometimes speak roughly. I do not know if
I should translate."

---

[1] *Naljorpa* (written *rnal hbyorpa*), literally : " He who has attained
perfect serenity," but usually interpreted : an ascetic possessing
magic powers.

" Please do," I replied. " I am here to take notes ; especially of anything at all curious and original."

" Well, then—excuse me—he said, ' What is this idiot here for ? ' "

Such rudeness did not greatly astonish me as, in India also, certain *yogins* make a habit of insulting anyone who approaches them.

" Tell him I have come to ask why he mocked at the crowd seeking the benediction of the Dalai Lama."

" Puffed up with a sense of their own importance and the importance of what they are doing. Insects fluttering in the dung," muttered the *naljorpa* between his teeth.

This was vague, but the kind of language one expects from such men.

" And you," I replied, " are you free from all defilement ? "

He laughed noisily.

" He who tries to get out only sinks in deeper. I roll in it like a pig. I digest it and turn it into golden dust, into a brook of pure water. To fashion stars out of dog dung, that is the Great Work ! "

Evidently my friend was enjoying himself. This was his way of posing as a superman.

" Are these pilgrims not right, to profit by the presence of the Dalai Lama and obtain his blessing ? They are simple folk incapable of aspiring to the knowledge of the higher doctrines——"

But the *naljorpa* interrupted me.

" For a blessing to be efficacious, he who gives it must possess the power that he professes to communicate.

" Would the Precious Protector (the Dalai Lama) need soldiers to fight the Chinese or other enemies if he possessed such a power ? Could he not drive anyone he liked out of the country and surround Tibet with an invisible barrier that none could pass ?

" The Guru who is born in a lotus [1] had such a power, and his blessing still reaches those who worship him, even though he lives in the distant land of the Rakshasas.

" I am only a humble disciple, and yet——"

It appeared to me that the " humble disciple " was maybe a little mad and certainly very conceited, for his " and yet " had been accompanied by a glance that suggested many things.

My interpreter meanwhile was visibly uneasy. He profoundly respected the Dalai Lama and disliked to hear him criticized. On the other hand, the man who could " create stars out of dog dung " inspired him with a superstitious fear.

I proposed to leave, but as I understood that the lama was going away the next morning, I handed Dawasandup a few rupees for the traveller to help him on his way.

This present displeased the *naljorpa*. He refused it, saying he had already received more provisions than he could carry.

Dawasandup thought it right to insist. He took a few steps forward, intending to place the money on a table near the lama. Then I saw him stagger, fall backward and strike his back against the wall as if he had been violently pushed. He uttered a cry and clutched at his stomach. The *naljorpa* got up and, sneering, left the room.

" I feel as if I had received a terrible blow," said Dawasandup. " The lama is irritated. How shall we appease him ? "

" Let us go," I answered. " The lama has probably nothing to do with it. You, perhaps, have heart trouble and had better consult a doctor."

Pale and troubled, the interpreter answered nothing. Indeed there was nothing to be said. We returned, but I was not able to reassure him.

[1] Padmasambhâva, who preached in Tibet in the eighth century.

The next day Dawasandup and I left for Gangtok

The mule path that we followed dives right into the Himalayas, the sacred land which ancient Indian traditions people with famous sages, stern magicians, ascetics and deities.

The summer resorts established by foreigners on the border of these impressive highlands have not yet modified their aspect. A few miles away from the hotels where the Western world enjoys dancing and jazz bands, the primeval forest reigns.

Shrouded in the moving fogs, a fantastic army of trees, draped in livid green moss, seems to keep watch along the narrow tracks, warning or threatening the traveller with enigmatic gestures. From the low valleys buried under the exuberant jungle to the mountain summits covered with eternal snow, the whole country is bathed in occult influences.

In such scenery it is fitting that sorcery should hold sway. The so-called Buddhist population is practically Shamanist and a large number of *mediums* : Bonpos, Pawos, Bunting and Yabas of both sexes, even in the smallest hamlets, transmit the messages of gods, demons and the dead.

I slept on the way at Pakyong, and the next day I reached Gangtok.

As I neared this village-capital, I was greeted by a sudden and formidable hail-storm.

Tibetans think that meteorological phenomena are the work of demons or magicians. A hail-storm is one of their favourite weapons. The former use it to hinder pilgrims on their journey to holy places and the latter, by this means, defend their hermitages against intruders and keep off faint-hearted candidates for discipleship.

A few weeks after my arrival, the superstitious Dawasandup confessed that he had consulted a *mopa* (diviner) about the unexpected attack of hail upon the otherwise gloriously sunny day of my arrival.

The oracle declared that the local gods and the holy lamas were not hostile to me, but that, nevertheless, I should meet with many difficulties if I attempted to live in the " Land of the Religion," as Tibetans call their country.

A prediction very generously fulfilled !

His Highness Sidkeong Namgyal, hereditaɪy prɪnce of Sikkim, was a veritable lama : abbot of a monastery of the Karma-Khagyud sect and a *tulku* [1] believed to be the reincarnation of his uncle, a lama of saintly memory.

As usual, he had donned the monastic garb while still a child, and spent a part of his youth in the monastery of which he was now the head.

The British Government having chosen him, in preference to his elder brother, as successor to the mahârajah his father, he was put in charge of an anglicized Indian as guardian and teacher.

A short stay at Oxford and a trip round the world completed his heterogeneous education.

Sidkeong tulku [2] knew English better than his muther tongue : Tibetan. He spoke Hindustani fluently and, also, a little Chinese. The private villa he had built in his father's gardens resembled an English country house imposed on a Tibetan temple. The same contrasts were repeated within. The ground floor was furnished according to English taste, while upstairs there was an oratory with Lamaist images and a Tibetan sitting-room.

The young prince was very open-minded. He immediately became interested in my researches and facilitated my task with great zeal.

The first part of my stay in Sikkim was devoted to visiting the monasteries scattered through the forests.

---

[1] *Tulku*, a lama of high rank whom foreigners call a " living Buddha." See Chapter III, " The Living Buddhas."

[2] In Tibetan language, titles or other honours follow the name.

Picturesquely situated, usually on the spur of a mountain, their aspect impressed me deeply. I liked to imagine these rustic dwellings inhabited by thinkers liberated from worldly ambitions and struggles, who passed their days in peace and deep meditations.

I did not, however, find the monasteries quite what I expected. The monks of Sikkim are for the most part illiterate and have no desire to be enlightened, even about the Buddhism which they profess. Nor, indeed, have they the necessary leisure. The *gompas* of Sikkim are poor, they have but a very small income and no rich benefactors. Their *trapas* are compelled to work for their living.

Foreign authors call all members of the Lamaist clergy indiscriminately lamas, but this is not the custom in Tibet. The only monks who have a right to the title of lama[1] are the ecclesiastical dignitaries such as the *tulkus*, the abbots of large monasteries, the heads of the great monastic colleges and monks who hold high university degrees. All other monks, even those who have been ordained as *gelong*, are called *trapas* (students). Nevertheless, it is usual to give the courtesy title of lama to aged and learned monks when addressing them.

In Sikkim, a number of *trapas* whom their colleagues held to be learned men were capable of celebrating a few religious rites. They taught the novices to recite the liturgy and received as fees gifts in kind, more rarely a little money and, often, merely the domestic service of their pupils. However, the exercise of their priestly functions was the main source of their income.

Orthodox Buddhism strictly forbids religious rites, and the learned lamas acknowledge that they cannot bestow spiritual enlightenment, which can only be acquired by personal intellectual effort. Yet the majority believe in the efficacy of certain ritualistic

[1] Written *blama*, which means " superior "—" excellent."

methods of the healing of the sick, securing material prosperity, the conquest of evil beings and the guidance of the spirits of the dead in the other world.

The funeral ceremonies were the principal duty of the Himalayan monks. They celebrated these rites with zeal, even with pleasure ; for they include one or two banquets offered by the family of the dead to the monks of the monastery to which he had been attached. The officiating *trapas* also receive presents of money and in kind at the house of the dead man.

Now, the peasant clergy of these forests are generally poor and ill-fed, and it is difficult for them to suppress a thrill of delight when the death of a rich villager promises them several days' feast.

Grown-up men usually dissimulate their feelings, but the child-novices who guard the cattle in the woods are amusingly frank.

One day, while I was sitting not far from some of these youthful herdsmen, a far-off sound of wind instruments reached us.

In an instant the boys who had been playing stopped, listening attentively. Again, we heard the same sound. The children had understood.

" The conches ! " said one of them.

" Some one is dead ! " another answered.

Then they kept silent, looking at each other, their eyes sparkling with pleasure.

" We shall have meat to eat," one of the boys whispered.

In many villages, the lamaist priest comes into competition with the sorcerer, though as a rule this leads to no animosity. Generally, each has more or less faith in the worth of his rival's methods. Although the lama is held in higher esteem than the *Bön* sorcerer, a follower of the ancient religion of the aborigines, or than the *ngagspa*—magician, assimilated to the official clergy—these latter are nevertheless, believed to be more skilful in dealing with the demons who harm living beings or the spirits of the dead.

An unforeseen incident led me to discover how the spirit of a dead man is drawn out of his body by the officiating lama and directed on the right road in the next world.

I was returning, that day, from an excursion in the forest when I heard a sharp brief cry, unlike that of any animal known to me. A few minutes later, the same cry was twice repeated. I advanced slowly and noiselessly in the direction of the sound and discovered a cabin which had been hidden by a slight rise in the ground.

Lying flat between the bushes, I could observe what was going on without being seen.

Two monks were seated under the trees, their gaze lowered in an attitude of meditation.

Hik! cried one upon a peculiar abnormal shrill note. *Hik!* repeated the other after a few minutes. And so they continued, with long intervals of silence, during which they remained motionless between the shrieks.

I noticed that a great effort seemed required to produce this sound, which apparently came up from their very entrails. After having watched them for some time, I saw one of the *trapas* put his hands upon his throat. His face expressed suffering, he turned his head to one side and spat out a stream of blood.

His companion said a few words that I could not hear. Without answering the monk rose and went towards the cabin.

I then noticed a long straw standing straight up on the top of his head. What did this ornament signify?

While the *trapa* entered the hut and his friend had his back to me, I escaped.

As soon as I saw Dawasandup, I questioned him. What were these men doing; why did they utter this strange cry?

That, he said, is the ritualistic cry that the officiating lama shouts beside a man who has just died, in order to free the " spirit " and cause it to leave the body through a hole that this magic syllable opens in the summit of the skull.

Only a lama who has received, from a competent master, the power of uttering that *hik !* with the right intonation and required force, is capable of success. After *hik !* he shouts *phat!* But he must be careful not to articulate *phat* when he is only practising, like the monks you overheard. The combination of these two sounds invariably leads to the separation of body and spirit, so that the lama who pronounced them correctly over himself would immediately die.

This danger does not exist when he is officiating, because he acts by proxy, in place of the dead—lending him his voice, so that the effect of the magic words is felt by the dead man, not by the lama.

Once the psychic power of drawing the spirit out of its corporeal envelope has been conferred, by a competent master, upon a disciple, the latter must practise the uttering of *hik !* in the right tone. It is known that this has been attained when a straw stuck in the skull stands up straight as long as desired. For by shouting *hik !* a slight opening in the skull is produced and the straw is placed in it. In the case of a dead man, the opening is much larger. It is sometimes large enough to introduce the little finger.

Dawasandup was much interested in all questions concerning death and the spirit-world. Five or six years after I knew him, he translated a classic Tibetan work on the peregrinations of the dead in the next world.[1]

Several foreigners, Orientalist scholars or British officials have employed Dawasandup and acknowledged his ability. However, I have good reasons to think

[1] The " Bardo Tôd Tol "

that none of them knew the real peculiarities of his character as I did.

Dawasandup was an occulist and even, in a certain way, a mystic. He sought for secret intercourse with the Dâkinîs [1] and the dreadful gods hoping to gain supernormal powers. Everything that concerned the mysterious world of beings generally invisible strongly attracted him, but the necessity of earning his living made it impossible for him to devote much time to his favourite study.

Born at Kalimpong, his ancestors were hillmen : Bhutanis or Sikkimeeses from the Tibetan stock of the invaders. He got a scholarship and was educated at the High School of Darjeeling, established for young men of Tibetan origin.

He entered the British Government service in India and became interpreter at Baxe Duar, on the southern frontier of Bhutan. There he met the lama whom he chose for spiritual guide.

I got some idea of this teacher from the accounts of Dawasandup, who venerated him deeply. He must have resembled many lamas whom I have met later on, harbouring in his mind a mixture of learning and superstitions, but, above all, a good and charitable man.

He was distinguished from his colleagues, however, by having had as master a veritable saint whose death is worth relating.

This holy lama was an anchorite who practised mystic contemplation in a secluded spot in Bhutan. As it is often the case, one of his disciples shared his hermitage and served him.

One day a pious benefactor came to see the ascetic and left him a sum of money to purchase winter pro-

---

[1] Feminine deities. Dâkinî is their Sanskrit name used also in Tibetan mystic literature. Their Tibetan name is *mkah hgroma*, pronounced *Kandoma*. They are often styled " mothers " and are said to impart esoteric profound doctrines to their devotees.

visions. His disciple, urged on by covetousness, stabbed him and ran off with the silver. The aged lama was still alive, and came to his senses soon after the murderer had gone. His wounds caused him excruciating suffering, and to escape this torture he sank into meditation.

Concentration of thought is carried so far by Tibetan mystics that it becomes anæsthetic and they do not feel anything ; or at a lower degree of power they can thus greatly lessen their pains.

When another disciple of the lama went to visit him a few days later he found him rolled up in a blanket and motionless. The smell from the festering wounds and the blood-stained blanket caught his attention. He questioned his master. The hermit then told him what had happened, but when the man wished to get a doctor from the nearest monastery he was forbidden to do so.

" If the lamas and villagers happen to hear about my condition they will search for the culprit," said the ascetic. " He cannot have got far. They would find him and, probably, condemn him to death. I cannot permit this. I wish to give him more time to escape. One day he will, perhaps, return to the right path and, in any case, I shall not have been the cause of his death. So do not tell anyone what you have seen here. Now go, leave me alone. While I meditate, I do not suffer, but when I become conscious of my body my pain is unbearable."

An Oriental disciple does not discuss an order of this kind. The man prostrated himself at his guru's [1] feet and left. A few days later the hermit, all alone in his hut, passed away.

Although Dawasandup greatly admired the conduct of the holy lama, such moral summits were not for him. He humbly confessed it.

[1] *Guru*, in Sanskrit, the spiritual father and guide. This word is used by Tibetan mystics, especially in book language.

Drink, a failing frequent among his countrymen, had been the curse of his life. This increased his natural tendency to anger and led him, one day, within an ace of murder. I had some influence over him while I lived at Gangtok. I persuaded him to promise the total abstinence from fermented beverages that is enjoined on all Buddhists. But it needed more energy than he possessed to persevere. It was impossible for him to resist his surroundings ; where men say that to drink, and leave one's reason at the bottom of the cup, is the proper thing for a faithful disciple of Padma-sambhava.[1]

When I met Dawasandup he had left the Government service to become head master of the Tibetan school at Gangtok. He was too extraordinary for words in this rôle.

His passion for reading literally tyrannized the man. Wherever he went he carried a book with him and, absorbed in it, he lost himself in a kind of ecstasy. For hours he would forget where he was. His learned translations, his long conversations with lamas and the celebrating of occult rites constantly distracted him from attending to his school. Indeed, he often seemed to have forgotten its very existence.

Sometimes for a whole month he did not set foot in the schoolroom, abandoning his scholars to the care of an under master, who followed his example in neglecting them, as far as he dared without risking his job.

Left to themselves, the boys played and wandered in the woods, forgetting the little they had learned.

However, the day would come when Dawasandup, severe as a Judge of the Dead, suddenly appeared before

[1] Padmasambhava belonged to the degenerate sect of tantric Buddhism. Yet, nothing proves he was naturally intemperate, as some of his followers wish to make us believe, to justify their drunkenness.

his pupils, who trembled in every limb, knowing full well what they had to expect.

First, they had to stand in line in front of their examiner, who then questioned a boy at one or the other end of the line.

If the child gave an incorrect answer, or none at all, his comrade next in line might answer, and if his solution was right, he was ordered to slap the ignorant in the face and take his place.

The victim was again questioned. If he did not show more learning than the first time, the third in line was called up, and if successful, would be told to slap his comrade and take his place.

An unlucky urchin, stupefied by these repeated brutalities, reached the end of the row, having received a dozen blows.

Not infrequently it happened that several boys, standing side by side, were incapable of reciting their lessons. In that case, the most " erudite " of the group distributed all the slaps, and if all the children showed themselves equally ignorant, Dawasandup himself chastised them all.

Certain pupils hesitated to give a friend a hard blow and only made a pretence of striking him, but Dawa-sandup was on the look out.

" Come up here ! " he would say, with a little ferocious laugh. " You do not know how it is done, my boy. I'll teach you." And bang ! his large hand would strike the poor lad full in the face. Then the boy had to demonstrate, on his friend's cheek, that he had learned the lesson given by his terrible teacher.

Sometimes the faults to be punished were not connected with the pupil's work. In that strange school, devoid of all discipline, the inventive mind of Daw-asandup discovered transgressions to rules which had never been made. In these cases, he used a specially long and heavy stick, ordering the culprit to stretch out his arm and keep his hand open. Then the boy received on his palm the number of strokes fixed by his master.

As he manœuvred his weapon, Dawasandup executed a kind of savage war dance, marking each stroke with a leap and a wild exclamation of " han ! " So, with the active though unwilling co-operation of the victim, whose pain caused him to stamp, writhe and yell, the punishment looked like a devilish ballet.

Arriving unexpectedly at the school one day, I witnessed one of these scenes, and the children, who became familiar with me, frankly described their teacher's educational methods.

After a few days of this active professorship, Dawasandup would again abandon his pupils.

I could tell many other stories about my good interpreter, some quite amusing, in the style of Boccaccio He played other parts than those of occultist, schoolmaster and writer. But, peace to his memory. I do not wish to belittle him. Having acquired real erudition by persevering efforts, he was sympathetic and interesting. I congratulate myself on having met him and gratefully acknowledge my debt to him.

I may add that Dawasandup is the author of the first, and up to now, only English-Tibetan dictionary, and that he ended his days as professor of Tibetan at the university of Calcutta.

My joy was intense when the prince *Tulku* announced that a real Tibetan doctor of philosophy from the famous university of Trashilhumpo [1] was coming to live at the Enche monastery, near Gangtok, and that he also expected another lama—a native from Sikkim, who had studied in Tibet—to return shortly to his country.

I soon was able to meet these two men and found them learned and distinguished scholars.

[1] Near Shigatze, the capital of the Tsang province.

The doctor of philosophy's name was Kushog [1] Chösdzed, and he belonged to the family of the ancient kings of Tibet. He had been some years in prison for some political offence, and attributed his delicate state of health to poisoned food absorbed during his incarceration.

The prince of Sikkim held men of learning in high esteem. He was glad to receive the refugee and appointed him abbot of the Enche *gompa*, with the further duty of teaching grammar and sacred literature to about twenty novices.

Kushog Chösdzed was a Gelugspa, that is to say a follower of the reformed sect founded by Tsong Khapa, about A.D. 1400, familiarly known as the sect of the " Yellow hats."

Foreign writers who describe the doctrines and religious practices of the " Yellow hats " as completely opposed to those of the " Red hats " would have recognized their error on finding, at Enche Monastery, a Gelugspa abbot presiding over monks of the Red sect and chanting the liturgy with them.

I do not know whether this lama gave himself assiduously to meditation and should be classed as a mystic, but he certainly possessed extraordinary erudition. His memory resembled a miraculous library, where each book was ready at the asking, to open at the desired page. Without the slightest effort he could quote texts by the dozen, on any matter connected with Lamaism, Buddhist philosophy and Tibetan history or secular literature.

This is, however, not an unusual feat in Tibet, but his perfect understanding and subtle comprehension of shades of meaning was quite uncommon.

Whether from fear of being thought obtrusive or from pride of birth (his rank being higher than that of his protector), the lama seldom visited the prince at his

[1] *Kushog*, Tibetan equivalent of Sir.

villa, and only to consult with him about affairs concerning the monastery.

Sometimes he came to see me, but I generally went up to his *gompa*, which stood on a spur of the mountain that dominated Gangtok.

After several-conversations, the lama, suspicious as are most Orientals, devised an amusing stratagem to test my knowledge of Buddhism and the extent of my understanding of its doctrines. One day when I was seated in his room, he took out of a drawer a long list of questions and with exquisite politeness asked me to answer them at once. The subjects treated were abstruse and had certainly been chosen with the intention of embarrassing me.

I passed the trial honourably, my examiner seemed content. He then confessed that up to this moment he had not believed me to be a Buddhist and that, not being able to discover my reasons for questioning the lamas about their religion, he had feared that my designs were evil.

After this he seemed quite reassured and manifested great confidence in me.

The second lama who arrived shortly after this at Gangtok came from the monastery of Tolung Tserphug, situated in the region of Lhasa. He had studied there in his youth, and returned later as secretary to the Head of the sect of the Karmapas, one of the most important " Red hat " sects.

He was called Bermiag Kushog (the Honourable of Bermiag) because he was the son of the Lord of that place, one of the rare members of the Sikkimeese nobility who belonged to the aboriginal race called the Lepchas.

Like Kushog Chösdzed, he had received the higher ordination of *gelong* and was a celibate. He was chaplain to the mahârajah and, as such, occupied an apartment in the palace.

Nearly every afternoon he crossed the gardens and went to the villa where the crown-prince lived. There, in the sitting-room furnished according to English taste, we had long conversations on topics quite foreign to Westerners.

I like to recall these talks which gradually enabled me to lift the veil that hides the real Tibet and its religious world.

Sidkeong Tulku, always wearing his brocade robes, presided, seated on a couch. A table was placed in front of him, and I sat opposite, in an arm-chair. We were each provided with a little bowl of fine Chinese porcelain, with a silver saucer and a cover shaped like a pagoda roof, studded with coral and turquoises.

At a short distance from the prince, the Honourable of Bermiag, majestically draped in his garnet-coloured toga, had an arm-chair and a bowl with a silver saucer, but without a cover. As for Dawasandup, who was often present, he squatted tailor fashion (in the East they say " like a lotus ") at our feet and his bowl, placed upon the rug, had neither cover nor saucer.

The complicated and very strict Tibetan etiquette was thus obeyed.

While that learned and fluent orator, Bermiag Kushog, talked, we were lavishly supplied with Tibetan tea, the colour of faded roses and flavoured with butter and salt. Rich Tibetans always have a bowl of this tea near at hand. A popular expression to describe wealthy people is : " Their lips are always moistened with tea or beer." However, tea only appeared in these reunions, out of respect for my orthodox Buddhist principles.

A young attendant brought in a large silver teapot. He carried it around shoulder high and lowered it to the level of our cups with studied gestures, as if he was performing some religious rite. A few sticks of incense burning in a corner of the room, spread a penetrating fragrance unlike any I had ever smelt in India or in China. Sometimes, a slow solemn melody, at once melancholy and subdued, reached us from the distant palace temple. And Bermiag lama continued talking, describing the lives and thoughts of some sages or magicians who had lived or were living to-day, in the forbidden land, whose frontier was so near. . . .

To Kushog Chösdzed and to Bermiag Kushog I owe my first initiation into the creeds held by the Lamaists regarding death and the beyond : creeds unknown to most foreigners.

As one of these lamas was " Red hat," and the other belonged to the " Yellow hat " sect, by listening to both, I was sure of acquiring information that represented the general opinion and not that of any one particular sect or creed.

Moreover, in the years that followed, I had numerous occasions, in different parts of Tibet, of questioning other lamas on this subject. For the convenience of the reader, I will put together some of this information in the following summary.

Death and the Beyond. The profane generally imagine that Buddhists believe in the reincarnation of the soul and even in metempsychosis. This is erroneous. Buddhism teaches that the energy produced by the mental and physical activities of a being brings about the apparition of new mental and physical phenomena, when once this being has been dissolved by death.

There exist a number of subtle theories upon this subject and the Tibetan mystics seem to have attained a deeper insight into the question than most other Buddhists.

However, in Tibet, as elsewhere, the views of the philosophers are only understood by the élite. The masses, although they repeat the orthodox creed : " *all aggregates are impermanent* ; no ' *ego* ' *exists in the person, nor in anything,*" remain attached to the more simple belief in an undefined entity travelling from world to world, assuming various forms.

The ideas of the Lamaists regarding the condition of man immediately after death differ from those held by the Buddhists of the southern countries : Ceylon, Burma, Siam. They affirm that a certain time elapses between his death and his rebirth among one or other of the six kinds of recognized sentient beings.[1]

According to popular belief, the class of beings in which one is reborn and the more or less happy conditions in which one is placed among them, depend upon the good and evil actions one has accomplished during one's previous existence.

The more enlightened lamas teach that man—or any other being—by his thoughts and actions, creates affinities which, quite naturally, lead him to a kind of existence in keeping with the nature of these affinities.

Others say that, by his actions, and above all, by his mental activity, he modifies his very substance and so acquires the characteristics of a god, an animal, or of any kind of being.

So far, these views differ very little from those expressed among Buddhists. The following lamaist theories are more original.

In the first place, the great importance given to cleverness by certain Mahâyâna Buddhist sects is still more emphasized by Lamaists.

" He who knows how to go about it could live comfortably even in hell," is a very popular saying in Tibet. This explains more clearly than any definition or description all that the lamas mean by *thabs*, i.e. " method."

Thus, while most of their co-religionists believe that the fate of the dead is mathematically fixed in accordance with their moral character, the Lamaists declare that he who knows the proper " method " is capable

[1] See page 260.

of modifying for the better his *post-mortem* fate. In other words, he may cause himself to be reborn in the most agreeable conditions possible.

They say : " as agreeable *as possible*," because in spite of cleverness, the weight of past actions has considerable force. In fact, it is often so powerful that all the efforts of a dead being, or of an initiate devoted to his welfare, are unable to stop the " spirit " from precipitating itself into a miserable rebirth. We shall have an illustration of this difficulty a little later.

Starting with the idea that " method," the " savoir-faire," is of an essential importance, the Lamaists think that after having learned the art of living well, one must learn the art of dying well and of " doing well " in other worlds.

Initiates acquainted with mystic lore, are supposed to know what awaits them when they die, and contemplative lamas have foreseen and experienced, in this life, the sensations that accompany death. They will, therefore, neither be surprised nor troubled when their present personality disintegrates. *That* which is to continue, entering conscious into the next world, will be already familiar with the roads and bypaths, and the places to which they lead.

What is this " *that* " which continues its way after the body has become a corpse ? It is a special " consciousness " among the several distinguished by Lamaists. The " consciousness " of the " I," or according to another definition " the will to live."

I shall use the term " spirit " for the traveller whose peregrinations in the next world we are to follow. This term is far from conveying exactly the idea which learned Tibetans embody in the words *Yid kyi rnampar shespa*. But it has the advantage of being familiar to Westerners and, indeed, there is none more suitable in any European language.

I said that—according to Tibetans—a mystic initiate

is capable of keeping his mind lucid during the disintegration of his personality, and that it is possible to him to pass from this world to the next fully conscious of what is happening. It follows that such a man does not need the help of anyone in his last hours, nor any religious rites after his death.

But this is not the case for ordinary mortals.

By ordinary mortals, we must understand anyone, monk or layman, who has not mastered the " science of death," and these are, naturally, the great majority.

Lamaism does not abandon these ignorants to themselves. While they are dying, and after they are dead, a lama teaches them that which they have not learned while they were alive. He explains to them the nature of the beings and things which appear on their way ; he reassures them, and, above all, he never ceases guiding them in the right direction.

The lama who is assisting a dying man is careful to prevent him from falling asleep, or from fainting or falling into a coma. He points out the successive departure of the special " consciousness " attached to each sense, viz. consciousness of the eye, consciousness of the nose, of the tongue, of the body, of the ear. That is to say he calls attention to the gradual loss of sight, smell, taste, touch and hearing.

Then, the task of the lama is to make the " spirit " spring out of its envelope through the top of the head ; for if it leaves by any other road, the future well-being of the man will be greatly jeopardized.

This extraction of the " spirit " is produced by the ritualistic cry of *Hik !* followed by *Phat !* Before uttering the cry, the lama must concentrate his thoughts and identify himself with the man who has just died. He must make the effort which the man himself ought to have made, to cause the " spirit " to ascend to the summit of the skull with sufficient force to produce the fissure through which it can escape.

Initiates who are capable of making the "spirit" rise for themselves, utter the liberating cries of *Hik !* and *Phat !* when they feel their end approaching, and so free themselves without help.

They are also able to commit suicide in this way and it is said that certain mystics have done so.

The disembodied "spirit" then begins a strange pilgrimage. The popular belief is that a journey really takes place through lands that really exist and are peopled with real beings. But the more learned Lamaists consider the journey as a series of subjective visions, a dream that the "spirit" himself weaves under the influence of his character and his past actions.

Certain Lamaists assert that, immediately after the "spirit" has been disincarnated, it has an intuition, fugitive as a streak of lightning, of the Supreme Reality. If it can seize this light, it is definitely set free from the "round" of successive births and deaths. It has reached the state of *nirvâna.*

This is rarely the case. Generally the "spirit" is dazzled by this sudden light. He shrinks from it, pulled backward by his false conceptions, his attachment to individual existence and to the pleasure of the senses. Or, else, the significance of what he has seen escapes him, just as a man, absorbed by his preoccupations, will fail to notice what is going on around him.

The ordinary man who has died while in a faint, does not immediately understand what has happened when he becomes conscious again. For several days he will " talk " to people living in his former dwelling-place and he will be astonished that no one answers him or seems to be aware of his presence.

A lama of the monastery of Litang, in Eastern Tibet, told me that some dead men had communicated through the intermediary of *pawos* (mediums) the fact that they had tried to use objects belonging to them. They wanted to take a plough to work their fields or to reach their clothes which were hanging on a hook and put them on. They were irritated at not being able to carry on the life to which they were accustomed.

In such cases, the " spirit " of the dead is disoriented. What can have happened to him ? He notices an inert body similar to his own and sees the lamas chanting around him. Is it possible that he is dead ?

Simple people believe that the disincarnated " spirit " must go to a sandy spot and observe his footprints on the ground. If these footprints are reversed, that is to say if the heels are in front and the toes turned backwards, he can no longer doubt that he is dead.

We may well ask how a " spirit " can possess feet ?— It is not really the " spirit " which is provided with limbs, but the " ethereal double " to which he is still attached. For Tibetans, like Egyptians, believe in the " double."

During life, in a normal state, this " double " is closely united with the material body. Nevertheless, certain circumstances may cause their separation. The " double " can, then, leave the material body and *show* itself in different places ; or *being itself invisible*, it can accomplish various peregrinations. With some people this separation of the " double " from the body happens involuntarily, but Tibetans say that those who have trained themselves for the purpose can effect it at will.

The separation, however, is not complete, for a strand subsists, connecting the two forms. The link persists during a certain length of time after death. The destruction of the corpse generally, but not necessarily, brings about the destruction of the " double " in the end. In certain cases, it may survive its companion.

In Tibet, one meets people who have been in a state of lethargy, and are able to describe the various places in which, they say, they have travelled. Some have only visited countries inhabited by men, while others can tell of their peregrinations in the paradises, the

purgatories or in the *bardo*, an intermediary region
where " spirits " wander after death, while waiting to
be reincarnated.[1]

These curious travellers are called *delogs*, which
means : " one who has returned from the *beyond*."
Though the *delogs* vary in their descriptions of places
and events, they usually agree in depicting the feelings
of the pseudo-dead as definitely pleasant.

A woman whom I met in a village of Tsarong had,
some years ago, remained inanimate for a whole week.
She said she had been agreeably astonished by the
lightness and agility of her new body and the extraordinary rapidity of its movements. She had only to
wish herself in a certain place to be there immediately ;
she could cross rivers, walking upon the waters, or pass
through walls. There was only one thing she found
impossible—to cut an almost impalpable cord that
attached her ethereal being to the material body which
she could see perfectly well sleeping upon her couch.
This cord lengthened out indefinitely but, nevertheless,
it sometimes hampered her movements. She would
" get caught up in it," she said.

A male *delog*, whom my son had met in his youth,
gave a similar description of his state.

Evidently, the *delog* is not really a dead man, so that
nothing can prove that the sensations he experiences
in his lethargy are the same as those felt by the dead.
Tibetans, however, do not seem to be troubled by this
distinction.

When the dying man has taken his last breath, he is
dressed by putting his clothes on backwards—the front
of the gown fastened on his back. Then he is tied up,
with his legs crossed, or his knees bent and touching
his breast. In the villages, the body, dressed in this
way, is usually placed in a cauldron. As soon as the
corpse has been taken out for its journey to the ceme-

[1] The existence of such a region is denied by orthodox Buddhists.

tery, this cauldron is hastily washed, and soup or tea is often prepared in it for the funeral guests who do not seem troubled by fear of infection from the corpse.

In Tibet, funeral ceremonies occupy many days, and though the high altitude of the central and northern provinces retards decomposition, in the hot and damp valleys, corpses kept for a week or longer spread a putrid odour.

This does not in the least affect the appetite of the officiating *trapas*, who continue to advise the dead, signalling the roads he should follow and those he should avoid in the next world. They take their meals facing the departed one. One may even say they eat *with* him, for the chief monk invites him by name as follows : " Spirit, come here, immediately, and feed yourself."

In the wooded regions of Tibet, the bodies are burned. The inhabitants of the vast barren northern and central regions, where cowdung is the only fuel available, abandon the corpses to the beasts of prey, either in cemeteries reserved near the villages, or anywhere on the mountain solitudes.

The bodies of high religious dignitaries are sometimes preserved by the double process of salting and cooking in butter. These mummies are called *mardong*. Swathed in clothes, their faces painted with gold, they are placed in mausoleums of massive silver, studded with precious stones. A pane of glass is sometimes fitted in these cases, on a level with the head, so that the gilded face can be seen. Other Grand Lamas are incinerated with butter and their bones preserved in rich caskets. All funeral monuments, in Tibet, take the form of *chorten*, which are imitations of the stûpas which the ancient Buddhists of India built over their holy dead, or other precious relics.

In obedience to Buddhist beliefs in the excellence of charitable deeds, Lamaists find, in the funerals, a fitting occasion for a supreme act of charity. The dead

man wished—or is supposed to have wished—that his
body should serve as his last gift, to nourish those
tormented by hunger.

A work entitled : A guide for the " spirit " of the
dead in the next world,[1] expounds the subject as
follows :

(1) The body is transported to the top of a mountain.
It is dismembered, the four limbs being cut off with a
well-sharpened knife. The entrails, the heart, the lungs
are laid out on the ground. The birds, wolves and
foxes feed themselves upon them.

(2) The body is thrown into a sacred river. The
blood and the humours are dissolved in the blue water.
The fish and the otters eat the flesh and the fat.

(3) The body is burned. Flesh, bones and skin are
reduced to a heap of cinders. The *Tisas* [2] are nourished
by the odour.

(4) The body is hidden in the earth. Flesh, bones
and skin are sucked by worms.

Families who can afford to pay the officiating monks,
have the religious service repeated every day, for six
weeks following the funerals. After this, an effigy is
made with a light frame of sticks, supporting clothes
that belonged to the deceased. A sheet of paper
represents the face. The portrait of the dead person
is sometimes sketched upon it ; more often a printed
paper sheet is bought, ready made, in a monastery.
There are two models : one being the picture of a
man, the other that of a woman. The name of the
departed is written under the drawn portrait or the
printed picture.

There is one more, final, religious ceremony, at the
close of which the officiating lama burns the paper

---

[1] Tse hdas kyi rnamshes thog grang.

[2] The *Tisas* are demi-gods who feed upon odours ; but while
some of them nourish themselves with sweet fragrances, others
prefer odours which are offensive to us, such as that of burnt flesh.

sheet, or face of the dead person. The clothes in which the effigy was dressed are given to the lama as part of his fee.

After this symbolic incineration, the ties which might still have attached the deceased to this world are considered to be definitely severed.

Tibetans keenly desire avoiding any intercourse with the dead. Peasants use especially precise words to get rid of them. Just before the corpse is carried out of the house, a meal is served to him and an aged member of the family harangues him, in these words :

" So-and-so, listen. You are dead, be sure of that. You have nothing more to do here. Eat copiously for the last time. You have a long road to run and several mountain passes to cross. Take strength and do not return ever again."

I heard an even stranger discourse.

After having duly told the dead man that he no longer belonged to this world and bidding him never to reappear, the orator added :

" Pagdzin. I must tell you that your house has been destroyed by fire, everything you possessed is burned. Because of a debt you had forgotten, your creditor has taken your two sons away as slaves. Your wife has left with a new husband. As it would sadden you to see all this misery, be careful not to return."

I listened in astonishment to this extraordinary list of calamities.

" How did this series of misfortunes happen ? " I asked an assistant.

" Nothing at all has happened," he answered, smiling maliciously. "The farm and the cattle are intact and the widow is sitting quietly at home with the sons. We invented that tale to disgust Pagdzin so that he will not think of returning to his home."

This seemed rather a naïve stratagem for people

who credit the " spirit " with the faculty of seeing what is going on in our world.

In liturgical terms far more solemn than those employed by the villagers, the lama also advises the departed one to follow his road without looking backward. But this counsel is for his own good, while the common people only think of avoiding the occult presence of a ghost which they consider dangerous.

During the celebration of these various ceremonies, the " spirit " travels through the *Bardo*.

He beholds, in turn, radiant beautiful beings and hideous forms. He sees diversely coloured paths and a crowd of strange visions. These apparitions frighten him, he is bewildered and wanders at random among them.

If he is able to hear and to follow the advices of the officiating lama, he can take a road that will lead him to be reborn among the gods, or in some other pleasant condition—just as the initiate may, who has entered consciously into the *Bardo* after a careful study of its " map."

But men who have not learned anything about the *Bardo*, and who enter it while absorbed in their regret at leaving the material world, can hardly profit by the counsels given to them.

So they miss the opportunity of escaping the mathematically rigid consequences of their actions. The roads to celestial happiness are behind them. The wombs of human and of animal beings are offered them and, deceived by their hallucinations, they fancy these to be pleasant grottoes or palaces. Thinking they will find an agreeable resting-place, they enter one or another of them and thus determine for themselves the conditions of their rebirth. This one will become a dog, while another will be the son of distinguished human parents.

According to other beliefs, the great mass of people

who have not obtained *post-mortem* spiritual illumination, by seizing the meaning of the vision which arose
before them immediately after death, travel like a
frightened flock of sheep through the phantasmagoria of
Bardo, until they reach the court of Shinje, the Judge
of the Dead.

Shinje examines their past actions in a mirror or
weighs them under the form of white and black pebbles.
According to the predominance of good or of evil
deeds, he determines the species of beings among
whom the " spirit " will be reborn and the particular
conditions that shall accompany this rebirth, such as
physical beauty or ugliness, intellectual gifts, social
standing of the parents, etc.

There is no question of " skilfulness " in saving oneself here, for the judge is impartial and inflexible.

In fact, even at the time when " skilfulness " may be
helpful, it only acts within the limit permitted by the
power of past actions. I have already mentioned this
limitation and will, now, give an amusing illustration
of it which is characteristic of Tibetan humour.

A Grand Lama had passed his whole life in idleness.
Although he had been given excellent tutors in his
youth, had inherited from his predecessors an important
library and had, moreover, always been surrounded
by men of learning, still, he scarcely knew how to
read. This lama died.

In these times there lived a strange man, a miracle-
worker and rough-speaking philosopher, whose eccentricities—sometimes coarse—often exaggerated by
his biographers, have given birth to a number of
stories in the style of Rabelais, much appreciated in
Tibet.

Dugpa Kunlegs, for such was his name, travelled
under the guise of a vagabond. Having arrived at the
bank of a brook, he saw a girl who had come there to
draw water.

Suddenly he attacked her, and without saying a word he tried to violate her.

The lass was robust and Dugpa Kunlegs was approaching old age. She defended herself so vigorously that she escaped him, and, running back to the village, told her mother what had happened.

The good woman was most astonished. The men of the country were well behaved, none of them could be suspected. The brute must be a stranger. She made her daughter minutely describe the wicked wretch.

While listening to the girl, the mother wondered. The description of the man corresponded, in all points, to that of Dugpa Kunlegs, this eccentric and saintly lama whom she had met during a pilgrimage. There was no doubt possible. Dugpa Kunlegs, himself, had wished to abuse her daughter.

She began to reflect on the strange behaviour of the holy one. The common moral principles which rule the conduct of ordinary men do not apply to men of supernormal wisdom—she thought. A *doubtob* [1] is not bound to follow any law. His actions are dictated by superior considerations which escape the vulgar observer. . . .

So she said to her daughter :

" The man you have seen is the great Dugpa Kunlegs. Whatever he does is well done. Therefore, return to the brook, prostrate yourself at his feet and consent to anything he wishes.

The girl went back and found the *doubtob* seated upon a 'stone, absorbed in his thoughts. She bowed down before him, excused herself for having resisted him when she had not known who he was, and declared that she was entirely at his service.

The saint shrugged his shoulders.

" My child," he said, " women awake no desire in

[1] A sage and wonder-worker.

me. However, the Grand Lama of the neighbouring
monastery has died in ignorance, having neglected all
occasions of instruction. I saw his ' spirit ' wandering
in the *Bardo*, drawn towards a bad rebirth, and, out
of compassion, I wished to procure him a human body.
But the power of his evil deeds has not permitted this.
You escaped, and while you were at the village, the
asses in that field near by, coupled. The Grand Lama
will soon be reborn as a donkey."

The majority of the dead men heed the desire of their
families, as expressed during the funeral, and do not
return. The latter conclude that their fate, in the next
world, has been definitely settled and, probably, to
their satisfaction.

However, some departed ones are less discreet. They
frequently appear in dreams to their relatives or their
friends and strange things happen in their former
dwellings. Tibetans believe that this shows the
" spirit " to be unhappy and calling for help.

There are lama diviners who can be consulted in
such cases. They order the rites to be celebrated, the
gifts to be bestowed upon the clergy, and holy books
to be read, to comfort the unhappy " spirit."

Nevertheless, many people, especially in those remote
regions near the frontiers, fall back on the practices
of the ancient Böns[1] for such cases. They think that the
dead man, himself, should be listened to. So a *medium*,
male or female (*pawo* or *pamo*), is summoned to lend his
voice to the departed one.

Spiritualistic seances, in Tibet, do not resemble those
of the Western countries. Neither darkness nor silence
are required, sometimes they are held in the open air.

The *pawo* begins chanting, accompanying himself
with a little drum and a bell. He dances, first slowly,
then faster and faster, and, finally, trembles convul-

[1] The shamanist aborigines.

sively. A being of another world, god, demon or spirit
of a dead person, has taken possession of him.

In a kind of frenzy, he utters broken sentences, which
are supposed to convey that which the invisible being
wishes to communicate to the assistants.

Since it is of the first importance to know exactly
who is speaking through the *medium*, and what he is
saying, the most intelligent men of the village are
called upon to listen attentively.

It sometimes happens that different gods or spirits
take possession of the *medium* one after another. Once
in a while, the latter, under the impulsion given to
him by one of these beings, will suddenly attack one
of the public and beat him mercilessly. This correction
is always accepted without any resistance being offered.
Tibetans imagine that it is meant to drive out a demon
that has lodged himself in the man without his being
aware of it. This undesirable guest has, however, been
discovered by the spirit animating the *medium*.

The departed ones who suffer in the next world
usually limit their performances to giving an account
of their misfortunes.

At a seance, where I was a spectator, I heard one
say : " I met a demon upon my road who dragged me
into his dwelling. He made a slave of me. He forces
me to work hard, without stopping, and ill-treats me.
Have pity on me ! Set me free so that I may reach
the ' Paradise of the Great Bliss.' "

The mother of the man who was supposed to be
speaking, as well as his wife and children, wept bitter tears.

Families who receive supplications of this kind, think
of nothing but how to liberate the unfortunate captive.

It is a complicated affair.

First, one must get into communication with the
demon and negotiate the ransom of his prisoner.

The chosen intermediary is often a Bön sorcerer. He
informs the relatives of the unhappy " spirit " that his

demoniacal master demands the sacrifice of a pig or a cow, before setting him free.

Having offered the victim, the Bön enters into a trance. His " double " is supposed to visit the dwelling-place of the demon.

He travels ; the way is long and hard, full of obstacles. This, the sorcerer indicates by his contortions. But unlike the *pawo* he remains seated, moving only his head and his bust. A flow of hurried words are uttered, telling the various incidents of his adventure.

He is even more difficult to understand than the *pawo*. The cleverest listeners find it hard to make out the sense of his words.

The Bön has accomplished his task ; now he has seized the " spirit " and prepares to take him away. The demon has received the ransom demanded, but he usually breaks faith and tries to hold on to his slave. The sorcerer fights him, one can see him struggling and panting, one can hear his screams.

The family and friends of the dead men follow the phases of the drama with the greatest anxiety. They are overjoyed when the sorcerer declares that he has been successful, and has led the " spirit " to an agreeable place.

But the first attempt does not always succeed. I have witnessed several performances where the sorcerer, after having simulated extraordinary efforts, declared that the " spirit " had been taken away from him by the demon.

In this case, all rites, sacrifices . . . and the payment of the Bön's fees, must begin all over again.

When a lama is called upon to save a " spirit " from slavery, no sacrifice is performed for redemption and the rites that are celebrated ignore all negotiation. The lama, who is learned in the magic ritual, considers himself powerful enough to compel the demon to release his victim.

Under the influence of Buddhism, the inhabitants of Tibet proper have given up sacrificing animals. This is far from being true of Tibetans living in the Himalayas who have only a thin coating of Lamaism and have remained practically Shamanists.

The beliefs of the learned lamas and of contemplative mystics differ greatly from those held by the masses about the fate of the " spirit " in the next world.

To begin with, they consider all the incidents of the journey in the *Bardo* as purely subjective visions. The nature of these visions depends on the ideas the man has held when he was living. The various paradises, the hells and the Judge of the Dead appear to those who have believed in them.

A *gomchen* of Eastern Tibet told me the following story upon this subject.

A painter whose principal work was that of decorating temples, often painted the fantastic beings with human bodies and animal heads, who are supposed to be the attendants of Shinje. His son, who was still a very young child, often stayed beside him while he worked and amused himself looking at the monstrous forms appearing in the frescoes.

Now it happened that the boy died, and entering the *Bardo*, met the terrible beings whose images were familiar to him. Far from being frightened, he began to laugh.—" Oh ! I know you all," he said. " My father makes you on the walls." And he wished to play with them.

I once asked the lama of Enche what would be the *post-mortem* subjective visions of a materialist who had looked upon death as total annihilation.

" Perhaps," said the lama, " such man would see apparitions corresponding to the religious beliefs he held in his childhood, or to those, familiar to him, held by the people among whom he has lived. According to the degree of his intelligence and his *post-mortem* lucidity, he would, perhaps, examine and analyse these visions and remember the reasons which, during his life-time, made him deny the reality of that which now appears to him. He might, thus, conclude that he is beholding a mirage.

"A less intelligent man in whom belief in total annihilation was the result of indifference or dullness, rather than of reasoning, will, perhaps, see no vision at all. However, this will not prevent the energy generated by his past actions from following its course and manifesting itself through new phenomena. In other words, it will not prevent the rebirth of the materialist."

My many copy-books filled with notes, showed that I had worked a great deal since I had come to Sikkim. I thought I might allow myself a holiday. Summer was approaching, the warmer temperature tempted me to undertake a trip in the north of the country.

The road I chose was an excellent mule track leading from Gangtok to Kampa-dzong and on to Shigatze, in Tibet. Rising gradually from the travellers' bungalow of Dikchu buried in the tropical jungle, on the bank of the Tista, it follows a tributary of this river up to its source, passing through enchanting landscapes.

At about 50 miles from Gangtok, and at a height of 8,000 feet, this road crosses a village called Lachen, which occupies a prominent place in my experiences of Lamaist mysticism.

This little group of cottages is the most northern in Sikkim, the last which the traveller meets on his way towards the high passes of the Tibetan border. It is inhabited by sturdy hillmen, who combine a little farming, in the valley, with the rearing of yaks [1] higher up on the Tibetan tableland, where they spend a part of the year under tents.

[1] Yak, the hairy Tibetan ox.

Perched on a mountain slope, a humble monastery dominates the villagers' dwellings.

I visited it the day after my arrival, but finding nothing of interest in the temple, I was about to leave when a shadow darkened the luminous space of the wide-open door : a lama stood on the threshold. I say " a lama," but the man did not wear the regular monastic garb, neither was he dressed as a layman. His costume consisted of a white skirt down to his feet, a garnet-coloured waistcoat, Chinese in shape, and through the wide armholes, the voluminous sleeves of a yellow shirt were seen. A rosary made of some grey substance and coral beads hung around his neck, his pierced ears were adorned with large gold rings studded with turquoises, and his long thick braided hair touched his heels.[1]

This strange person looked at me without speaking, and as at that time I knew but little of the Tibetan language, I did not dare to begin a conversation. I only saluted him and went out.

A young man, my general factotum, was waiting for me on the terrace of the monastery. As soon as he saw the lama descending the steps of the peristyle, behind me, he prostrated himself thrice at his feet, asking for his blessing.

This astonished me, for the lad was not usually lavish with such signs of respect, and honoured none, in this way, but the prince *tulku* and Bermiag Kushog.

" Who is this lama ? " I asked him as I returned to the travellers' bungalow.

" He is a great *gomchen*," the boy replied. " One of his monks told me, while you were in the temple.

---

[1] Later on, I learned that this is the costume of the anchorites who are proficient in *tumo* (see Chapter VI) and various other branches of the secret lore. The rosary is made of 108 small round pieces of bone, each one cut out from a different human skull.

He has spent years alone, in a cave high up in the
mountains. Demons obey him and he works miracles.
They say he can kill men at a distance and fly through
the air."

What an extraordinary man ! I thought.

My curiosity had been greatly excited by the stories
regarding Tibetan *gomchens* I had read with Dawasandup. I had also heard a great deal from the prince
tulku and from various lamas, about the way of living
of the Tibetan hermits, the curious doctrines they
profess and the wonders they can perform.

Now I had, most unexpectedly, come across one of
them. This was a lucky opportunity. But how could
I talk with the lama ? My boy was utterly ignorant
of Tibetan philosophical terms, he would never be
able to translate my questions.

I was annoyed and excited. I slept badly, troubled
by incoherent dreams. I saw myself surrounded by
elephants who pointed at me musical trunks from
which came out deep sounds like those of long Teban
trumpets. This strange concert woke me. My room
was plunged in darkness. I no longer saw the elephants
but I continued to hear the music. After listening
attentively, I recognized religious tunes. The *trapas*
were playing on the terrace of the temple. Who were
they serenading in the night ? . . .

Whatever might come of it, I wished to risk an
interview with the *gomchen*. I sent a request that he
would see me and the next day, accompanied by my
boy, I returned to the monastery.

A primitive staircase led to the lama's apartment
situated above the assembly hall. In front of the
entrance door was a small loggia decorated with frescoes. While waiting to be invited in, I examined
these with some amusement.

On the walls, an artist, endowed with more imagination than professional skill, had represented the tor-

ments of the purgatories, peopling the latter with a host of demons and victims who grinned and writhed in the most comical attitudes.

In the middle of a panel, lust was undergoing punishment. A naked man, abnormally thin, faced an unclothed woman. Her huge, disproportionate belly gave to this " belle " the appearance of an Easter egg mounted on two feet and topped with a doll head. The lecherous sinner, incorrigible slave of his passions, forgetting where he was and how he had been led there, hugged the infernal creature in his arms, while flames springing out from her mouth and from a secret recess scorched him.

At a small distance from this couple, a sinful woman suffered her chastisement. Bound, in a reversed posture, to a triangle pointing downward, she was compelled to accept the caresses inflicted upon her by a green devil with teeth like a saw and a monkey's tail. In the background, other demons, variously coloured, were seen running forward to take their turn.

The *gomchen* lived in a kind of dark chapel, lighted only at one end by a small window, the ceiling supported by wooden pillars painted red. According to the Tibetan custom the altar served as book-case.

In a niche, among the books, stood a small image of Padmasambhâva, with ritual offerings placed before it : seven bowls filled with pure water, grain and a lamp.

Incense sticks burning on a small table mingled their mystic fragrance with odours of tea and melted butter. The cushions and rugs piled up for the master to sit upon were threadbare and faded, and the tiny gold star of the altar lamp shining at the back of the room showed up its dust and emptiness.

Through my boy acting as interpreter, I tried to ask several questions on subjects I had discussed with the lamas I had met at Gangtok, but it was useless. If only Dawasandup had been with me. The young man was dumbfounded and unable to find words to express ideas whose meaning he could not grasp.

I gave it up, and for a long time the lama and I sat facing each other in silence.

The next day I left Lachen, continuing my journey towards the north.

Here the scenery, which all along the track lower down had been charming, became simply marvellous. The azalea and rhododendron thickets were still decked with their bright spring garment. A shimmering torrent of blossoms submerged the valley and seemed to be pouring out, on the neighbouring slopes, a resistless flood of purple, yellow, red and pure white waves. Seen from a distance, my porters, whose heads only emerged from the bushes, seemed to be swimming in a sea of flowers.

A few miles farther, the fairy-like gardens gradually grew thin and scattered, till a few rosy patches only remained, here and there, where dwarf bunches of azaleas struggled obstinately for life against the dizzy heights.

The track now entered the fantastic region near the frontier passes.[1] In the intense silence of these wild majestic solitudes, icy, crystalline, purling brooks chatted gently. From the shore of a melancholy lake, a golden-crowned bird solemnly watched my caravan as it passed.

Up and up we went, skirting gigantic glaciers, catching occasional glimpses of crossing valleys filled by huge clouds. And then, without any transition, as we issued from the mists the Tibetan tableland appeared before us, immense, void and resplendent under the luminous sky of Central Asia.

Since then I have travelled across the country lying behind the distant mountain ranges which, at that moment, bound my horizon. I have seen Lhasa,

[1] The Koru la and the Sepo la, both above 15,000 feet.

Shigatze, the northern grassy solitudes with their salt lakes as large as seas ; Kham, the country of brigand-knights and magicians ; the unexplored forests of Po and the enchanting valleys of Tsarong where the pomegranates ripen, but nothing has ever dimmed, in my mind, the memory of my first sight of Tibet.

A few weeks later the weather changed, the snow began to fall again. My provisions were on the verge of giving out, porters and servants grew irritable and quarrelsome. One day I had to use my riding-whip to separate two men who were fighting with knives for a place near the camp fire.

After a few short excursions into Tibetan territory I left the frontier. I was not equipped for a long journey and, moreover, the land that lay in front of me was forbidden ground.

Again I crossed Lachen, saw the *gomchen* and talked with him about his hermitage that was a day's march distant, higher up in the mountains. He had lived there for seventeen years. These plain details my boy could easily translate and I myself could follow a certain amount of his conversation.

However, I did not risk mentioning the demons, said by popular opinion to be his servants. I knew my young interpreter was too superstitious to dare to approach this subject and, probably, also the lama would not have answered such inquiries.

I returned to Gangtok, sad at having missed the opportunity of learning things of real interest regarding the mystery world of Tibetan anchorites, which I had skirted by chance. I did not, in the least, foresee the curious consequences of my trip.

A little while after this, the Dalai Lama left Kalim-pong. His army had beaten the Chinese and he was to go back to Lhasa in triumph. I went to bid him farewell at a hamlet situated below the Jelap pass.

I arrived ahead of him at the bungalow where he

was to stop. There I found many noblemen of the
Sikkimeese court in great distress. They were in
charge of the preparations for the short stay of the
Lama-king, but, as is usual in the East, everything had
come too late. Furniture, rugs, hangings were not in
place and the distinguished guest might appear at any
minute.

Everything was in confusion in the small house, with
masters and servants wildly rushing about. It amused
me to lend a helping hand and arrange the cushions
that would serve the Dalai Lama for a bed. Some of
the assistants assured me that this would bring me good
luck, now and in lives to come.

Here I had another opportunity of talking with
the Tibetan sovereign. His thoughts seemed entirely
directed towards political affairs.

As usual he blessed the devotees with his duster made
of ribbons, but one felt that his mind had already
crossed the mountain pass that marks the frontier and
was busy organizing the profits of his victory.

The following autumn I left Sikkim for Nepal and,
later on, spent nearly a year in Benares. I had made
a long stay there in my youth, and returned with
pleasure.

I gratefully accepted the kind offer of the members
of the Theosophical Society to rent me a small apartment in their beautiful park. The ascetic simplicity
of this lodging was in harmonious keeping with the
atmosphere of the holy city of Shiva and quite suited
my taste.

In these congenial surroundings, I assiduously
resumed the study of the Vedanta philosophy, somewhat forsaking Lamaism which I did not seem to be able
to investigate more thoroughly than I had already done.

I had no thought of leaving Benares, when an unexpected combination of circumstances led me one
morning to take a train going towards the Himalayas.

CHAPTER II

A GUEST OF THE LAMAS

AT Gangtok I again met Bermiag Kushog. The Lama of Enche had left for Shigatze, in Tibet, and only returned some months later. Dawasandup had been called upon, as interpreter, to follow the Sino—Tibetan political conference that was convoked in India. The maharajah having died, his son Sidkeong *tulku* succeeded him and, consequently, had less time to devote to religious studies. Unexpected obstacles prevented me from completing the journey which I had planned. Everything worked against my desires.

Gradually hostile forces seemed to gather around me. I seemed to be obsessed by invisible beings who incited me to leave the country, insinuating that I should be able to advance no farther, either in my study of Lamaism or upon the actual soil of Tibet. By a sort of clairvoyance at the same time, I saw these unknown enemies triumphant and rejoicing, after my departure, at having driven me away.

I attributed these phenomena to fever or neurasthenia due to brain fatigue and the annoyance at my plans being upset. Some people would, perhaps, have seen in this the effect of occult activities. Whatever it was, I could not overcome this painful state bordering on hallucination. Calming drugs did not relieve me, I thought that a change of scene might be more efficacious.

While I was racking my brain to think of a place where I might stop without leaving the Himalayas, the new maharajah, the lama *tulku,* without guessing that he was more than realizing my desires, offered me an apartment in the monastery of Podang, about 10 miles away from Gangtok, in the misty forests.

The apartment consisted of an immense room on the first floor of the temple and a huge kitchen where, according to Tibetan custom, my servants were to sleep.

Two large bay-windows let in all the light of the sky, and with equal hospitality they admitted wind, rain or hail through large gaps on both sides, for the framework was too narrow and only joined the walls at the top.

In one corner of this hall I placed my books upon a wide wainscot. I opened my folding table and chair, and this was my " work room." In another corner I hooked my tent to the beams and set up my camp bed. This was my bedroom. The middle of the apartment, too well aired by cross ventilation, became a kind of reception-room for my visitors, when the weather was fine.

The religious music which I heard at Podang twice a day, before dawn and at sunset, enchanted me. The small orchestra consisted of two *gyalings* (a kind of hautboy), two *ragdongs* (a huge Teban trumpet) and two kettle-drums.

A bell striking a special rhythm, peculiar to Eastern temples, was sounded as prelude. After a few moments' silence the deep-toned *ragdongs* rumbled for a while, then the *gyalings* by themselves sang a slow musical phrase supremely moving in its simplicity. They repeated it with variations, supported by the bass notes of the *ragdongs* in which finally joined the kettle-drums that imitated the thunder rolling in the distance.

The melody flowed as smoothly as the water of a deep river, without interruption, emphasis or passion. It produced a strange, acute impression of distress, as if all the suffering of the beings wandering from world to world, since the beginning of the ages, was breathed out in this weary, desperate lamentation.

What musician, inspired without his knowing, had found this *leit motiv* of universal sorrow? And how, with this heterogeneous orchestra, could men devoid of any artistic sense render it with such heart-rending fervour?—This remained a mystery which the musician monks would have been unable to explain. I had to be content to listen to them, while watching the dawn come up behind the mountains, or in the darkening of the sunset sky.

Beside attending the daily services, I had the opportunity during my stay at Podang to witness the annual Ceremony of the Demons. In Tibet, later on, I saw the same rites celebrated with much greater display of clerical paraphernalia, but, to my mind, this diminished the picturesque character which they assumed when performed in the shadow of the Himalayan forests. Sorcery loses much of its prestige when seen by broad daylight and in a crowd.

First, the *trapas* took Mahākala out of the cabinet in which he had been shut up a full year, with offerings and charms.

In every lamaist monastery there exists a temple, or a room reserved as a dwelling-place for the ancient deities of the aborigines or those imported from India. The latter have considerably lost rank in entering the Land of Snows. Unconscious of their irreverence, Tibetans have turned them into mere demons and sometimes treat them harshly.

Mahākala is the most famous among the exiled Hindu deities. His original personality is a form of Shiva in his function of Destroyer of the World. Having become a harmful spirit, he is held in slavery by the lamas who compel him to render them various kinds of services and do not hesitate to punish his lack of zeal.

A popular tradition has it that a celebrated lama,

head of the Karmapa sect, attached Mahākala to him
as attendant. When this lama was at the Chinese
court, he offended the Emperor, who had him tied to
the tail of a horse. Dragged behind the animal, and in
peril of death, the great Karmapa called on Mahākala
to help him. But the latter did not immediately
appear. When the lama had freed himself by means
of magic words which separated his beard from his
chin, he saw Mahākala coming toward him too late to
be of any use, and in his anger he hit the poor devil
such a blow that though several centuries have now
passed his cheek remains swollen even to-day.

Of course, the *trapas* of Podang were not powerful
enough to take such liberties, Mahākala inspired them
with real terror.

Here, as in some other monasteries, grim wonders
were said to happen. Sometimes blood sweated
through the boards of the shrine where Mahākala was
shut up, and at other times, on opening it, the remains
of a human heart or brain were found. These signs—
according to the *trapas*—betoken the occult activity of
the terrible deity.

When the mask which represents Mahākala—and in
which he is supposed to reside—was taken out of the
shrine, it was placed in a dark chapel reserved for other
kindred malevolent deities. Two novices watched it,
repeating without interruption the magic words which
prevent him from escaping. Lulled by their monotonous chant, the boys fought with all their might
against sleep during the long hours of the night, convinced that if they stopped for an instant repeating the
mysterious formula their dreadful captive would take
advantage of it to free himself and they would become
his first victims.

In the neighbouring hamlets, the peasants were
greatly perturbed by the slight semblance of liberty
given to Mahākala. They locked their door early in

the evening and mothers bid their children not to stay out after sunset.

Less important demons supposed to be wandering around the country, seeking to do harm, were attracted by the incantations of the lamas and compelled to enter a sort of cage woven of light wood and coloured threads. Then this pretty house was solemnly carried out of the monastery and precipitated, with its prisoners, into a flaming brazier.

But the demons are immortals—fortunately for the sorcerers whose living depends upon them. Next year the same rites must be performed all over again.

A learned lama belonging to a wealthy family of Sikkim had just returned from Tibet. He became head of the monastery of Rhumteck in succession to his brother who had died recently. Custom demanded that he should celebrate certain rites meant to assure the welfare of the dead in the next world, at Podang, the chief monastery of his sect in Sekkim.

The late head lama was an old acquaintance of mine. I had met him at Kalimpong where he had come in the train of the heir prince to pay a visit to the Dalai Lama.

He was a jolly fellow, a veritable " bon vivants " ; who did not worry himself with philosophic problems, kept two wives at home, and appreciated old brandy to the extent of drinking several bottles a day. In possession of a large income, he would buy anything he fancied right and left although ignorant of its use. It is in this way that, one day, the big powerfully built head lama came to see me wearing the hat, trimmed with pink ribbons, of a three-years-old girl.

The new abbot, popularly called " the gentleman from Tibet "—Pöd Kushog—because he usually lived in this country, was quite different from his brother. He had spent his youth studying in various Tibetan monasteries, and even in Lhasa he enjoyed the reputation among erudite lamas of being a distinguished grammarian. He had also taken high Orders and remained a celibate, which is rare among the Himalayan clergy.

The funeral services over which he presided lasted for a whole week. Happy days for the *trapas* of Podang, who feasted and received gifts !

These ceremonies being ended, in the first month of the year [1] Pöd Kushog proceeded to the annual blessing of the monastery. Escorted by a choir of *trapas* chanting a litany of good wishes, he walked round the buildings and through the corridors, throwing consecrated grain into each room as he passed by.

A few handfuls of barley, cast with a gracious smile and the liturgic wish *tashi shog !* (may prosperity be), rattled against my " tent-bedroom " and sprinkled the table and the books in my " study."

Prosperity ! prosperity ! . . . Duly exorcised and blessed, the monastery should become a branch of the Paradise of the Great Bliss (Nub Dewachen). Yet the monks did not feel quite safe. Secretly doubting their occult powers and even those of the learned grammarian they feared that a few devils might have escaped exter-mination and be waiting in hiding to begin doing mischief again. They begged the help of one whom they trusted more.

One evening, the *gomchen* of Lachen appeared with all the trapping of a magician : a five-sided crown, a rosary-necklace made of one hundred and eight round pieces, cut out of so many skulls, an apron of human bones bored and carved, and in his belt the ritualistic dagger (phurba).

Standing in the open, near a flaming fire, he drew magic signs in the air with his sceptre-dorje and stabbed the air as he recited incantations in a low voice.

I do not know which invisible demons he was fighting,

[1] The Tibetan year begins in February.

but in the fantastic light of the leaping flames, he certainly looked like a demon himself.

My remedy had proved efficacious : whether change of place had killed the microbes of fever, or the diversion of new scenes had cured the brain fatigue, or my unyielding will-power had conquered conscious beings of the occult world, I, at any rate, was freed from the obsession that had tortured me.

Yet a strange thing happened during my stay at Podang.

Sidkeong *tulku* having become maharajah, wished to make his subjects renounce their superstitions in favour of orthodox Buddhism. For this purpose, he had invited an Indian monk, who belonged to the Theravadin philosophic school, to preach in his country. The missionary had to fight against such anti-buddhistic customs as sorcery, the cult of spirits and the habit of drinking fermented drinks. This monk, Kali Kumar by name, was already at work.

The maharajah-lama, as abbot of Podang, had an apartment in the monastery where he stayed on the rare occasions when he officiated at the head of his monks. He came for two days, during my stay in the *gompa*.

We were taking tea together, late in the afternoon, and talking of Kali Kumar's mission and the way in which he might hope to free the hillmen from their inveterate superstitions.

" It is impossible," I said, " to know exactly what the historical Padmasambhâva, who preached in Tibet centuries ago, was like. But it is certain that his followers have made him the hero of legends that encourage drunkenness and absurd, pernicious practices. Under his name, they worship an evil spirit— even as you do," I added laughingly, pointing out an image of the great magician standing at the far end of the room with an altar lamp burning at its feet.

"It is necessary," I continued, when, suddenly, I could say no more. A third invisible presence had interrupted me. Yet no one had spoken, there was complete silence in the room, but I keenly felt the influence of some occult force.

"Nothing you can do will succeed," said a soundless voice. "The people of this country are mine . . . I am more powerful than you. . . ."

I listened in amazement to these silent words, and I had almost decided that they were only the expression of my own doubts regarding the success of the proposed reforms, when the maharajah replied.

He replied to that which *I had not said*, arguing with the invisible adversary of his plans.

"Why should I not succeed," he went on to say. "Possibly it will take some time to change the ideas of the peasants and the lower clergy. The demons which they feed will not easily become resigned to die of hunger, but, nevertheless, I shall get the better of them."

He was mockingly alluding to the animal sacrifices offered to the evil spirits by the sorcerers.

"But I have not said——" I began and stopped short, for I thought that, in spite of the brave declaration of war the prince had made on the demons, he was not entirely free from superstition and consequently it was better not to tell him what had happened.

However, I do not wish to leave the reader with this impression of Sidkeong *tulku*. He had probably liberated himself from superstition more fully than I supposed.

According to his horoscope, in which Tibetans place complete faith, the year of his death was noted as dangerous for him. To counteract hostile influences, several lamas—among whom was the *gomchen* of Lachen— offered to celebrate the rites prescribed for the purpose.

He thanked them and refused their ministry, saying

that if he must die, he felt capable of passing into another life without their ceremonies.

I think he must have left the reputation of being an impious man. As soon as he was dead, all innovations and religious reforms that he had started were abolished. Preaching was stopped and beer was supplied in the temples again. A lama informed the country clergy that they should return to their former habits.

The invisible adversary triumphed as he had predicted he would.

Although my head-quarters were at Podang, I had not entirely given up my excursions across Sikkim. Thus it happened that I met two *gomchens* from Eastern Tibet who had recently come to live in the Himalayas.

One of them dwelt in Sakyong, and for this reason he was called Sakyong *gomchen*. It is not considered polite, in Tibet, to address a person by his name. All who are not treated as one's inferiors are designated by some title.

Sakyong *gomchen* was picturesque in his ways and open-minded. He haunted the cemeteries and shut himself up for months in his house to practise magic rites. Like his colleague from Lachen, he did not wear the regular monastic garb, and instead of cutting his hair short he wore it rolled up on the top of his head after the fashion of Indian yogins. For anyone except a layman to wear his hair long in Tibet, is the recognized distinction of those ascetics or anchorites who are called *naljorpas* and are believed to seek salvation through the mystic " Short Path." [1]

Up to then, my conversations with lamas had been chiefly concerned with the philosophical doctrines of Mahayanist Buddhism from which Lamaism is derived. Sakyong *gomchen* held them in slight esteem and moreover was but little conversant with them. He was fond of paradoxes. " Study," he said, " is of no use

[1] See Chapter VII.

in gaining true knowledge, it is rather an obstacle.
All that we learn in that way is vain. In fact, one
only *knows* one's own ideas and one's own visions. As
for the real causes that have generated these ideas they
remain inaccessible to us. When we try to grasp
them we only seize the ideas that we, ourselves, have
elaborated about these causes.

Did he clearly understand what he said, or was he
merely repeating what he had read or heard expressed
by others ? . . .

At the request of the prince *tulku*, Sakyong *gomchen*
also went on a round of preaching. I had the opportunity of watching him delivering a sermon. I say
watching rather than *hearing*, for at that time I was far
from being capable of understanding all what he said
in Tibetan. In this rôle of apostle he was really very
fine, the vehemence of his speech, his gestures, the
varied expressions of his countenance proclaimed him
a born orator, and the frightened faces, bathed in tears,
of his listeners was proof enough of the impression he
produced.

The *gomchen* of Sakyong is the only Buddhist I have
ever seen preaching in such impassioned way. For orthodox Buddhism excludes gestures and vocal effects as
unbefitting in expounding a doctrine which appeals
only to calm reason.

I, one day, asked him : " What is the Supreme
Deliverance (tharpa) ? " He answered : " It is the
absence of all views and all imagination, the cessation
of that mental activity which creates illusions." [1]

Another day, he said : " You should go to Tibet and
be initiated by a master of the ' Short Path.' You are
too much attached to the doctrines of the *nienthös* (the
Buddhists of the Theravadin school). I foresee that

---

[1] That mental activity which Tibetans call *togpa*, ratiocination,
in contradistinction to *togspa* (understanding).

you would be capable of grasping the secret teaching." [1]

" And how could I go to Tibet, since foreigners are not admitted ? " I asked.

" Pooh ! many roads lead to Tibet," he replied lightly. " All the learned lamas do not live in U and Tsang (the central provinces with Lhasa and Shigatze as capitals). One can find other, yet more learned, teachers in my country." [2]

The ideas of getting into Tibet by way of China had never occurred to me, nor did the *gomchen's* suggestion, that day, awaken any echo in my mind. My hour had probably not yet come.

The second *gomchen* whom I got to know was of an uncommunicative character and rather haughty in his manners. Even the customary formulas of politeness which he was compelled to utter were tinged with a peculiar icy coldness.

Like the *gomchen* of Sakyong he was called after the place where he lived—Daling *gomchen*.

He always wore the regular monastic robes and toga but with the addition of ear-rings of ivory, and a silver *dorje* studded with torquoises stuck in his hair.

This lama spent the whole summer of every year in a cabin built for him on the top of a woody mountain.

A few days before his arrival, his disciples and the villagers round about would carry into the hermitage enough provisions for three or four months. After this, they were absolutely forbidden to approach the

[1] Secret teaching regarding methods of spiritual training and not regarding a supposed esoteric Buddhist doctrine as a few foreigners unacquainted with Buddhist literature believe. There exists no such thing as esoteric Buddhism. All theories expounded in the mystic circles are extant in books. That which is taught secretly to initiates, are ways to make the mind fit to reach enlightenment or, at lower degrees, ways to develop supernormal powers.

[2] As it has been said, the *gomchen* was a native of Eastern Tibet.

gomchen's dwelling. The lama had no difficulty in getting them to respect his solitude. The country people did not doubt that he practised dreadful rites to trap the demons and compel them to give up their mischievous designs against the persons or the possessions of those who worshipped him. His protection greatly reassured them, but they feared that if they went near his hut they might chance to meet some malignant beings answering unwillingly the *gomchen's* summons and not in pleasant mood. Moreover, the mystery which always surrounds the conduct, as well as the character, of the *naljorpas*, inspired them with prudence.

Little inclined as this lama was to answer my questions the desire expressed by the prince—to whom he owed his appointment as head of the small monastery of Daling—compelled him to depart somewhat from his reserve.

Among other subjects that I approached in my talk with him was that of the food permitted to a Buddhist. "Should we interpret the command not to kill, sophistically and continue to eat meat and fish?" I asked.

The *gomchen*, like most Tibetans, was not a vegetarian. He expounded a theory on this subject which I heard again in other parts of Tibet and which is not altogether lacking in originality.

"Most men," he said, "eat like beasts, to satisfy their hunger without pondering upon the act they are accomplishing nor upon its consequences. Such ignorant people do well to abstain from eating meat and fish.

"Others consider what becomes of the material elements they absorb when eating animals. They know that the assimilation of these elements involves the assimilation of the psychic elements which are inherent in them. Anyone who has acquired that knowledge may, at his risk and peril, contract these associations and endeavour himself to obtain results useful to the victims sacrificed.

" The question is to find out whether the animal elements which he absorbs strengthen the animal propensities of the man, or whether this man will be capable of transmuting these elements into intellectual and spiritual forces, so that the substance of the animal passing into the man will be reborn in the form of human activity."

I then asked him if this explained the esoteric sense of the belief common among Tibetans, that the lamas can send the spirits of the slaughtered animals to the Paradise of the Great Bliss.

" Do not think that I can answer your question in a few words," he replied. " The subject is intricate. Animals have several ' consciousnesses,' just as we have ourselves, and as it also happens in our case, these ' consciousnesses ' do not all follow the same road after death. A living being is an assemblage, not a unity. But one must have been initiated by a proper master before being able to realize these doctrines."

Often the lama cut his explanations short by this declaration.

One evening, when the prince, Daling lama and I were together in the bungalow of Kewzing, the conversation was about mystic ascetics. With a repressed enthusiasm that was most impressive, the *gomchen* spoke of his master, of his wisdom, of his supernormal powers. Sidkeong *tulku* was deeply moved by the profound veneration of the lama for his spiritual teacher.

At that time the prince was full of cares on account of his contemplated marriage with a Birman princess.

" I regret very much that I cannot meet this great *naljorpa*," he said to me in English. " For he, certainly, would give me good advice."

And addressing the *gomchen* he repeated, in Tibetan :

" I am sorry that your master is not here. I really need the advice of some such clairvoyant sage."

But he did not mention the question he wished to ask, nor the nature of his preoccupations.

The lama with his usual coldness of manner asked : " Is the subject serious ? "

" It is extremely important," the prince replied.

" You can perhaps receive the desired advice," said Daling *gomchen*.

I thought that he meant to send a letter by a messenger and was about to remind him the great distance that would have to be covered, when his aspect struck me.

He had closed his eyes and was rapidly turning pale, his body stiffening. I wished to go to him, thinking he was ill, but the prince, who had observed the sudden change in the lama, held me back, whispering :

" Don't move. *Gomchens* sometimes go into a trance quite suddenly. One must not wake them, for that is very dangerous and might even kill them."

So I stayed seated watching the lama who remained motionless. Gradually his features changed, his face wrinkled, taking on an expression I had never seen him wear before. He opened his eyes and the prince made a startled gesture.

The man we were looking at was not the *gomchen* of Daling, but some one we did not know. He moved his lips with difficulty and said in a voice different from that of the *gomchen* :

" Do not be disturbed. This question will never have to be considered by you."

Then he slowly closed his eyes, his features changed again and became those of Daling lama who slowly recovered his senses.

He eluded our questions and retired in silence, staggering and seeming to be broken with fatigue.

" There is no sense in his answer," the prince concluded.

Whether by chance or for some other reason, it unfortunately proved that there had been a meaning in these words.

The matter troubling the young maharajah was about his fiancée and an affair with a girl who had borne him a son which he did not wish to break off when he married. But, truly, he needed not to ponder over his course of conduct toward the two women, for he died before the day arranged for the marriage.

I happened also to see two hermits of a peculiar type which I did not meet again in Tibet where, on the whole, the natives are more civilized than in the Himalayas.

I was returning with the prince *tulku* from an excursion to the frontier of Nepal. His servants, knowing that he liked to show me the " religious curiosities " of his country, pointed out the presence of two hermits in the mountains near the village where we had spent the night.

The peasants said that these men had hidden themselves so cleverly that no one had seen them for several years. A supply of food was placed from time to time under a rock, at a chosen spot where the anchorites would take it at night. As to the huts they had built themselves, none knew where they were, nor did anyone try to discover them. For if the hermits were anxious to avoid being seen, the superstitious villagers were even more anxious to keep at a distance from them and turned away from the wood they inhabited.

Sidkeong *tulku* had freed himself from fear of sorcery. He ordered his servants together with a number of peasants to beat up the forest and bring the hermits to him. The latter should be well treated and presents promised to them, but great care must be taken that they did not escape.

The hunt was strenuous. The two anchorites, surprised in their quiet retreat, tried to run away, but with twenty men on their track they were finally captured.

They had to be forcibly made to enter the small temple where we were waiting with several lamas—among whom was the *gomchen* of Sakyong. Once there, no one could get a word out of them.

I have never seen such strange human creatures. Both men were frightfully dirty, scarcely covered by a few rags, their long hair, thick as brushwood, covered their faces and their eyes shot out sparks like a brazier.

While they looked around them like wild beasts newly caught in a cage, the prince caused two large wicker baskets to be brought. These were filled with tea, meat, barley-flour, rice and sundries. He told the hermits that he meant to give all this to them. But in spite of this agreeable prospect they remained silent.

A villager then said that he thought he had understood that when the anchorites came to live on that hill they were under a vow of silence.

His Highness, who was a prey to sudden attacks of truly Oriental despotism, replied that they might at least bow to him as it is the custom and adopt a more respectful attitude.

I saw his anger rising and, to avoid trouble brewing for the wild " holy ones," I begged him to allow them to retire.

He first resisted my request, but I insisted.

In the meantime I had told one of my servants to bring two bags of crystallized sugar taken from my luggage—Tibetans are very fond of it—I placed one bag in each basket.

" Open the door, and let these animals out," the prince commanded at last.

As soon as they saw a chance of escape, the hermits pounced on the baskets. One of them hastily pulled something from under his rags, plunged his claw-like hand in my hair ; and then both of them flew away like hares.

I found a little amulet in my hair which I showed to my friends and, later on, to some lamas who were conversant in the science of charms. All agreed in telling me that far from being harmful, the amulet secured me the company of a demon who would drive away any dangers on my road and serve me. I could only be pleased. Perhaps the hermit had understood that I begged for him and his companion to be set free, and his strange gift was a token of gratitude.

My last excursion with the lama prince led me again toward the north of the country. I revisited Lachen and saw its *gomchen*. I was now able to converse with him, but there was no time for long talks as we only stopped for one day on our way to reach the foot of the Kinchindjinga mountain.[1]

On the way, we camped on the side of a pretty lake in the desolate valley of Lonak, not far from the highest pass in the world : the Jongson pass (about 24,000 feet high) where the frontiers of Tibet, Nepal and Sikkim meet.

We spent a few days near the gigantic moraines from which spring the snow-covered peaks of the Kinchindjinga. Then Sidkeong *tulku* left me to return to Gangtok with his retinue.

He made fun of my love for high solitary places which led me to continue my journey with the young Yongden and a few servants. I can see him, even now. This time he was not dressed as a genie of the Arabian Nights, but in the kit of a Western alpinist. Before disappearing behind a rocky spur, he turned back toward me waving his hat and crying from far off :

" Come back soon. Don't stay away too long ! "

[1] Altitude 28,150 feet. The altitude of the Mount Everest, the highest mountain of the world, is 29,000 feet.

I never saw him again. He died mysteriously a few months later, while I was stopping at Lachen.

The Lonak valley was too near Tibet for me to possibly resist climbing one of the passes leading to that country. The Nago pass (over 18,000 feet) was the most easily accessible. The weather was fair but cloudy and a little snow fell as we were starting.

The landscape, viewed from the top of the pass, did not resemble that which I had seen two years earlier, so gloriously luminous. Now the twilight cast a purple greyish veil over the immense tableland extending, majestically void, from the foot of the mountain toward other ranges standing out indistinctly in the distance. But softly enshrouded in the first evening's shadows the forbidden solitudes looked still more mysterious and irresistibly attractive.

I should have been content to wander aimlessly across this extraordinary region, but I had a goal. Before leaving Gangtok one of the native officials had called my attention to the monastery of Chörten Nyima.

" The monasteries you have seen in Sikkim are very different from those of Tibet," he had told me. " Since you cannot travel freely in Tibet, go at least to see Chörten Nyima. Though this *gompa* is very small, you will get some idea of a true Tibetan monastery."

So I was going to Chörten Nyima.

The monastic habitations of that place fully justified the name *gompa* (a dwelling in the solitude) given, in Tibetan language, to monasteries. It is impossible to fancy any more solitary site. The region in which the monks' houses have been built is not only un-inhabited but the high altitude makes a desert of it.

Sandy cliffs curiously carved by erosions, a large valley ascending toward a mountain lake, high snowy peaks, a limpid brook on a bed of mauve, greyish green or rosy coloured pebbles formed around the *gompa* an impassible, wholly mineral scenery from which emanated a serenity beyond expression.

Legends and prodigies are naturally in their right place in such a setting. They are not lacking at Chörten Nyima. This very name, which means "Sun shrine," was derived from a wonder. Once upon a time a Chörten containing precious relics was miraculously transported through the air, on a ray of sun, from India to that spot.

In ancient traditions it is related that Padmasambhâva the apostle of Tibet has hidden in the vicinity of Chörten Nyima a number of manuscripts regarding mystic doctrines which he thought it was premature to disclose, for in the eighth century, when Padmasambhâva visited Tibet, Tibetans possessed no intellectual culture. This master foresaw that long after he had left this world, lamas, predestined by their former lives, would bring these writings to light again. Several works are said to have been found in this region and some lamas are still hunting to discover others.

According to Tibetans, one hundred and eight *chörtens* and one hundred and eight springs exist round about Chörten Nyima. All of them are not visible. A large number can only be seen by those whose mind is particularly pure. Wishes made beside these springs, after one has placed an offering in the water at the very spot where it wells up out of the earth, cannot help being fulfilled.

Chöd do (stone offerings) either standing up or piled in the shape of cairns bristle all over the country, and when erected by pious pilgrims to honour Padmasambhâva, these primitive monuments are believed to be indestructible.

The monastery, which must at one time have been somewhat important, is falling in ruins. As in many other places in Tibet, we may see here a result of the destitution of the ancient sects which have not followed the reforms of Tsong Khapa, whose disciples, nowadays, form the state clergy.

I found only four nuns at Chörten Nyima who belonged to the Nyingma sect (" ancient sect," the oldest of the " red caps "). They lived as celibates but without having been fully ordained and did not wear monastic robes.

Numerous examples of strange contrasts are to be seen in Tibet, but what most astonished me was the tranquil courage of the womenfolk. Very few Western women would dare to live in the desert, in groups of four or five or sometimes quite alone. Few would dare under such conditions to undertake journeys that last for months or even years, through solitary mountain regions infested by wild beasts and brigands.

This shows the singular character of Tibetan women. They do not ignore these real dangers and they add to them by imagining legions of evil spirits taking on thousands of strange forms, even that of a demoniacal plant which grows on the edge of precipices, seizes hold of travellers with its thorny branches and drags them into the abyss.

In spite of these many reasons for staying safely in their native villages, one finds here and there in Tibet, communities of less than a dozen nuns, living in isolated convents situated at a great height, some of them blocked in by the snow for more than half of the year.

Other women live as hermits in caves, and many women pilgrims travel, alone, across the immense territory of Tibet carrying their scanty luggage on their backs.

Visiting the *Lhakhangs* (houses of the gods, where their images are placed) still existing among the ruined buildings of the monastery, I found a room containing a collection of small images made of coloured clay and representing the fantastic beings which surround the " spirits " of the dead as they cross the *Bardo*.[1]

[1] See Chapter I : Death and Hereafter.

Above them, in the attitude of a Buddha meditating, Dorjee Chang was seated naked, his blue body symbolizing space, that is to say, in mystic symbology : Emptiness.

One of the nuns surprised me by explaining their meaning.

" All these are non-existent," she said, pointing out the monstrous forms of the *Bardo's* phantoms. " Mind evokes them out of the void and can also dissolve them into the void."

" How do you know that ? " I asked, doubting that the good woman could have evolved this theory by herself.

" My lama has told it to me," she answered.

" And who may your lama be ? "

" A *gomchen* living near the Mo-te-tong lake."

" Does he come here sometimes ? "

" No, never. The lama of Chörten Nyima lives at Tranglung."

" Is he too a *gomchen* ? "

" No, he is a *ngagspa* (magician) and a householder, he is very rich and works many kinds of wonders."

" For instance ? . . ."

" He can cure people or animals or cause them to become ill, even at a distance. He can stop, or bring, rain and hail at will . . . Listen to what he did a few years ago :

" When it was harvest time, the lama ordered the villagers to cut and store his grain. Some of them made answer that they would certainly store his barley, but not until they had lodged their own grain.

" The weather was unsettled and the peasants were afraid of hail-storms, frequent at that time of the year. So instead of begging the lama to protect their fields while they were working for him, a number of them remained obstinate, meaning to cut their own barley first.

" Then the lama used his magic powers. He performed a *dubthab* rite, called up his tutelary deities and animated some *tormas*.[1] As soon as he had ended uttering the magic words, the *tormas* flew away and travelling, like birds, through the air, they circled about, entered the houses of those who had refused to obey immediately and caused much damage. But they passed by the houses of the men who had first harvested the lama's barley, without doing any harm.

" Since then, no one dares to disregard the orders of the lama."

Oh ! to talk with this magician who shot avenging cakes through space ! . . . I was dying with desire to meet him.

Tranglung was not far from Chörten Nyima, the nuns said a day's march would bring me there. But that day's march led through forbidden territory. I had, once more, ventured to cross the border to visit Chörten Nyima, should I push on farther and show myself in a village ? If it was known, was I not likely to be turned out of Sikkim ? There was no question of starting a regular journey across Tibet. I was not at all prepared for this, and as the matter was only one of paying a short visit to a sorcerer, I did not think it worth while compromising my chance of continuing my Tibetan studies in the Himalayas.

So I decided to return after leaving a present for the nuns and another to be sent to the lama of Tranglung.

My regrets were later on wiped off the slate. For two years later I met the sorcerer and was several times his guest at Tranglung.

Autumn was coming on, snow had invaded the passes, nights under the tent became hard. I recrossed the frontier and was delighted to find myself in a house, beside a flaming fire.

[1] Ritualistic cakes.

The house was one of those bungalows built by the British administration for the convenience of foreign travellers, all along the roads of India and the neighbouring countries under British control. Thanks to them, trips that would otherwise have to be organized expeditions, can be easily accomplished.

The Thangu bungalow, 12,000 feet high and about 14 miles to the south of the Tibetan frontier, stood in a pretty solitary place surrounded by forests.

I felt comfortable there and stayed on, little inclined to hasten my return to Gangtok or to Podang. There was not much more for me to learn from the lamas I had been associated with. Perhaps in normal times I would have left the country for China or Japan, but the war which had begun in Europe just as I was leaving for Chörten Nyima, made it rather dangerous to cross seas ploughed by submarines.

I was considering where I should spend the winter, when a few days after my arrival at Tangu, I learned that the *gomchen* of Lachen was in his hermitage, half a day's march from the bungalow.

I immediately decided to pay him a visit. The excursion could not help being interesting. What was this " cave of the clear light " as he called it, and what sort of life did he live there?—I was curious to know.

I had sent back my horse when leaving for Chörten Nyima and made the journey on a yak.[1] I expected to hire a beast at Lachen for my return to Gangtok. Seeing me without a horse, the keeper of the bungalow proposed to bring his own. The animal, he said, was very sure-footed and would climb the rough steep path that led to the *gomchen's* cave perfectly well.

I accepted and the next day was mounted on a small, not too ugly, beast with a red coat.

Horses are bridled and bitted but yaks are not, and when one rides the latter, one's hands are free. I had

[1] The long-haired grunting Tibetan ox.

kept this habit, and thinking of other things, was putting on my gloves, forgetting to hold the reins as I should have done, especially as I was unfamiliar with the horse's character. While I continued dreaming, the animal rose on his fore feet and kicked his heels at the clouds. Shot through the air, I fell down on a piece of ground, luckily covered with grass, below the path. The hard blow made me unconscious.

When I came to myself again, a sharp pain in my back made it impossible to get up.

As to the red horse, his fit of kicking over he had not budged. Quiet as a lamb, with his head turned toward me, he watched with attentive interest the people busying themselves about me and carrying me into my room.

The keeper of the bungalow was most grieved at my reproaches.

" This horse has never before acted like that, I assure you. It is not vicious," he said. " I should not have offered it to you if I had not been sure of it. I have ridden it for several years.

" Watch me. I shall make it trot a little."

Through the window I saw the beast standing quite still.

His master approached it, spoke to it, took hold of the bridle, placing his foot in the stirrup and sprung, not as he intended, into the saddle, but into the air, where a good kick had hurled him.

Less lucky than I had been, he fell upon rocks.

Men ran to help him. He was badly wounded in the head and bleeding freely, but escaped with no bones broken.

Between his groans, he kept repeating, as he was carried home : " Never, never before has this horse acted in that way ! "

This is very astonishing, I thought, as I lay stiff and bruised on my bed.

While I was pondering on this strange manifestation of an animal supposed to be so gentle, my cook came in :

" Reverend lady, this is not natural," he said. " I have questioned the keeper's servant. His master told the truth ; the horse has always been quiet. The *gomchen* must be at the bottom of this. He has demons around him.

" Do not go to his hermitage. Harm will come to you. Return to Gangtok. I shall find you a chair and porters if you cannot ride on horseback."

Another of my men lighted incense sticks and a small altar lamp. Yongden who, at that time, was only fifteen, wept in a corner.

This stage setting looked as if I was dying. I started to laugh.

" Come, come, I am not dead yet," I said. " The demons have nothing to do with the horse. The *gomchen* is not a wicked man. Why are you afraid of him ? Send up dinner early and then let us all go to sleep. To-morrow, we will consider what is to be done."

Two days later the *gomchen*, having heard about my accident, sent me a black mare to take me to him.

No incident marked the trip. Through mountain paths that wound about the woody height, I reached a clearing at the foot of a very steep and barren mountain-side that was crowned by an indented ridge of black rocks.

A little farther up a number of flags showed the place of the hermitage.

The lama came half-way down to welcome me. Then he led me through the loops of the winding path not to his own dwelling, but to another hermitage about a mile away below his own.

He had a large pot of buttered tea brought there and a fire lighted on the ground, in the centre of the room. The word room might prove misleading, for it was

not in a house that the *gomchen* showed me this hospitality, we were in a small-sized cave closed by a wall of
uncemented stones, in which two narrow gaping holes
less than ten inches high served for windows. A few
boards, roughly hewn with an axe, and bound together
with strips of supple bark, formed the door.

I had left Thangu late and it was dusk when I arrived
at the hermitage.

My servants spread my blankets on the bare rock,
and the *gomchen* took them to sleep in a hut which, he
said, was just beside his cave.

Left to myself, I stepped out of my lair. There was
no moon. I could only dimly see the white mass of a
glacier against the shadow at the end of the valley,
and the sombre mountain-tops that towered above my
head toward the starry sky. Below me lay a mist of
darkness from which ascended the roar of a distant
torrent. I did not dare to go far in this blackness ;
the path was only large enough for a foothold and
skirted the void. I had to put further explorations off
until to-morrow.

I went in and lay down. I had scarcely time to roll
myself in my blankets before the light flickered and
went out. The servants had forgotten to fill the lantern
with kerosene. I could find no matches at hand and
being unacquainted with the formation of my prehistoric dwelling I did not dare to move for fear of
hurting myself on some pointed rocks.

A bitter breeze began to blow in through the
" windows " and the cracks of the door. A star peeped
at me through the gap facing my ascetic couch : " Do
you feel comfortable ? " it seemed to say. " What do
you think of a hermit's life ? "

Indeed, its ironical twinkling mocked me !

" Yes, I am all right," I answered. " Thousand
times better than all right . . . ravished, and I feel
that the hermit's life, free of what we call ' the goods

and pleasures of the world,' is the most wonderful of all lives."

Then the star left off mockery. It shone more brightly and growing larger, lighted the whole cave.

> " That I may be capable of dying in this hermitage
> And my wish will be accomplished," [1]

it said, quoting the verses of Milarespa. And an expression of doubt dulled its grave voice.

The next day I went up to the hermitage of the *gomchen*.

This too was a cave, but larger and better furnished than mine. The whole ground under the arched rocky roof had been enclosed by a wall of uncemented stones and provided with a solid door. This entrance room served as a kitchen. At the back of it a natural opening in the rock led into a diminutive grotto. There the *gomchen* had his living-room. A wooden step led to the entrance, for it was higher than the kitchen, and a heavy multi-coloured curtain hid the doorway. There was no aperture to ventilate this inner chamber ; a fissure in the stone through which air may have entered was closed with a glass pane.

The furniture consisted of several wooden chests piled up behind a curtain which formed the back of the anchorite's couch, which was made of large hard cushion placed on the ground. In front of it were two low tables, mere slabs of wood set up on feet, painted in bright colours.

At the back of the grotto, on a small altar, were placed the usual offerings : copper bowls filled with water, grain and butter lamps.

Scrolls of religious painting completely covered the

[1] These verses belong to a poem composed by Milarespa in the eleventh century, while he was living in a cave. It is popular in Tibet and means : If I am capable of living in this hermitage until death, without being tempted to return to the world, I shall have reached my spiritual goal.

rocky uneven walls. Under one of these was hidden the small cabinet in which lamas of the tantric sects keep a demon prisoner.

Outside the cave, half sheltered under protuberant rocks, two cabins had been built that served to store the provisions.

As you can see, the *gomchen's* dwelling was not entirely lacking in comfort.

This eyrie commanded a romantic and absolutely solitary site. The natives held it to be inhabited by evil spirits. They said that some men who had formerly ventured there looking for stray cattle or to work as wood-cutters had strange encounters which sometimes led to fatal consequences.

Such spots are often chosen as dwelling-places by Tibetan hermits. Firstly they deem them a suitable ground for spiritual training. Secondly, they think that they find, there, the opportunity of using their magic powers for the good of men and animals, either by converting malignant evil spirits or by forcibly preventing their harmful activity—at least, simple people ascribe that charitable desire to these " holy ones."

Seventeen years earlier, the lama whom the mountaineers called *Jowo gomchen* (Lord contemplative anchorite) had established himself in the cave where I saw him. Gradually the monks of the Lachen monastery had improved it, till it became as I have just described it.

At first the *gomchen* had lived in total seclusion. The villagers or herdsmen who brought his provisions, left their offerings in front of his door and retired without seeing him. The hermitage was inaccessible during three or four months every year, for the snows would block the valleys that led to it.

When he grew older he kept a young boy with him as attendant, and when I came to live in the cave below his he called near him his initiated consort. As he belonged to the " red hat sect " the *gomchen* was not bound to be a celibate.

I spent a week in my cave, visiting the *gomchen* each day. Though his conversation was full of interest, I was still far more interested in watching the daily life of a Tibetan anchorite.

A few Westerners such as Csöma de Köros or the French Rev. Fathers Huc and Gabet have sojourned in lamaist monasteries, but none has lived with these *gomchens* about whom so many fantastic stories are told.

This was reason enough to incite me to stay in the neighbourhood of the *gomchen*. Added to this was my keen desire to myself experience the contemplative life according to lamaist methods.

However, my wish did not suffice, the consent of the lama was needed. If he did not grant it, there would be no advantage in living near his hermitage. He would shut himself up and I could only look at a wall of rock behind which " something was going on."

So I presented my request to the lama in a manner that agreed with Oriental customs. I begged that he would instruct me in the doctrine he professed. He objected that his knowledge was not extensive enough and that it was useless for me to stay in such an inhospitable region to listen to an ignorant man, when I had had the opportunity of long talks with learned lamas elsewhere.

I strongly insisted, however, and he decided to admit me, not exactly as a pupil, but on a trial as a novice, for a certain time.

I began to thank him, when he interrupted me.

" Wait," he said, " there is a condition ; you must promise me that you will not return to Gangtok, nor undertake any journey toward the south without my permission." [1]

The adventure was becoming exciting. The strangeness of it aroused my enthusiasm.

" I promise," I answered without hesitating.

A rough cabin was added to my cave. Like that of the *gomchen*, it was built of planks roughly hewn with an axe. The mountaineers of this country do not know how to use a saw, nor did they, at that time, care to learn.

A few yards away, another hut was built, containing a small private room for Yongden and a lodging for our servants.

In enlarging my hermitage, I was not altogether yielding to sybaritic tendencies.

It would have been difficult for me to fetch water and fuel and to carry these burdens up to my cave. Yongden, who had just left school, was no more experienced than I at this kind of work. We could not do without servants to help us, therefore an ample supply of provision and a store-house was indispensable since we were facing a long winter during which we should remain completely isolated.

Now these things seem to me small difficulties, but at that time I was making my " début " in the rôle of anchorite, and my son had not yet began his apprenticeship as explorer.

The days passed. Winter came, spreading a coat of immaculate snow on the whole country and, as we had expected, blocking the valleys that led to the foot of our mountain.

The *gomchen* shut himself up for a long retreat. I did the same thing. My single daily meal was placed

---

[1] To go southward meant to go to Gangtok or to Kalimpong, where a few foreigners reside, and even if avoiding these places, to follow a road sometimes frequented by Western tourists coming to these hills from India.

behind a curtain at the entrance of my hut. The boy
who brought it and who later carried away the empty
plates left in silence, without having seen me.

My life resembled that of the Carthusians without the
diversion which they may find in attendance at religious
services.

A bear appeared in search of food and after its first
feelings of astonishment and defiance were over, grew
accustomed to coming and waiting for bread and other
eatable things that were thrown to it.

At last, toward the beginning of April, one of the
boys noticed a black spot moving in the clearing beneath
us and cried out : " a man ! " just as early navigators
must have cried " land ahead ! " We were no longer
blocked in ; letters arrived that had been written in
Europe five months before.

Then it was springtime in the cloudy Himalayas.
Nine hundred feet below my cave rhododendrons
blossomed. I climbed barren mountain-tops. Long
tramps led me to desolate valleys studded with trans-
lucent lakes. . . . Solitude, solitude ! . . . Mind and
senses develop their sensibility in this contemplative life
made up of continual observations and reflections.
Does one become a visionary or, rather, is it not that
one has been blind until then ? . . .

A few miles farther north, beyond the last range of
the Himalayas which the clouds of the Indian monsoon
cannot cross, the sun shone in the blue sky over the
high Tibetan tableland. But, there, the summer was
rainy, cold and short. In September the tenacious
snows already covered the neighbouring heights and
soon our yearly imprisonment began again.

What were the fruits of my long retreat. I should
have found it difficult to explain, yet I learnt a number
of things.

Apart from my study of the Tibetan language with
the help of grammars, dictionaries and talks with the

gomchen, I also read with him the lives of famous Tibetan mystics. He would often stop our reading to tell me about facts he had himself witnessed, which were akin to the stories related in the books. He would describe people he had known, repeating their conversations and telling me about their lives. Thus, while seated in his cabin or in mine, I visited the palaces of rich lamas, entered the hermitages of many an ascetic. I travelled along the roads, meeting curious people. I became, in that way, closely acquainted with Tibet, its inhabitants, their customs and their thoughts : a precious science which was later on to stand me in good stead.

I never let myself be taken in by the illusion that my anchorite's home might become my final harbour. Too many causes opposed any desire of staying there and of laying down, once and for all, the burden of foolish ideas, routine cares and duties to which, like other Westerners, I still fancied myself to be bound.

I knew that the personality of a *gomchenma* which I had taken on, could only be an episode in my life as a traveller, or at the best, a preparation for future liberation.

Sadly, almost with terror, I often looked at the thread-like path which I saw, lower down, winding in the valleys and disappearing between the mountains. The day would come when it would lead me back to the sorrowful world that existed beyond the distant hill ranges, and so thinking, an indescribable suffering lay hold of me.

Besides more important reasons, the impossibility of keeping my servants any longer in this desert, compelled me to leave my hermitage. Yet, before parting once more from Tibet, I wished to visit one of its two great religious centres : Shigatze, which was not a great distance.

The famous monastery of Tashilhunpo lies near

this town. It is the seat of the Grand Lama whom foreigners call the Tashi Lama. Tibetans call him *Tsang Penchen rimpoche*, " the Precious learned man of the province of Tsang." He is considered to be an emanation of Ödpagmed, the mystic Buddha of infinite light, and at the same time, a reincarnation of Subhuti, one of the foremost disciples of the historical Buddha. From a spiritual point of view, his rank equals that of the Dalai Lama. But as spirit, in this world, must often yield precedence to temporal power, so the Dalai Lama autocrat of Tibet is the master.

Foreseeing the possible consequences of this journey I put off starting for Shigatze until I was definitely ready to leave the Himalayas.

I went from my hermitage to Chörten Nyima where I had stayed before. From there I left for Shigatze accompanied by Yongden and a monk who was to act as our servant. We were all three on horseback. Our luggage was placed in large leather saddle-bags, as is customary in Tibet ; a pack-mule carried two small tents and our provisions.

The distance was not great. One could easily accomplish the trip in four days. I intended, however, to travel very slowly so as not to miss anything of interest on my way, and above all, that I might absorb in body and spirit as much as possible of Tibet whose heart I was at last about to penetrate, but probably might never see again.

Since my first visit to Chörten Nyima I had met a son of the lama sorcerer who sent ritualistic cakes flying through the air to punish his disobedient neighbours, and I had been invited, if circumstances permitted, to visit him.

Tranglung, the village where he lived, was no more on the straight road leading from my hermitage to Shigatze than Chörten Nyima, but as I have just said, I intended to profit by all opportunities of seeing in-

teresting things that my adventure in forbidden land
might bring me.

We reached Tranglung at the end of the afternoon.
The village was quite different from any that Tibetan
settlers have built in the Himalayas. It was, indeed,
surprising to find such a complete contrast at so short
a distance. Not only the tall stone houses differed
from the cottages made of wood with thatched roofs
I had been accustomed to see in Sikkim, but the climate,
the soil, the landscape, the people's cast of features and
general look had changed. I was really in Tibet.

We found the sorcerer in his oratory, a huge room
without any windows, scantily enough lighted through
the roof. Near him were several men to whom he was
distributing charms which consisted in toys like small
pigs' heads, made of pink-coloured clay and wrapped in
woollen threads of different shades.

The peasants listened with rapt attention to the
lama's endless instructions on the ways to use these
objects.

When they had gone, the householder-lama, with a
gracious smile, invited me to take tea with him. A
long conversation ensued. I was burning to ask my
host about the flying cakes, but a direct question would
have been against all rules of politeness.

During the few days I remained there, I was told
about a peculiar domestic drama and had the rare
honour of being consulted by an authentic sorcerer.

Here, as in a large number of families in Central
Tibet, polyandry was practised. On the wedding day
of the lama's eldest son, his brothers' names had been
mentioned in the marriage deed and the young girl
had consented to take them all as husbands.

As in most cases, at that time some of the " bride-
grooms " were mere children who had, of course,
not been consulted. They were, nevertheless, legally
married.

Now the sorcerer of Tranglung had four sons. I was not told what the second son thought about his partnership with his elder brother. He was away in journey and most likely all was right with him.

The third son, whom I knew personally, was also travelling somewhere. It was he who had upset the peace of the family.

He was much younger than his first two brothers, being only twenty-five, and he obstinately refused to fulfil his conjugal duties toward the collective wife.

Unfortunately for the lady, this purely nominal husband was far more attractive than the elder two. Not only was he rather better looking than his brothers, but he surpassed them in social position, eloquence, learning, and may be in various other accomplishments that I could not discover.

While the two elders were but wealthy farmers, the third brother enjoyed the prestige attached, in Tibet, to clergy. He was a lama, and more than a common lama. He was a so-called *naljorpa* initiated in occult doctrines, he had the right to wear the five-sided hat of the tantric mystics and the white skirt of the *respas* who are adepts in *tumo*, the art of keeping warm without fire in even the coldest weather.[1]

It was this distinguished husband who refused to fulfil his part, and the offended wife could not resign herself to be disdained.

What made the matter worse was that the young lama courted a girl in one of the neighbouring villages and meant to marry her.

The law of the country permitted him to do so, but if he persisted in this marriage and thus broke up the unity of the family, the young husband would have to leave his father's house and establish a new home for his bride. The priestly son of my host, indeed, did not shrink from the responsibility, and even relied con-

---

[1] Regarding *tumo*, see Chapter VI.

fidently on his earnings as a sorcerer to make that home comfortable.

But by so doing would he not be setting himself up as a rival to his father ? Although the old lama did not express his thought in words, I could read in the expression of his face that he feared a competitor in that obstinate son who refused to please a healthy, sturdy woman of forty, probably not too ugly.

I could not dispute this point, for the wife's features were hidden under a thick coating of butter and soot that made her as black as a negress.

" What on earth is to be done ? " groaned the aged mother of the family.

I had no experience in such matters. Though I had met polyandrist ladies in the west, as a rule no family council was called in to settle the imbroglios that result from their affairs. And in my travels I had only been asked for advice by polygamist gentlemen whose homes had become a seat of war.

Since polygamy is also legal in Tibet, I suggested that the young lama might be persuaded to bring his bride home.

Luckily for me, I was then wearing the respected monastic robe, for only this prevented the jealous, disdained wife from throwing herself upon me.

" Reverend lady," cried the old mother as she wept, " you do not know that our daughter-in-law wanted to send her servants to beat the girl and to disfigure her. We had a hard task to prevent her from doing so. Think of people of our rank doing such thing ! We should be dishonoured for ever afterwards ! "

I could find nothing more to say, so I remarked that it was time for my evening meditation and asked permission to retire to the oratory which the lama had courteously lent to me for the night.

As I was leaving the room I noticed the youngest son, a lad of eighteen, the husband number four. He was seated in a dark corner and looking at the common wife with a strange half-smile, as if he were saying— " Wait a little, old lady, I have worse things in store for you."

During the following days I wandered idly from village to village, sleeping at night in the peasants' houses. I did not try to hide my identity as I was obliged to later on, on the road to Lhasa. No one here seemed to notice that I was a foreigner or, at any rate, no one seemed to attach any importance to the fact.

My road passed the monastery of Patur which appeared to me immense compared with those of Sikkim. One of the ecclesiastic officials invited us to an excellent meal in a dark hall where we enjoyed the company of several monks.

Nothing there, with the exception of the massive buildings several stories high, was entirely new to me. Nevertheless, I understood that Lamaism as I had observed it in Sikkim was only a pale reflection of that which exists in Tibet.

I had vaguely imagined that beyond the Himalayas the country would become wild, but now I began to realize that on the contrary I was coming into touch with a truly civilized people.

Among the various incidents of the journey, the Chi River, swollen by the rains and the melting snows, was difficult to ford in spite of the help of three villagers who took our horses across one by one.

Beyond the village called Kuma extends a long track of desert land. According to the description of our servant who knew the road well I hoped to camp pleasantly near thermal springs, getting a hot bath and warm earth for bedding. A sudden storm compelled us to set up our camp hastily before reaching this desired paradise. First hail attacked us, then the snow began to fall so hard that it soon came nearly up to our knees.

A neighbouring brook overflowed into our camp. I had to spend the night fasting and standing up most of the time on the small island that was the only spot, under my tent, not invaded by the muddy water. So much for the comfortable sleep I had expected.

At last, at a turning of the road where I had stopped to look at a drunken man wallowing in the dust, my eyes suddenly fell on a glorious vision. In the bluish gloaming, the enormous monastery of Tashilhunpo stood in the distance : a mass of white buildings crowned with golden roofs that reflected the last dim rays of the setting sun.

I had reached my goal.

A strange idea had grown up in my mind. Instead of looking for a shelter in one of the inns of the town, I sent my servant to the lama who was responsible for entertaining the monks' visitors or the native students from the Kham province. How could a foreign woman traveller, unknown to him, awaken his interest, and what reason could she have for requesting his good offices ? I had not asked myself this question. I acted entirely on impulse and the result was excellent.

The distinguished official sent a *trapa* to order two rooms for me in the only house next to the monastery. There I settled myself.

The very next day, according to the protocol the requests for an audience with the Tashi Lama were begun. I had to give details of my native country and satisfied them by saying that my birthplace was called Paris.

Which Paris ?—South of Lhasa there is a village called Phagri, that name being pronounced Pari. I explained that " my Paris " was a little farther away from the Tibetan capital and stood westward, but I insisted on the point that starting from Tibet, one could reach my country without crossing the sea and that, consequently, I was not a *Philing* (stranger).

This was a play upon the word *philing* which literally means a continent over sea.

I had stayed so long in the proximity of Shigatze that it was impossible to be unknown there, and, moreover, the fact of having lived as a hermit made me somewhat famous in the country. An audience was immediately granted and the mother of the Tashi Lama invited me to be her guest.

I went over every corner of the monastery and, to pay for my welcome, I offered tea to the several thousand monks living there.

The number of years that have elapsed and the chances I have taken, since that time, to visit the large lamaseries, or even to dwell in them, have dulled my impressions, but when I went round Tashilhunpo, I was deeply struck by every thing I saw.

A barbaric splendour reigned in the temples, halls, and palaces of the dignitaries. No description can give an idea of it. Gold, silver, turquoises, jade were lavishly used on the altars, the tombs, the ornamented doors, the ritualistic implements and even on mere household objects for the use of wealthy lamas.

Should I say that I admired this opulent display? No, for it seemed unrefined and childish : the work of powerful giants whose minds had not grown up.

That first contact with Tibet would even have impressed me unfavourably if I had not had ever present before me the vision of its calm solitudes, and known that they conceal ascetic sages who spurn the vulgarities that are the insignia of grandeur in the eyes of the masses.

The Tashi Lama was most kind to me every time I saw him and showered me with attentions. He knew quite well where *my* Paris was and pronounced the word France with a perfect French accent.

My zeal for the study of Lamaism pleased him very much. He was willing to help my researches in any way. Why should I not stay in Tibet? he asked me.

Why, indeed? Desire was not lacking, but I knew that however great and honoured he was in the country, the gracious Grand Lama had not enough temporal power to obtain permission for me to live in Tibet.

Nevertheless, if I had, at that moment, been as free of ties as I was when I undertook my journey to Lhasa, I might have attempted to avail myself, in some secluded spot, of the protection which was offered to me. But I had not foreseen such an offer. My luggage, notes, collections of photo negatives (why should one think these things important?) had been left behind, some in the care of friends in Calcutta, others in my hermitage. How many things remained for me to learn, how great was the mental transformation necessary to enable me to become, a few years later, a joyful tramp in the wilds of Tibet.

While at Shigatze I met the masters who had educated the Tashi Lama : his professor of secular sciences and he who had initiated him into the mystic doctrines. I also came to know a contemplative mystic, the spiritual guide of the Tashi Lama, highly revered by him, who —if we must believe the stories told about him—ended his life, a few years later, in a miraculous way.[1]

During my visit to Shigatze, the temple that the Tashi Lama meant to dedicate to the future Buddha Maitreya, the lord of infinite compassion, was nearing completion.

I saw the huge image placed in a hall with galleries that allowed the devotees to circle around it on the ground floor on a level with the feet and successively ascending the first, second and third galleries, up to its belt, its shoulders and its head.

Twenty jewellers were setting the enormous ornaments that were to adorn the gigantic Maitreya. They were re-setting the jewels presented by the ladies belonging

[1] See the end of Chapter VIII.

to the nobility of Tsang, the mother of the Tashi Lama at their head, with the gift of all her sets of precious stones.

I spent delightful days in the palaces of the Tashi Lama in Shigatze and the neighbourhood. I talked with men of widely different characters. The novelty of what I saw and heard, the special psychic atmosphere of the place, enchanted me. I have seldom enjoyed such blissful hours.

At last, the dreaded moment came. Taking with me books, notes, presents and the robe of a graduate lama that the Tashi Lama had bestowed on me as a kind of diploma of Doctor *honori causa* of the Tashil-hunpo university, I left Shigatze, gazing sadly at the immense monastery as it disappeared behind the same turning of the road from which it had first appeared to me.

I went on to Narthang to visit the largest of the printing establishments in Tibet. The number of engraved wooden plates used for the printing of the various religious books was prodigious. Set up on shelves, in rows, they filled a huge building.

The printers, spattered with ink up to their elbows, sat upon the floor as they worked, while in other rooms monks cut the paper according to the size required for each kind of book.

There was no haste ; chatting and drinking of buttered tea went on freely. What a contrast to the feverish agitation in our newspaper printing-rooms.

From Narthang I sought out the hermitage of a *gomchen* who had been good enough to send me an invitation. I found the anchorite's abode in a desolate place on a hill, near the lake Mo-te-tong. It consisted of a spacious cave, to which one room after another had been added, till it looked like a small fort.

The present *gomchen* had succeeded his master who himself had succeeded his own spiritual father, famous

as a wonder-worker. Gifts of devotees to three gener-
ations of lama magicians had led to the accumulation,
in the hermitage, of a good number of objects affording
comfort, and life could be passed there quite pleasantly ;
that is, from the point of view of a Tibetan, born in
the wilds and accustomed since his youth to live as the
disciple of an anchorite.

Such was the case of my host. He had never been to
Lhasa nor to Shigatze, nor travelled anywhere in Tibet,
and knew nothing of the world outside his cave. His
master had lived there for more than thirty years, and
when he died the present hermit had walled himself in.

By walled in, one must understand that one door
only gave access to the hermitage enclosure, and this
door the lama never approached. Two lower rooms
under the rock—kitchen, store-room and servant's
quarter all together—opened on an inner courtyard
closed in, on the side which gave on to the precipice
by a high wall. Above these rooms an upper cave was
the private apartment of the lama, which was reached
by a ladder and a trap-door in the floor. This chamber
stood on a small terrace, also closed by walls. So the
recluse could take a little exercise or sun himself without
being seen by anyone outside and without himself
seeing anything but the sky overhead.

The anchorite mitigated the severity of his seclusion
by receiving visitors and chatting with them, but he
added to its austerity by never lying down to sleep,
spending the nights in a *gamti*.

There exist, in Tibet, special seats which are called
gamti (box seat) or *gomti* (meditation seat). These are
square boxes, each side being about 25 or 30 inches
long and one of the sides being higher to form the back
of the seat. At the bottom of the box a cushion is
placed on which the ascetic sits cross-legged. Often he
does not allow himself to lie against the back of the seat,
and in order to support his body, either while sleeping

or during long meditation, he uses the " meditation rope " (*sgomthag*). It is a sash usually made in woollen cloth, which one passes under the knees and behind the nape of the neck, or with which one encircles the knees and the back. Many *gomchens* spend days and nights in that way, without reclining or stretching their limbs to sleep.

They doze sometimes but never fall fast asleep, and except during these short periods of drowsiness, they do not stop their meditation.

I had several interesting conversations with the hermit and then I turned back towards the frontier.

The British resident at Gangtok had already sent a letter by peasants from Sikkim ordering me to leave Tibetan soil. I had not obeyed because I wanted to end my trip as I had planned it, but now I had accomplished my object, and as I had foreseen the consequences of a prolonged incursion on the forbidden territory, I was ready to bid farewell to the Himalayas.

A second letter commanding me to leave the vicinity of the Tibetan border found me already on the road to India *en route* for the Far East.

CHAPTER III

A FAMOUS TIBETAN MONASTERY

ONCE more I have crossed the Himalayas, proceeding downward to India.

It is sad to leave the bewitching region where during several years I have lived a most fantastic and captivating life : though, wonderful as this entrance house of Tibet proved to be, I know that I am far from having obtained even a glimpse of all the strange mystic doctrines and practices which are hidden from the profane in the hermitages of the " Land of Snow." My journey to Shigatze has also revealed me the scholastic Tibet, its monastic universities, its immense libraries. How many things are left for me to learn ! And I am leaving . . .

I go to Burma and spend days of retreat on the Sagain hills with the Kamatangs, the contemplative monks of one of the most austere Buddhist sects.

I go to Japan where I dive into the calm of the Tōfoku-ji, a monastery of that Zen sect which, for centuries, has collected the intellectual aristocracy of the country.

I go to Korea. Panya-an ; the " monastery of wisdom " concealed in the heart of the forest opens its door to me.

When I went there to beg temporary admittance, heavy rains had washed the path away. I found the Panya-an monks busy repairing it. The novice sent by his abbot to introduce me stopped before one of the workers as muddy as his companions, bowed respectfully and said a few words to him. The digger, leaning on his spade, looked at me intently for a while, then nodded his consent and began to work again, without taking any more notice of me.

"He is the head of the hermitage," my guide told me. "He is willing to give you a room."

The next day when I returned to Panya-an, I was led to a completely empty cell. My blanket spread on the floor was to be my couch, while my dressing-case could be used as a table. Yongden was to share the room of a young novice of his age, which, excepting for a few books on a shelf, was as little furnished as mine.

The daily routine included eight hours of meditation divided in four periods of two hours—eight hours of study and manual work—eight hours devoted to sleep, meals and recreation according to individual tastes.

Each day, a little before 3 a.m., a monk went round the houses, striking a wooden instrument to waken his brothers.

Then, all met in the assembly room, where they sat in meditation facing the wall.

Diet was truly ascetic . . . rice and some boiled vegetables without any flavouring. Even the vegetables were often missing and the meal consisted of plain rice alone.

Silence was not compulsory as it is amongst the Trappist, but the monks seldom spoke. They did not feel the need of talking nor of spending their energy in outward manifestations. Their thoughts remained fixed on secret introspections and their eyes had the inward gaze of the Buddha's images.

I go to Peking. I live in Peling-sse, formerly an imperial mansion, now a Buddhist monastery. It is situated next the large Lamaist temple and near the stately temple of Confucius, several miles distant from the Legations. There, Tibet calls to me again.

For years I have dreamt of far-away Kum-Bum

without having dared hope I would ever get there. Yet the journey is decided. I will cross the whole of China to reach its north-western frontier into Tibetan land.

I join a caravan composed of two rich lamas and their respective retinues, who are returning to Amdo, a Chinese trader of the remote Kansu province with his servants, and a few monks and laymen who are glad to benefit from the protection that numbers ensure on the unsafe roads.

The journey is most picturesque. Besides other incidents my travelling companions supply abundant matter for amazement.

One day, the gigantic head of our caravan entertains some Chinese harlots at the inn where we have put up. Slender and short, clad in pale-green pants and pink coats, they enter the lama's room like a family of Tom Thumbs going into the Ogre's den.

The "lama" is a *ngagspa*, a follower of the very heterodox sect of the magicians, scarcely belonging to the clergy, and a married man.

A harsh and noisy bargaining takes place with the door wide open. The cynical, yet candid terms of the borderer of Koko-nor wilderness are translated into Chinese by his imperturbable secretary-interpreter. Finally, five Chinese dollars are accepted as honorarium ; one of the dolls stays over night.

Our libertine companion is also hot tempered. Another day he quarrels with a Chinese officer. The soldiers of a neighbouring post invade our inn, guns in hand. The lama calls his retainers, who arrive with their own guns. The inn-keeper falls prostrate at my feet beseeching me to intervene.

With the help of the Chinese trader, a member of our travelling party, who knows Tibetan and acts as my interpreter, I succeed in convincing the soldiers that it is beneath their dignity to pay the least attention to the stupid actions of a barbarian from the Koko-nor wilds.

Then I remonstrate with the lama against a man of his rank compromising himself with vulgar soldiers.

Peace is restored.

I become acquainted with civil war and robbery. I endeavour to nurse wounded men left without help. One morning I see a bunch of heads—those of newly beheaded robbers—hung above the door of our inn. That sight arouses philosophical thoughts about death in my placid son, which he quietly expounds to me.

The road ahead of us is blocked by the fighting troops. I think I shall be able to avoid the vicinity of the battles by going to a town named Tungchow situated several miles away from the direct road to Sian-fu.

The day after my arrival Tungchow is besieged. I could watch storming enemies climbing the city walls on high ladders, while defenders hurled stones down on them. I seemed to be living in an ancient picture depicting the wars of olden times.

I escape from the besieged town during a tempest when the army remains sheltered on the other side of the walls. My cart rushes madly through the night ; we arrive at the shore of a river beyond which we expect to be in safety. We call the ferry-man. For answer, shots are fired at us from the other bank.

I have an amusing remembrance of a tea-party with the governor of Shensi. The enemy surrounds the city. Tea is served by soldiers with guns on their shoulders and revolvers in their belts, ready to resist an attack that m y occur at any minute. Yet, the guests talk calmly with that exquisite and apparently serene courtesy which is one of the fruits of the old Chinese education.

We discuss philosophical questions, one of the officials speaks French perfectly and acts as my interpreter. Whatever the feelings of the governor and his party may be in this tragic situation, their faces remain smiling. The conversation around the tea-table is that of litterati enjoying the intellectual game of exchanging subtle thoughts in a dispassionate way.

How wonderfully refined and civilized are the Chinese and how lovable, in spite of the faults that can be found in them !

I came out, at last, from the troubled area. I am in Amdo, settled in the precinct of the Pegyai Lama's palace, in the Kum-Bum monastery. . . . Again, I plunge into Tibetan life.

> " Salutation to the Buddha.
> In the language of the gods and in that of the lus,[1]
> In the language of the demons and in that of the men,
> In all the languages which exist,
> I proclaim the Doctrine."

A few lads stand on the flat roof of the assembly hall, they have hastily recited the liturgic formula and, simultaneously, lift the conches to their lips. Each of them take turn at breathing, while his companions continue to blow. And so is produced an uninterrupted bellowing whose sonorous waves, rising and falling in successive crescendi and diminuendi, spread over the still sleeping monastery.

Above the peristyle of the hall the young novices, wrapped in the clerical toga, are silhouetted on the bright starry sky like a row of unearthly dark beings who have alighted to call the dead from their slumbers. And, truly, the silent *gompa* with its many low-roofed whitewashed houses appears, in the night, as a vast necropolis.

The musical summons dies away. Moving lights appear through the windows of the princely *garbas* [2] and noises arise from the *tashas* [3] squatting around

---

[1] Snake demi-gods who live in the lakes and the ocean and are said to be the owners of fabulous wealth.

[2] Grand Lama's mansions.   [3] Houses of ordinary monks.

them. Doors open, a hurried stamping of feet is heard
in all the streets and avenues of the monastic city :
the lamas are going to the morning assembly.

As they reach the precincts of the hall, the sky grows
pale, the day breaks. Taking off their felt boots,
which they leave outside, piled here and there, each
of them hastens towards his place.

In large monasteries, the gathering monks number
several thousands. A strange, shabby, ill-smelling crew,
offering a strange contrast to the sumptuousness of the
gold brocade vests worn by the dignitaries and the
jewelled cloak and rod of office of the *tsogs chen shalngo*,
the elected ruler of the *gompa*.

Hanging from the high ceiling, from the galleries
and against the tall pillars, scrolls of painting show
countless Buddhas and deities, while a host of other
worthies, saints, gods and demons, may be vaguely
discerned on the frescoes which decorate the walls of
the dark edifice.

At the bottom of the hall, behind rows of butter
lamps, shine softly the gilded images of former Grand
Lamas and the massive silver and gold reliquaries which
contain their ashes or mummified bodies. A mystic
atmosphere envelops men and things, veiling all vulgar
details, idealizing the attitudes and the faces. Whatever knowledge one may have acquired regarding the
shortcomings of many of the monks assembled there,
the sight of the assembly itself is most impressive.

Now, every one is seated cross-legged, motionless,
the lamas and officials on their thrones whose heights
vary according to their rank, and the common ecclesiastic folk on long benches nearly on the level of the
floor.

Chanting begins, deep toned in a slow rhythm.
Bells, wailing *gyalings*,[1] thundering *ragdong*,[2] tiny drums

---

[1] A musical instrument like a hautboy.
[2] A kind of huge Theban trumpet.

and big drums on which the cadence is beaten, at times accompany the psalmody.

The little novices, seated at the extremity of the benches near the door, hardly dare to breathe. They know the hundred-eyed *chöstimpa*[1] soon detects any chatting or playful gestures, and fear-inspiring are the rod and whip that are hung at hand, next his high seat.

Chastisement, however, is not for little boys only, and full-grown members of the religious Order may well receive at times their good share of it.

I have witnessed queer performances of that kind. One of them took place in a monastery of the Sakya sect during a solemn festival.

Several hundred monks were assembled in the *tso-khang* (assembly hall) and the usual liturgy and music was going on, when three men communicated something to each other by gesture. As they were not seated on the front bench, they thought themselves sufficiently screened by the monks placed in front of them. The slight motion of their hands and the looks they exchanged would, they believed, not be noticed by the *chöstimpa*. But most likely, the patron gods of the lamaseries invest these stern officials with a supernormal keenness of sight : the *chöstimpa* had seen the culprits and started towards them.

He was a tall, dark Khampa[2] with athletic features, and standing on his high seat, as on a pedestal, looked like a bronze statue. Majestically, he took down his whip, descended from his throne and strode across the hall with the air of a destroying angel.

He passed before me, tucking his toga above his elbows. The whip which he clutched in his large hand was made of several leather ropes, each the size of a forefinger and ended by a knot.

[1] An official who enforces discipline in the *gompa*, especially during the religious ceremonies.
[2] A native of Kham, in Eastern Tibet.

Having reached the place where the culprits awaited their unavoidable chastisement, he grasped their necks from behind, one after the other, lifting them brutally from the bench.

It being impossible even to think of escape, the resigned fellows moved to the passage between the rows of monks and there prostrated themselves, their forehead against the floor.

A few strokes of the whip sounded on the back of each one and the fearful personage, with the same supreme dignity of demeanour, returned to his seat.

However, only minor offences, as breach of silence, incorrect attitude, etc., are punished in the assembly hall. More severe penalties are carried out elsewhere.

A much appreciated intermission cuts the long service : tea is brought in steaming hot, flavoured with butter and salt, according to the Tibetan taste. It is carried in large wooden buckets whose bearer walks along the rows. Each *trapa* produces his own bowl, kept till then under his vest next his skin. The bowls are of special patterns which vary according to the sects. No china or silver ornamented bowls are allowed at the assembly. The highest dignitaries must use a plain wooden one. Yet even that rule, meant as a symbolic remembrance of the renunciation and poverty enjoined by the original Buddhist discipline, is avoided by the astute lamas. The bowl of the richest among them is truly in wood, but some of these wooden utensils, made of special timbers out of the excrescences that grow on the trunk of certain trees, are highly prized and may cost as much as the equivalent of £6 in local currency.

In wealthy *gompas*, the tea is generously buttered and the monks bring with them, to the assembly, a small pot in which they blow a certain quantity of the butter that rises to the surface of the liquid. This they use at home or sell to be put again in tea or to fill the lamps used in the house. Not the altar lamps, for which new butter is required.

Trapas bring also some *tsampa* [1] from their own houses, and this flour, together with the tea provided free, constitutes their breakfast.

Upon certain days, *tsampa* and a piece of butter are distributed with the tea, or a soup served instead of tea, or even the meal includes both tea and soup.

The inmates of the famous lamaseries enjoy a rather large number of these special breakfasts offered by rich pilgrims or by wealthy Grand Lamas belonging to the monastery itself.

On such occasions, hills of *tsampa* and huge heaps of pieces of butter, sown in sheep's stomachs, fill the *gompa's* kitchen to overflowing. The spectacle is still "greater" when it is a question of soup, for then a number of sheep's carcasses amounting sometimes to several hundred are cut up for the gargantuan broth.

While living in Kum-Bum and in other monasteries— though, as a woman, I was not allowed to take part at the monastic banquet—a pot full of the special dainty of the day was brought to my house whenever I wished.

It was in that way that I became acquainted with a certain Mongolian dish made of mutton, rice, Chinese dates, butter, cheese, curds, sugar-candy, and various other ingredients and spices, all boiled together.

This was not the only sample of their culinary science with which the lamaist " chefs " treated me.

A distribution of money takes place, sometimes, during the meal. Mongolians greatly outdo Tibetans in their liberality to the clergy. I have seen some of them leave more than ten thousand Chinese dollars at the Kum-Bum monastery during their visit.

So, day after day, in the frosty morning or the warm summer dawns, that peculiar lamaist matins is per-

---

[1] Flour made with roasted barley, which is the staple food of all Tibetans.

formed in countless *gompas* all over the immense terri-
tories [1] of which Tibet itself is but a small part.

Each morning, half-awake lads, together with their
elders, are bathed in that curious atmosphere which
is a blend of mysticism, gastronomic preoccupations
and anticipations of a dole. That beginning of the
day in the *gompa* gives us an idea of the character of
the whole lamaist monastic life. In the latter we find
also, always present, the same ill-assorted elements :
subtle philosophy, commercialism, lofty spirituality and
eager pursuit of coarse enjoyments ! And these are
so closely interwoven that one endeavours in vain to
completely disentangle them.

Youngsters brought up amongst these conflicting
streams of influence yield to one or other of them
according to their natural propensities and the way
in which they are directed by their masters. Out of
that early, rather incoherent monastic training, issue
a small élite of litterati, a number of idle, dull, sleepy
fellows, wanton braggarts, and a few mystics who
resort to lonely hermitages and life-long meditations.

The majority of the Tibetan *trapas* and *lamas* do
not, however, belong exclusively to any of these different classes, they rather harbour in their mind—at
least in potentiality—all of these various characteristics,
and, according to the circumstances, one or another
appear on the stage to play its part.

Plurality of personalities in the apparently single
individual is, of course, not peculiar to Tibetan lamas,
but it exists in them in a remarkably high degree, and
on that account their discourses and behaviour provide
the attentive observer with continual matter for wonder.

Tibetan Buddhism differs widely from Buddhism as
seen in Ceylon, Burma and even China or Japan. So,
also, lamaist monastic dwellings have their own quite

[1] The whole of Mongolia, parts of Siberia, of Manchuria and
even of European Russia.

peculiar aspect. As I have already mentioned, in Tibetan language, a monastery is called a *gompa*,[1] that is to say a " house in the solitude," and this name is entirely justified.

Proudly isolated on summits beaten by the wind, amidst wild landscapes, Tibetan *gompas* look vaguely aggressive, as if bidding defiance to invisible foes, at the four corners of the horizon. Or, when squatting between high mountain ranges, they often assume a disquieting air of laboratories where occult forces are manipulated.

That twofold appearance corresponds to a certain reality. Though nowadays the thoughts of the monks may be mostly occupied by mercantile and other vulgar cares, Tibetan *gompas* were not, originally, intended for such earthly-minded folk.

The hard conquest of a world other than that perceived through the senses, transcendental knowledge, mystic realizations, mastery over occult forces, such were the aims for the pursuit of which were built the lamaist towering citadels and those enigmatic cities concealed in the maze of snowy hills. Yet nowadays mystics and magicians must be looked for mostly out of the monasteries. In order to escape an atmosphere that has become too much permeated by material cares and pursuits, they emigrate to more remote, inaccessible places, and the discovery of hermitages entails, sometimes, all the hardships of a real exploration. Nevertheless, with a very few exceptions, anchorites begin life as novices in the regular religious Order.

The boys whom their parents destine for a clerical life are taken to the monastery at the age of eight or nine. They are given as wards to a monk of their own family parentage or, failing a relative in the monastery, to some intimate friend. As a rule, the

1 Spelling *dgon pa*.

tutor of the novice is his first teacher and, in many cases, his only one.

However, wealthy parents, who can afford generous recognition to the tuition of an erudite monk, either entrust the guardianship of their sons to such a one, or make an arrangement to the effect that the lads be sent to him to be taught at appointed hours. Sometimes, also, they beg for their sons the favour of being admitted as boarders in the house of an ecclesiastic dignitary. In that case, the latter will more or less supervise the youths' education.

These novices are supported by their parents, who send to their tutor's house the usual supply of butter, tea, *tsampa* and meat.

Beside substantial provisions, rich Tibetans send to their sons various dainties : cheese, dried fruits, sugar, molasses, cakes, etc. Such treasures play a great part in the everyday life of the boys lucky enough to possess them. They allow of countless bartering, and many services can be bought from poor and gourmand fellow-students with a handful of shrunk, stone-like apricots, or a few bits of desiccated mutton.

Young Tibetans begin, in that way, the apprenticeship in the tricks of trade while they are spelling out the first pages of religious treatises. One may guess that their progress in the former science is, often, more rapid than in the latter.

Entirely destitute boys become *geyog*,[1] that is to say that in exchange for menial work, they get teaching and sometimes also food and clothing at the house of a monk. Needless to add that, in this case, lessons are, as a rule, rare and brief ! The professor, who is often illiterate or nearly so, can only teach the lads to memorize parts of the liturgic recitations, which they mangle dreadfully, and whose meaning they will never understand.

[1] " Servant of virtue " or " virtuous servant."

Numbers of *geyog* remain without being taught anything at all. It is not that their work as servants is
heavy, but the carelessness natural to their age prevents
them from asking for lessons which are not imposed
on them, and they spend their many leisure hours
playing with other little fellows of their own condition.

As soon as they are admitted to a monastery the
novices have a share in the income of the *gompa* [1] and
in the gifts made by the devotees to the community.

If, when growing older, the novice feels inclined to
study and if circumstances allow, he may seek admission to one of the monastic colleges. There are four
of them in all, large lamaseries.

As for the youths who belong to smaller *gompas*
where no such colleges exist, they may at any time
get leave to go and study elsewhere.

The subjects taught are : Philosophy and Meta-
physics in the *Tsen ñid* college ; Ritual and Magic
in the *Gyud* college ; Medicine, according to Chinese
and Indian methods, in the *Men* college ; and the
Sacred Scriptures in the *Do* college.

Grammar, arithmetic and several other sciences are
taught outside of these schools by private professors.

Both junior and senior students of philosophy hold
discussions at regular dates. Often the latter take
place in the open, and in all large lamaseries a shady
garden, surrounded by walls, is reserved for that
purpose.

Ritualistic gestures accompany the controversies and
are a lively part of it. There are peculiar ways of
turning one's rosary around one's arm, clapping one's
hands and stamping when putting a question : there
are other prescribed ways of jumping when giving an

[1] As I have given in another book, *My Journey to Lhasa*, a large
number of details regarding the organization of the lamaseries,
their source of revenues, information about their tenants, etc., I
omit them here.

answer or replying to one interrogation by another. And so, though the words exchanged are usually but quotations, and only do honour to the memory of the controversialists, their antics and challenging attitudes create the illusion of passionate debates.

Yet, all members of the Philosophical College are not mere parrots. Amongst them one finds eminent litterati and subtle thinkers. They too can quote for hours from countless books, but they are also able to descant on the import of the old texts and bring forward the results of their own reflections.

A noteworthy feature of these public contests is that, at the end of them, he who has been acknowledged the victor is carried round the assembly riding on the shoulders of his defeated opponent.

The College of Ritualistic Magic is generally the most sumptuously housed of the *gompa's* scholastic institutions, and its Fellows, called *gyud pas*, are held in high esteem. They are believed to know the special technique which enables one to propitiate the fierce deities and subjugate evil spirits ; and the protection of their monasteries is entrusted to them. The *gyud pas* belonging to the two great *Gyud* Colleges that exist at Lhasa, act in the same capacity on behalf of the State. Their appointed duty is to attract prosperity to Tibet and its ruler, as well as to shelter them from all bad influences and malignant undertakings.

Gyud pas are also entrusted with the task of honouring and serving the aboriginal gods or demons, whose good will or neutrality had been previously won by promising them perpetual worship and attendance to their needs. They must, also by their magic art, keep the untamed evil spirits bound in captivity.

Though for lack of another word in the English language we are compelled to refer to the *gompas* as monasteries, they do not in the least resemble a Christian monastery. Excepting the fact that the inmates of

the *gompa* are celibates and that the monastery owns
property, I hardly see a point in common between
the Christian and the Lamaist religious Orders.

As to celibacy, it must be remembered that all
monks of the *Ge-lugs-pa* sect, familiarly called " yellow
cap " sect, are celibate. But in the various " red cap "
sects celibacy is only enjoined on fully ordained monks
called *gelongs*. Married lamas or *trapas* keep, outside
of the *gompa*, a home where their family lives. They
have also a dwelling-place in their respective monasteries where they stay occasionally, at the time of
religious festivals or when retiring for a period of
religious exercises or meditation. Wives are never
allowed to cohabit with their husbands in the enclosure
of a monastery.

Lamaseries are meant, just as the *vihāras* of Ceylon
or the monasteries of any Buddhist country, to house
people who pursue a spiritual aim. That aim is neither
strictly defined nor imposed and common to all *gompa's*
dwellers. Humble or lofty, as it may be, the goal of
each monk remains his secret and he may endeavour
to reach it by any means he chooses. No devotional
exercises in common, nor uniform religious practices
are enjoined on the inmates of the lamaseries. The
only rules that exist are of a lay character, relating
to the good order, the keeping up of the monastery,
or the attendance of the members of the *gompa* to
daily or occasional meetings. These assemblies themselves have nothing to do with the celebration of a
cult in which each one present joins for his own sake
and from which he expects good fruits for himself.
When lamaist monks meet in the assembly hall, it is,
beside hearing communications from the monastic
authorities, to read parts of the Scriptures for the
benefit of the monastery, the State, or the supporters
and occasional benefactors of the *gompa*. Such readings
are credited with happy results in bringing prosperity,

averting illness and calamities, and keeping away malevolent beings.

As for the ritualistic ceremonies, all of a magic nature, they are also performed for some aim in which the celebrants have no share. It is even believed that none can perform them for his own sake. The most proficient *gyud pas* are compelled to call a colleague when they wish to have these rites celebrated on their behalf.

Magic for personal purposes, meditation and exercises connected with spiritual life, are accomplished privately by each monk in his own dwelling. None but the teacher whom he has chosen has the least right to interfere in that matter. No one either has any right to ask any account of the lama's views. He may believe whatever doctrine he deems true, he may even be an utter unbeliever ; this concerns himself only.

There is no church or chapel in the lamaist monasteries, for, as it has been explained, no worship is done in which the laity joins or even merely attends.

Beside the assembly hall there exist a number of *lha khangs*, that is to say " god's houses." Each of them is dedicated to a deity or to some Buddhist worthies, historical or mythical. Those who wish it pay courteous visits to the images of these exalted persons. They light a lamp or burn incense in their honour, salute them with three prostrations and depart. Favours are often begged during such visits, but not always, and a number of these polite meetings are the outcome of disinterested reverence.

Before the images of the Buddha boons are not requested, for Buddhas have passed beyond the " world of desire " and, in fact, beyond all worlds. But vows are taken and spiritual wishes expressed such as : " May I be, in this life or in the next one, able to distribute a quantity of alms, to contribute efficaciously

to the welfare of many," or "may I be able to understand the meaning of Buddha's doctrine and to live
accordingly."

There are a larger number than one would suppose
who, when raising a small lamp in the gesture of an
offering before the Buddha's image, ask for no more
than spiritual insight. Though they may make but
little practical effort to reach it, the mystic ideal of
salvation through enlightenment remains alive amongst
Tibetans.

To the complete spiritual freedom of the lamaist
monk corresponds a nearly equal material liberty.

The members of a monastery do not live in community, but each one in his own house or apartment,
and each one according to his own means.

Poverty is not enjoined to them as it was to the
early Buddhist monks. I must even say that the lama
who voluntarily would practise it would enjoy no special
regard on that account; quite the opposite. Anchorites
only may indulge in that kind of "eccentricity."

Yet, absolute renunciation, as India—and may be
India alone—has thoroughly understood it, is not an
ideal altogether foreign to Tibetans,[1] nor do they fail
to pay homage to its loftiness. Stories of youths of
good family who leave their home and take to the
life of religious mendicants (and especially, the story
of Siddhartha Gautama, the Buddha, who gave up
his estate and princely rank) are listened to with the
deepest reverence and admiration. But these stories,
relating to facts which took place in times long gone,
are regarded as belonging to another world that has
no connection whatever with that of their wealthy
and honoured lamas.

One may be ordained in any grade of the religious
Order without becoming a member of a monastery,

[1] The ascetic poet Milarespa (eleventh century), the most
popular of Tibetan saints, is an instance.

though this seldom happens, and only when the candidate is of an age to know what he is doing and intends
to live as an anchorite.

Admission in a *gompa* does not confer any right to
free lodging therein. Each monk must build his dwelling or purchase it from a previous owner, unless he
inherits it from a relative or from his own teacher.
Poor monks rent a room or two in the house of a more
wealthy colleague. In the case of students and of
learned or old *trapa*, lodging is often granted free to
them in the houses of rich lamas.

The poorest ones who, beside a shelter, need also
board, engage themselves in the service of wealthy
members of the monastery. Their condition depends
on their ability ; some may be clerks, others cooks, or
stable boys. Those who succeed in becoming stewards of
a *tulku*, often become important and wealthy persons.

Learned monks belonging to poor families may earn
their livelihood as teachers, as artists if they are gifted
at painting religious pictures, as resident chaplains at
the houses of rich lamas or laymen, or by occasionally
performing religious ceremonies at householders' homes.
Besides these various professions, divination, astrology,
drawing horoscopes may be reckoned amongst their
sources of income.

The lama doctors create very favourable situations
for themselves if they show their skill by curing a
sufficient number of distinguished people. But even
with a smaller amount of success, the medical profession
is a lucrative one.

However, the profession which looks the most attractive to many is trade. The great majority of those
lamaist monks who are not especially religious minded,
become traders. If they lack the money needed to
undertake a business of their own, they engage themselves as secretaries, accountants, or even as mere
servants of a trader.

Transacting business, in a more or less unostentatious way, is to a certain extent allowed in the monasteries. As for those of their members who have a really big business they obtain leave from the authorities of the monastery to travel with their caravan, and open shops or branches wherever they like.

One may think that trade does not fit in very well with religious pursuits, but we must also remember a monk has very seldom chosen his own profession. Most of them are led to the monastery as little boys, and it would be unjust to reproach them for not following a mystic avocation which has never been their own choice.

Trading on a large scale is carried on by the lamaseries themselves as a means of increasing their income. They barter and sell the products of their land and cattle which they receive from their tenants. To these are added the revenue derived from the big collections called *kartik*. These collections take place at regular intervals, each year or every two or three years. The lamas resort, also, to occasional appeals when building a new monastery, or a new temple in an already established lamasery, and for various other purposes. Small monasteries merely send some of their monks in the neighbouring regions to beg alms, but in large *gompas*, going to *kartik* takes all the forms of an expedition. Groups of *trapas* may go from Tibet to Mongolia, spend months travelling across the country and return like triumphant warriors with hundreds of horses, cattle, gold, silver and goods of every description, all offerings from the devotees.

They have a peculiar custom of entrusting, for a time, a certain amount of money, or a quantity of goods, to an official of the monastery who must traffic with that capital so as to provide for certain special expenses out of his profit. As an instance, he must supply during one year, or more, the butter needed to keep burning the lamps of a particular *lha khang*, or he must give a fixed number of meals to the whole community or, again, support the expenses of building repairs, horse fodder, reception of guests and many other things. At the end of the period, be it one year or three, the capital entrusted to him must be given back. If the man who has received it, as a deposit, has been able to make more profit than was needed to cover his expenses, so much the better for him, he can keep the balance. But if he has expended more than his profit, he must pay it from his own pocket. In any case, the capital must remain intact.

The administration of a large monastery is as complicated as the administration of a town. Beside a population of several thousand men living between their walls, these *gompas* own large estates inhabited by tenants to whom they owe protection and over whom they have the right of justice. A number of elected officials, helped by clerks and a kind of police body, all clerics, assume the care of these temporal affairs.

A big personage called *tsogs chen shal ngo* is the elected head of the *gompa*. To him belongs the infliction of punishments on those who infringe monastic rules. It is he who grants leave, dispensations and admission to the *gompa*. He is assisted by several other officials. All of them wear ceremonial cloaks adorned with precious stones and carry massive silver sticks encrusted with golden ornaments and inlaid with turquoise and coral.

The policemen, called *dobdobs*, are well worth special mention. They are recruited amongst the athletic unlettered braggarts whose fathers have placed them as children in the monastery when their place ought rather to be in the barracks.

Brave with the wild rashness of brutes, always on the look out for quarrels and mischief, these impudent scoundrels have all the picturesque characteristics of medieval ruffians.

The badge which they favour is dirt. Grease, they think, increases the martial appearance of a man. A true brave never washes himself, nay more, he blackens his face with the greasy soot that sticks on the bottom of the cauldrons, till he looks like a real negro.

Sometimes poverty is responsible for the ragged garments worn by the *dobdob*, but he often deliberately tears his monastic robe, to look—he thinks—more terrible.

Nearly always when putting on a new dress, his first care is to make it greasy. Tradition commands it. However costly the material may be, the *dobdob* kneading butter in his black hands, spreads it all over his new clothes.

These strange fellows consider that nothing can be more elegant than a robe and a toga which has become as shining as velvet and stiff as armour, by the careful and constant application of dirt and filth.

The Miraculous Tree of Tsong Khapa

The monastery of Kum-Bum owes its celebrity to a miraculous tree. I borrow from the Kum-Bum chronicles the following details about it.

In 1555, the Reformer Tsong Khapa, founder of the Gelugspa sect,[1] was born in Amdo, in North-eastern Tibet, at the place where now stands the great lamasery of Kum-Bum.

A short time after the child's birth the Lama dubchen Karma Dorje prophesied that his career would be an extraordinary one and advised his parents to keep the spot where his mother had been delivered perfectly clean. A little later, a tree began to grow there.

Even to-day, beaten earth is used as the floor in

[1] " Yellow hats " sect. Literally *Gelugspa* means " those who have virtuous customs."

most houses of Amdo, and the natives sleep on cushions or carpets spread on that floor. This makes it easy to understand the tradition according to which the tree grew out of the blood that had been spilled during the confinement and cutting of the umbilical cord.

At first the sapling did not bear any peculiar signs on its leaves, but owing to its miraculous origin, it enjoyed some fame and was worshipped by people of the neighbourhood. A monk built a hut next to it and lived there. This was the beginning of the present large and rich monastery.

Many years later, when Tsong Khapa had already begun his reformation work, his mother, from whom he had been separated for a long time, wished to see him again and sent him a letter to call him back. At that time, Tsong Khapa lived in Central Tibet. During a mystic meditation, he understood that his journey to Amdo would benefit nobody, and therefore he only wrote to his mother. With his letter he gave to the messenger two pictures of himself intended for his mother and his sister, a picture of Gyalwa Senge,[1] Lord of Science and Eloquence, the patron of the intellectuals, and several pictures of Demchog, a deity of the tantric pantheon.

When these objects were being handed to the family of the reformer, the latter, exercising his magic powers from afar, caused the picture of the deities to appear on the leaves of the miraculous tree. The print was so neat, so perfect, according to the legend, that the most clever artist could not have drawn them better.

With the pictures, various other marks and the " Six Writings " (the formula in six syllables : *Aum mani padme hum*) appeared on the branches and the bark of the tree.

This is the origin of the name Kum-Bum : " hundred

[1] More generally denominated Jampeion. His Sanskrit name is Manjushri.

thousand images," by which the monastery became known.

In the account of their journey in Tibet, the French Fathers Huc and Gabet affirm that they have read the words *Aum mani padme hum !* on the leaves and the trunk of the tree.

Now, what kind of tree did these two travellers see ?

The monastery's chronicles relate that after the miraculous appearance of the images on the tree, the latter was wrapped in a piece of silk (a " robe ") and that a temple was built around it.

Was it an unroofed one ? The word *chörten* used in the text does not favour that opinion, for a *chörten* is a monument with a needle-like top and consequently *closed*.

Deprived of light and air, the tree could not but die. And as, according to the chronicles, the *chörten* was built in the sixteenth century, the Fathers Huc and Gabet at best could only have seen the dried skeleton of the tree. But their description applies to a living one.

The chronicles mention also that the miraculous tree remained unchanged in winter and summer, and that the number of its leaves was always the same.

We read again that, once upon a time, noises were heard inside the *chörten* in which the tree stood. The abbot of Kum-Bum entered it, cleaned the space around the tree, and found near to it a small quantity of liquid which he drank.

These details seem to indicate that the tree was in a closed room but seldom entered, while the wonder of keeping its leaves during the winter (the species to which belongs the Kum-Bum tree has caducous leaves) can only be applied to a living tree.

It is difficult to find one's way amongst these conflicting accounts.

To-day a *chörten* about 40 to 50 feet high (in which the original tree is said to be enshrined) stands in the middle of a gold-roofed temple.

Yet, when I lived at Kum-Bum the lamas said that the shrine had been erected only a few years ago.[1]

In front of that temple grows a shoot of the miraculous tree, surrounded by a railing, and is venerated to a certain extent.

Another larger tree, which is also believed to have originated from the miraculous tree, has been transplanted into a small garden before the temple of the Buddha. The leaves of these two trees are collected when they fall, and distributed to the devotees.

Perhaps it is one of these two which the Fathers Huc and Gabet saw. Foreign travellers who go to Kum-Bum, as a rule, do not know the history, or even the existence, of the tree hidden in the shrine.

Some Europeans residing in Kansu (the Chinese province on the border of which Kum-Bum is situated) have told to me that they have read *Aum mani padme hum!* on the leaves of the living trees. However, lamaist pilgrims and the monks of the monastery (about 3,000 men) do not notice anything peculiar about these leaves and even listen with scornful scepticism to accounts of the foreigners' visions of the sacred trees.

Nevertheless, their modern attitude is not supported by the old chronicles, which affirm that all people of Amdo saw the miraculous imprints on the tree when they first appeared, about four hundred years ago.

Living Buddha

Besides the various officials, there exist, in the *gompas*, another class of men who, as a rule, do not take any direct part in the business of the monastery and live more or less aloof in their sumptuous mansions. These are the lamas *tulkus*.

[1] Or rather rebuilt after a fire which destroyed it.

Tulkus occupy a prominent place in Lamaism, they constitute one of its most striking features which set it quite apart from all other Buddhist sects.

The real character of the lamas *tulkus* has never been correctly defined by Western authors and it would almost seem that they have never even suspected it. However, the theories regarding *tulkus* are well worth our attention, for they are far removed from any belief in incarnations or transmigrating spiritual entities and, as we will see, border upon the field of psychic phenomena.

The peculiar religious aristocracy which goes by the name of *tulkus* is not of very ancient origin. It is only after A.D. 1650 that it developed in the form which exists at present.

The fifth Grand Lama of the Gelugspa sect (Yellow caps), Lobzang Gyatso by name, had then been newly enthroned as temporal ruler of Tibet by a Mongolian prince and recognized as such by the Chinese emperor. Yet, these earthly honours failed to satisfy the ambitious lama, and he added to them by declaring himself to be an emanation of the Bodhisatva Chenrezigs. At the same time, he established his religious teacher as Grand Lama of Tashilhunpo, affirming that he was a *tulku* of Ödpagmed, a mystic Buddha of whom Chenrezigs is the spiritual son.[1]

The example set by the lama-king encouraged the creation of *tulkus*. Very soon, all monasteries of some importance deemed it a point of honour to have, at their head, an incarnation of one or another worthy. However, in setting himself up as a *tulku* of Chenrezigs, Lobzang Gyatso had not been entirely an innovator. Theories affording him some support can be traced in the mahâyânist speculations regarding the mystic

---

[1] Chenrezigs and Ödpagmed are, respectively, the Tibetan names of the mystic beings called in Sanskrit Avalokiteshvara and Amithaba.

Buddhas and their spiritual family of Bodhisatvas and human Buddhas who are said to emanate from them.

Moreover, since the death (about A.D. 1470) of Gedundub, the disciple of the reformer Tsong Khapa, his successors as head of the " Yellow caps " sect had been recognized as his reincarnations. So, the fifth Dalai Lama was therefore already a *tulku* of Gedundub when he became Chenrezigs' *tulku*.

But even earlier, in the eleventh century, Tibetans believed in *tulkus*. We read in the biography of Milarespa, that one of his disciples, called Bhiraja, convinced that a divine being was incarnated in his master, asked him to disclose his name. Milarespa himself believed that his own master, the lama Marpa, was the *tulku* of Dorjee Chang. He called him by that name repeatedly, not only in his poems, but when addressing him directly.

So, though recognized avatars were, at first, insolated cases and not in the regular lineal succession of incarnations, they have paved the way for the Dalai Lama-Chenrezigs and the thousands of lordly *tulkus* who are nowadays to be found all over the lamaist countries.

" Living Buddha " is a current appellation given by foreigners to lamas *tulkus*. Now, in spite of the many books on Buddhism which have been published in Western languages, there still remain a large number of Westerners who take the word Buddha for a proper noun : the name of the founder of Buddhism. To these people, the words " living Buddha " convey the idea of a reincarnation of Gautama the historical Buddha.

There is no Tibetan, even amongst the most ignorant villagers or herdsmen, who entertains such a false view. As for learned lamas, they agree with all other Buddhists, in declaring that the Buddha Gautama (Sakya Thubpa as he is called in Tibet) cannot be incarnated again. The reason of it is that Gautama has entered *nirvâna,* a state which precludes all possibilities of reincarnation, for that which is called *nirvâna* is precisely a setting free from the round of births and death.

So much for avatars of the historical Buddha. There have never been any in the past and none exist at present.

Can there be incarnations of *other* Buddhas?—In fact: no. And for the same reason—the Buddhas have entered *nirvâna*. It is, indeed, because they have realized that condition that they are Buddhas. However, while in Southern Buddhist countries the title of " Buddha " is exclusively given to the historical human Buddha, to his supposed predecessors and to his expected successor, Maitreya, Northern Buddhists have imagined a number of symbolic and mystic entities, certain of which are styled " Buddha." It is these who are said to manifest themselves through avatars, and their avatars may assume other forms than that of human being.

It follows that, according to popular belief, a *tulkus* is either the reincarnation of a saintly or peculiarly learned departed personality, or the incarnation of a non-human entity.

The number of the former greatly exceeds that of the latter. *Tulkus* of non-human entities are limited to a few avatars of mystic Buddhas, Bodhisatvas or deities, such as the Dalai Lama, the Grand Lama of Tashilunpo, the Lady Dorje Phagmo and, lower in rank, the *tulkus* of some autochthonous gods like Pekar.

Tulkus of gods, demons and fairies (khadhomas) appear especially as heroes of stories, yet some living men and women enjoy, as such, some local renown. This category of *tulkus* is not reckoned amongst the lamaist aristocracy ; one may think that it originated not in Lamaism, but in the old religion of Tibet.

Though Buddhism denies the existence of a transmigrating soul and considers the belief in a permanent *ego* as a most pernicious error, the large majority of unlearned Buddhists have lapsed into the old Indian doctrine which represents the *jîva* (self) periodically "changing his worn-out body for a new one, as we cast away a worn-out garment to clothe ourself in a new." [1]

Based on that belief, lines of successive reincarnations of human worthies [2] have been recognized. These are styled " rosary of births " or " rosary of bodies " [2] because they are linked together like the beads of a rosary.

When the *tulku* is considered as the incarnation of a god or the emanation of a spiritual entity who co-exists with him, the reason afforded by " the *self* changing his flesh garment" does not explain his nature. But average Tibetans do not think deeply, and for all practical purposes *tulkus* of celestial personages are considered as true reincarnations of their predecessors.

The ancestor of a line of purely human *tulkus* is called *ku kongma*, he is generally—but not necessarily— a lama.

Amongst the exceptions I may mention the father and mother of the reformer Tsong Khapa. Both reincarnate in male children who become monks and, as lamas, have their seat at Kum-Bum monastery. The lama who is held to be the reincarnation of Tsong Khapa's father is called Aghia tsang and is the lord of the monastery. When I lived at Kum-Bum, he was a boy in his tenth year.

There exist also nuns who are *tulkus* of departed saintly ladies or goddesses.

By the by, I may say that it is a cause of amusement for the observer to remark how intelligence and holiness often seem to become exhausted in a succession

---

[1] Bhagavad Gîtâ, II, 22.
[2] *Kyai treng* (spelt *skye hphreng*), or more politely *kutreng* (spelt *sku hphreng*).

of incarnations. It is not unusual to find an utterly stupid fellow as the supposed embodiment of some eminent thinker, or to see an earthly minded epicure recognized as the incarnation of a mystic anchorite famous for his austerity.

The reincarnation of the *tulkus* cannot astonish people who believe in a transmigrating *ego*. According to that view, we all are *tulkus*, for the *self*, now embodied in our present form, cannot but have existed previously in other forms. The only peculiarity with *tulkus* is that they are reincarnations of remarkable personalities, that they, sometimes, remember their previous lives and are able, at the time of death, to choose and make known the place of their next birth and their future parents.

However, some lamas see a complete difference between the process of reincarnation in the case of common men and that of the enlightened ones. Men, they say, who have practised no mental training, who live like animals, yielding thoughtlessly to their impulses, are like travellers who wander over the world without any fixed purpose. Such a man sees a lake in the east, and, being thirsty, hurries away to the water. When nearing the shore, he perceives the smell of smoke. This suggests the presence of a house or a camp. It would be pleasant, he thinks, to get hot tea instead of water, and a shelter for the night. So the man leaves the lake without having actually reached its shore and proceeds to the north, the smoke coming from that direction. On his way, before he has yet discovered any houses or tent, threatening phantoms spring up before him. Terrified, the wanderer turns away from the fearful beings and runs for life towards the south. When he deems that he has gone far enough to be safe, he stops to rest. Now, other wanderers pass who tell him of some blissful land of joy and plenty that they intend to reach. Full of enthusiasm, the vagrant joins the party and goes off to the west. And on the road he will be tempted many times to change his direction again before seeing the enchanted country.

So, continually roaming at random all his life, that simpleton will reach no goal whatever. Death will overtake him on the road, and the conflicting forces of his disordinated activity will be scattered to the four winds. The co-ordinated amount of energy [1] necessary to determine the continuation of a same current of force not having been produced, no *tulkus* can arise.

On the contrary, the enlightened one is likened to a traveller well aware of the goal which he means to reach, well informed, also, of its geographical position and the roads that lead to it. The mind unflinchingly fixed on his aim, indifferent to the various mirages and allurements of the roadside, this man controls the forces begotten by his concentration of mind and his bodily activity. Death may dissolve his body on the path, but the psychic energy of which that body is both creator and instrument, will remain coherent. Pushing forward towards the same goal, it will provide itself with a new material instrument, that is to say with a new form which is a *tulku*.

Here we meet with different views. Some lamas think that the subsisting subtile energy attracts elements of congenial essence and thus becomes the nucleus of a new being. Others say that the desembodied force joins an already existing being, whose material and mental dispositions, acquired in previous lives, provide a harmonious union.

Needless to say that several criticisms and objections may be brought forward against these theories, but the present book is meant only to relate lamaist opinions and not to discuss them. I can only say that all the views I have mentioned are consistent with a number of old Tibetan stories whose heroes determine, by an

[1] In Tibetan *Tsal* or *shugs*.

act of will,[1] the nature of their rebirth and the course of action of their future avatar. This shows that similar theories have been widely spread among Tibetans for a long time.

In spite of the part which a conscious purpose plays in bringing about the continuation of a line of *tulkus*, one must beware of thinking that the composition of the new personality is arbitrarily produced. The determinist idea is too strongly rooted in the mind even of the wildest Tibetan herdsmen to allow of such an idea. Laws are said to be at work during the whole process which proceeds according to natural attractions and repulsions.

More learned lamaists hold another view regarding the nature of *tulkus*. This is, in fact, the only truly orthodox one, which fully agrees with the very meaning of the term *tulku*.

The word *tulku* means a form created by magic, and in accordance with that definition, we must consider the *tulkus* as phantom bodies, occult emanations, puppets constructed by a magician to serve his purpose.

I cannot do better than quote, here, the explanation of *tulkus* given to me by the Dalai Lama.

As I have related it in the first chapter of the present book, I met the Dalai Lama in 1912 when he was living in the Himalayas, and asked him several questions regarding lamaist doctrine to which he first answered orally. Afterward, in order to avoid misunderstandings, he told me to write a list of new questions on the points which still appeared to me obscure. To these he gave written answers. The present quotation is taken from the document with which the Dalai Lama favoured me.

" A Bodhisatva [2] is the basis of countless magic

---

[1] According to lamaists, that will is determined, depends on causes.

[2] A being who has attained the high degree of spiritual perfection immediately below that of a Buddha.

forms. By the power generated in a state of perfect concentration of mind he may, at one and the same time, show a phantom (tulpa) [1] of himself in thousands millions of worlds. He may create not only human forms, but any forms he chooses, even those of inanimated objects such as hills, enclosures, houses, forests, roads, bridges, etc. He may produce atmospheric phenomena as well as the thirst-quenching beverage of immortality." (The latter expression I have been advised to take in both a literal and a symbolic sense.) " In fact," reads the conclusion, " there is no limit to his power of phantom creation."

The theory sanctioned in these lines by the highest authority of official Lamaism is identical with that expounded in the mahâyânist literature, where it is said that an accomplished Bodhisatva is capable of effecting ten kinds of magic creations. The power of producing magic formations, *tulkus* or less lasting and materialized *tulpas*, does not, however, belong exclusively to such mystic exalted beings. Any human, divine or demoniac being may be possessed of it. The only difference comes from the degree of power, and this depends on the strength of the concentration and the quality of the mind itself.

The *tulkus* of mystic entities co-exist with their spiritual parent. For instance, while the Dalai Lama, who is Chenrezigs' *tulku*, lives at Lhasa, Chenrezigs himself— so Tibetans believe—dwells in Nankai Potala, an island near the Chinese coast. [2]

The Dhyani Buddha Ödpagmed, of whom the Tashi Lama is the *tulku*, resides in the Western Paradise, Nub dewachen.

Men, also, may co-exist with their magic progeny. King Srong bstan gampo and the warrior chieftain

[1] Written *sprulpa*.
[2] Pu-to-shang island in the Choushan archipelago, off the coast of Chekiang.

Gesar of Ling are illustrations of this. In our own days it is said that when he fled from Shigatze, the Tashi Lama left, in his stead, a phantom perfectly resembling him who played his part so thoroughly and naturally that every one who saw him was deceived. When the lama was safe beyond the border, the phantom vanished.[1] The three men here mentioned are themselves *tulkus*, but according to lamaists, that circumstance does not preclude the further creation of emanations. These spring from one another and there exist denominations for emanations of the second or the third degree.[2]

It may happen that the self-same defunct lama, multiplying himself *post-mortem*, has several recognized *tulkus* who are contemporaries. On the other hand, there are lamas who are said to be *tulkus* of several entities. Before dismissing the subject, it may be interesting to remind ourselves that the followers of the docetae sect, in early Christianity, looked upon Jesus Christ as being a *tulku*. They maintained that Jesus who had been crucified was not a natural being, but a phantom created to play that part by a spiritual entity.

So, also, in contradiction with the orthodox tradition which tells that the historical Buddha Gautama is the incarnation of a Bodhisatva who came down from the Tushita heaven, some Buddhists have affirmed that he who is the real Buddha was never incarnate, but that he created a phantom which appeared in India as Gautama.[3]

In spite of the various more or less subtle theories

[1] See the account of the Tashi Lama flight in my book, *My Journey to Lhasa*.

[2] *Yang tulku* emanated from a *tulku* ; *gsum tulku* emanated from the *tulku* of a *tulku*.

[3] The Buddhist sect which held that view was that of the Vetullaka.

held about *tulkus* in learned Tibetan circles, they are considered, for all practical purposes, as real reincarnation of their predecessors and the formalities regarding their recognition have been devised accordingly.

It happens, not unfrequently, that a lama—often himself one of a line of *tulkus*—foretells, at his deathbed, the country or district where he will be reborn. Sometimes he adds various particulars about his future parents, the situation of their house and so on.

Contrary to the opinion prevailing in the southern schools of Buddhism, lamaists believe that a certain time of undetermined length elapses between the death and the rebirth of a being on the earth. In the interval, the main consciousness, that which causes the rebirth, is wandering in the labyrinth of the *bardo*,[1] seeking its way.

As a rule, it is about two years[2] after the death of a lama *tulku* that the treasurer, the head steward or other clerical officials of his household, begin to look for his reincarnation. By that time the child who is that supposed " reincarnation " is usually one or two years old. There are cases when the reincarnation is delayed, but these are very exceptional.

If the late lama left directions regarding his rebirth, his monks pursue their researches accordingly ; if such directions are lacking, they resort to a lama *tulku* astrologer[3] who points out generally in veiled and obscure sentences the country where investigations must be made and various signs by which the child may be known. When the *tulku* to be discovered is

---

[1] About *bardo*, see Chapter I.

[2] There are, however, no fixed customs regarding that matter, circumstances decide the turn given to the procedure.

[3] Called *tsispa*, a calculator. It is the *tsispa* who draws horoscopes, discloses hidden things, etc. Any ordinary monk may act as *tsispa*, but the discovery of a *tulku* is always entrusted to another *tulku*.

of a high rank, one of the State oracles may be consulted, and this is always done for the reincarnations of the Dalai Lama and the Tashi Lama.

Sometimes a young boy is quickly found whose birth-place and other characteristics answer the directions given by the late lama or the astrologer. In other cases, years elapse without finding anyone, and some " incarnations " even remain undiscovered. This is a cause of deep sorrow to the devotees of the *tulku*, and still more to the monks of his monastery, which, lacking its worshipful head, does not attract the same number of pious benefactors, suppliers of feasts and gifts. Yet, while some lament, that sad plight may be a cause of secret joy to a cunning steward who, during the absence of a legitimate master, manages the business of the *tulku* estate on his own authority and may thus find a way to make his own fortune.

When a child is discovered who nearly answers the prescribed conditions, a lama clairvoyant is again consulted, and if he pronounces in favour of the child the following final test is applied.

A number of objects such as rosaries, ritualistic implements, books, tea-cups,[1] etc., are placed together, and the child must pick out those which belonged to the late *tulku*, thus showing that he recognizes the things which were *his* in his previous life.

It sometimes happens when several children are candidates to a vacant *tulku* seat, that equally convincing signs have been noticed concerning each of them, and they all correctly pick out the objects owned by the defunct lama. Or it sometimes occurs that two or three clairvoyants disagree among themselves as to which is the authentic *tulku*.

[1] Each Tibetan owns a private bowl in which he alone drinks tea. That bowl may be the wooden one of the poor or the costly jade one with golden saucer and cover of the rich, or any of the intermediate kinds, but it is never lent to anyone to drink in.

Such cases are rather frequent when it is a question of succeeding to one of these grand *tulkus*, lords of big monasteries and large estates. Then many families are eager to place one of their sons on the throne of the departed grandee, which brings with it consideration and material profit.

Generally the parents of the *tulku* are allowed to live in the monastery till the child can dispense with his mother's nursing and care. Then a comfortable lodging is provided for them on the monastery land, but outside the *gompa's* enclosure, and they are plentifully supplied with all they need. If the monastery has no special mansion reserved for the parents of its grand *tulku*, the latter are well provided for at their own home.

Beside a grand lama *tulku*, who is the lord of the monastery, the *gompas* often include several other *tulkus* amongst their members. In the largest of these monastic cities, their number may amount to a few hundreds. Some of them rank high in the lamaist ecclesiastic aristocracy and, in addition to their seat in their parent monastery, they own mansions in other *gompas* and estates in Tibet or Mongolia. In fact, to be the near relative of even the least of them is a connection profitable enough to rouse covetousness in the heart of any Tibetan.

So countless intrigues are woven around the succession to a *tulku*, and, amidst the warlike folk of Kham or of the northern borderland, bloody feuds spring from such passionate competitions.

Countless tales are told throughout Tibet about extraordinary proofs of memory from previous lives and wonders worked by young *tulkus* to testify their identity. We find in them the habitual Tibetan mixture of superstition, cunning, comedy, and disconcerting events. I could relate dozens of them, but I prefer to confine myself to the relation of facts connected with people whom I have personally known.

Next the mansion of the Pegyai Lama, in which I lived at Kum-Bum, was the dwelling of a minor *tulku* called Agnai tsang.[1] Seven years had elapsed since the death of the last master of the place and none had been able to discover the child in whom he had reincarnated. I do not think that the steward of the lama's household felt greatly afflicted by that circumstance. He managed the estate and seemed rather prosperous.

Now it happened that in the course of a trading tour, he felt tired and thirsty and entered a farm to rest and drink. While the housewife made tea the *nierpa* (steward) drew a jade snuff-box from his pocket and was about to take a pinch of snuff when a little boy who had been playing in a corner of the room stopped him and putting his small hand on the box asked reproachfully :

" Why do you use my snuff-box ? "

The steward was thunderstruck. Truly, the precious snuff-box was not his, but belonged to the departed Agnai tsang, and though he had not perhaps exactly intended to steal it, yet he had taken possession of it.

He remained there trembling while the boy looked at him as his face suddenly became grave and stern, with no longer anything childish about it.

" Give it back to me at once, it is mine," he said again.

Stung with remorse, and at the same time terrified and bewildered, the superstitious monk could only fall on his knees and prostrate himself before his reincarnated master.

A few days later, I saw the boy coming in state to his mansion. He wore a yellow brocade robe [2] and

---

[1] Not to be mistaken for Aghia tsang, the grand *tulku* already mentioned.

[2] As he had not yet been admitted into the religious Order, he was not allowed to wear the ecclesiastic robes.

rode a beautiful black pony, the *nierpa* holding the bridle.

When the procession entered the house the boy remarked : " Why do we turn to the left to reach the second courtyard ? The gate is on our right side."

Now, for some reason, the gate on the right side had been walled up after the death of the lama and another one opened instead.

The monks marvelled at this new proof of the authenticity of their lama and all proceeded to his private apartment where tea was to be served.

The boy, seated on a pile of large hard cushions, looked at the cup with silver-gilt saucer and jewelled cover placed on the table before him.

" Give me the larger china cup," he commanded. And he described one, mentioning the very pattern that decorated it.

Nobody knew about such a cup, not even the steward, and the monks respectfully endeavoured to convince their young master that there was no cup of that kind in the house.

It was at that moment that, taking advantage of an already long acquaintance with the *nierpa*, I entered the room. I had heard the snuff-box story and wished to see for myself, my remarkable little new neighbour. I offered him the customary complimentary scarf and a few presents. These he received with a gracious smile but, apparently following the trend of his thoughts regarding the cup, he said :

" Look better, you will find it."

And suddenly, as if a flash of memory had dashed through his mind, he added explanations about a box painted in such a colour, which was in such a place in the store-room.

The monks had briefly informed me of what was going on and I waited with interest to see how things would turn out.

Less than half an hour later, the set, cup, saucer and cover, was discovered in a casket that was at the bottom of the very box described by the boy.

" I did not know of the existence of that cup," the steward told me later on. " The lama himself, or my predecessor, must have put it in that box which did not contain anything else precious and had not been opened for years."

I also witnessed a much more striking and fantastic discovery of a *tulku* in the poor inn of a hamlet, some miles distant from Ansi.

Roads going from Mongolia to Tibet cross, in that region, the long highway which extends from Peking to Russia over a whole continent. So I felt annoyed but not astonished when, reaching the inn at sunset, I found it crowded with visitors from a Mongolian caravan.

The men looked rather excited as if something unusual had just happened. Yet, with their customary courtesy still increased by the sight of the lamaist monastic garments which lama Yongden and I wore, the travellers immediately gave up a room for my party and made room for my beasts in the stable.

As Yongden and I remained in the courtyard, looking at the camels of the Mongolians, the door of one of the rooms opened and a tall handsome youth, poorly clad in a Tibetan robe, stood on the threshold and asked if we were Tibetans. We answered in the affirmative.

Then a well-dressed elderly lama appeared behind the young man and he, also, addressed us in Tibetan.

As usual, we exchanged questions about the country from which we came and where we were going. The lama said that he had intended going to Lhasa by the Suchow winter road, but now, he added, it was no longer necessary to take this journey. The Mongolian servants who were in the courtyard nodded their assent.

I wondered what could have caused these people to change their minds while *en route*, but as the lama retired to his room, I did not deem it polite to follow and ask explanations that were not offered.

However, later in the evening, when they had inquired about Yongden and me from our servants, the Mongolians invited us to drink tea with them and I heard the whole story.

The handsome young man was a native of the far distant Ngari province (in South-western Tibet). He seemed to be somewhat of a visionary. At least, most Westerners would have so described him, but we were in Asia.

Since his early youth, Migyur—this was his name—had been restless, haunted by the queer idea that *he was not where he ought to be*. He felt himself a foreigner in his village, a foreigner in his family. In dreams, he saw landscapes that did not exist in Ngari : sandy solitudes, round felt tents, a monastery on a hillock. And even when awake, the same subjective images appeared to him and superimposed themselves on his material surroundings, veiling them, creating around him a perpetual mirage.

He was only a boy when he ran away, unable to resist the desire of finding the reality of his vision. Since then, Migyur had been a vagrant, working a little here and there on his way, begging most times, wandering at random without being able to control his restlessness or settle anywhere.

To-day he had arrived from Aric, tramping aimlessly as usual.

He saw the inn, the encampment of the caravan, the camels in the courtyard. Without knowing why, he crossed the gate, and found himself face to face with the lama and his party. Then, with the rapidity of lightning, past events flashed through his mind. He remembered that very lama as a young man, his disciple, and himself as an already aged lama, both on that very road, returning from a pilgrimage to the holy places of Tibet and going home to the monastery on the hillock.

He reminded the lama of all these things, giving minute details regarding their journey, their lives in the distant monastery and many other particulars.

Now the aim of the Mongolians' journey was precisely to beg advice from the Dalai Lama as to the best way of discovering the *tulku* head of their monastery, whose seat had been unoccupied for more than twenty years, in spite of persevering efforts to find his reincarnation.

These superstitious people were ready to believe that the Dalai Lama, through his supernormal power, had detected their intention and out of kindness had caused their meeting with their reincarnated lord.

The Ngari wanderer complied immediately with the usual test, picking out without hesitation or mistake, among a number of similar objects, those that had belonged to the late lama.

No doubt subsisted in the mind of the Mongolians. On the morrow, I saw the caravan retracing its steps, moving away to the slow pace of the big camels and disappearing on the skyline into the Gobi solitudes. The new *tulku* was going to meet his fate.

CHAPTER IV

DEALING WITH GHOSTS AND DEMONS

The Lugubrious Communion

A RATHER large number of Tibetan occultists seem to delight in lugubrious musing and practices in which corpses play a prominent part. Vulgar sorcerers only seek by this means to acquire magic powers, but a number of more enlightened men affirm that esoteric teachings and a special kind of spiritual training is thus hidden under the veil of symbols and conventional language.

I need not say that this repugnant mysticism has nothing at all in common with Buddhism. It is also foreign to true Lamaism, though a few lamas secretly yield to its bizarre attraction. Its origin must be sought in the light of Tantric Hinduism and the doctrines of the ancient Bönpo shamanists.

The following story will be sufficient to illustrate this dark side of Tibetan occultism. It was told me at Cherku only a few years after the death of those concerned and by a man who had known them personally.

The lama who plays the principal part was the abbot of, Miniagpar Lhakhang near Tachienlu, known by the name of Chogs Tsang. He is the author of a number of prophecies regarding events which are to take place in Tibet, China and the world at large. He was regarded as having supernormal powers, among others of being able to cause death.

Chogs Tsang used to behave in a strange, often quite incomprehensible way, and was addicted to drinking. He lived for some time with the Tibetan chieftain of Tachienlu who bears the title of *gyalpo* (king).

Once, while talking and drinking with his host, the lama asked for the sister of the master of horse as his wife. This official, who happened to be present, refused his consent. The lama was so enraged that he violently threw the precious jade cup in which he had drunk on the ground, breaking it into pieces, and cursed the equerry, declaring that after two days he would die.

The *gyalpo* did not approve of the lama's request for his officer's sister and had no faith in the power of his curse. The equerry was young and healthy, he argued. Still the lama maintained that he would die and, indeed, two days later the man passed away.

Then the *gyalpo* and the parents of the young maid became frightened and hastened to bring the girl to the lama. But he refused to take her

" She would have been useful," he said, " for obtaining an object which would have benefited a large number of beings ; but the opportunity has passed, and I do not care for a wife."

This story resembles that of Dugpa Kunlegs, mentioned in the first chapter. It is a common theme of Tibetan tales.

Now one evening this same Chogs Tsang unexpectedly called up one of his *trapas*.

" Saddle two horses, we are going," he ordered him.

The monk remonstrated with the Lama, saying that it was already late and that it would be better to wait the next morning.

" Do not answer back," said Chogs Tsang laconically. " Let us go."

They start, ride in the night and arrive at some spot near a river. There they alight from their horses and walk towards the river bank.

Though the sky is completely dark a spot on the water is "lighted by sun rays," and in that illuminated place a corpse is floating up-stream, moving against the current. After a while it comes within reach of the two men.

"Take your knife, cut a piece of the flesh and eat it," commands Chogs Tsang to his companion. And he adds :

"I have a friend in India who sends me a meal every year at this date."

Then he himself begins to cut and to eat.

The attendant is struck with terror, he endeavours to imitate his master but does not dare to put the morsel into his mouth and hides it in his *ambag*.[1]

Both return to the monastery where they arrive at dawn.

The lama says to the monk :

"I wished you to share the favour and the most excellent fruits of this mystic meal, but you are not worthy of it. That is why you have not dared to eat the piece which you have cut off and hidden under your dress."

Hearing these words the monk repents of his lack of courage and puts his hand into his *ambag* to take his share of the corpse, but the piece of flesh is no longer there.

This fantastic story accords with certain information given me with great reserve by some anchorites belonging to the Dzogschen sect.

There exist, so they said, certain human beings who have attained such a high degree of spiritual perfection, that the original material substance of their bodies has become transmuted into a more subtle one which possesses special qualities.

Few people can discern the change which has come

[1] The breast pocket formed by the wide Tibetan robe tied with a belt.

over these exceptional men. A morsel of their transformed flesh, when eaten, will produce a special kind of ecstasy and bestow knowledge and supernormal powers upon the person partaking of it.

A hermit told me that when a *naljorpa*, through his clairvoyance, has discovered one of these wonderful beings, he sometimes begs from him the favour of being informed of his death in order that he may obtain a small portion of his precious body.

Might fervent candidates for this gruesome communion not sometimes grow too impatient and refuse to wait for the natural death of the holy one ?—Might they not hurry it forward ?—

One of those who disclosed this secret rite to me, almost seemed to confess that the thing had happened. However, he was careful to mention the attenuating circumstance that the victim consented to the sacrifice.

The Corpse Who Dances

Another mysterious rite is called *rolang* (the corpse who stands up). Traditions and ancient chronicles relate that, before the introduction of Buddhism into Tibet, it was practised by the Bönpo shamans during the funeral ceremony. However, the brief movement made by a dead body in such circumstances cannot be compared with what happens in the course of the horrible and grotesque *tête-à-tête* that Tibetan occultists depict.

There exist several kinds of *rolang*. These must not be mistaken for the *trong jug* [1] rite which causes the " spirit " of another being to pass into a corpse and apparently resuscitate it, though the corpse is not animated by its original occupant.

One of these lugubrious *rolang* was described to me as follows by a *ngagspa* who said he had practised it himself.

[1] Written *grong hjug*.

The celebrant is shut up alone with a corpse in a dark room. To animate the body, he lies on it, mouth to mouth, and while holding it in his arms, he must continually repeat mentally the same magic formula,[1] excluding all other thoughts.

After a certain time the corpse begins to move. It stands up and tries to escape; the sorcerer, firmly clinging to it, prevents it from freeing itself. Now the body struggles more fiercely. It leaps and bounds to extraordinary heights, dragging with it the man who must hold on, keeping his lips upon the mouth of the monster, and continue mentally repeating the magic words.

At last the tongue of the corpse protrudes from its mouth. The critical moment has arrived. The sorcerer seizes the tongue with his teeth and bites it off. The corpse at once collapses.

Failure in controlling the body after having awaked it, means certain death for the sorcerer.

The tongue carefully dried becomes a powerful magic weapon which is treasured by the triumphant *ngagspa*.

The Tibetan who gave me these details described most vividly the gradual awakening of the corpse : the first conscious look which brightened its glazed eyes and its feeble movements slowly growing in strength until he became unable to prevent the agitation of the jumping monster and needed all his strength to hold it. He described his sensations when he could feel the tongue issuing from the mouth of the corpse and touching his own lips, and realized that the terrible moment had come when, if he failed to conquer it, the horrible being would kill him.

Had that fantastic struggle not been purely subjective ? Had it not taken place during one of these trances which are frequently experienced by Tibetan *naljorpas*, which they also voluntarily cultivate ? I

[1] This differs according to the masters.

doubted and asked to see " *the tongue.*" The sorcerer showed me a desiccated blackish object which might have been " a tongue," but it was not sufficient to prove the origin of the hideous relic.

Be that as it may, numbers of Tibetans believe that the *rolang* rite really takes place.

Beside corpses being revived by special rites, Tibetans believe also that any corpse is liable to rise suddenly and harm the living. It is for this reason that dead bodies are continually watched by some one who recites the liturgic words which prevent that sham resurrection.

A *trapa* from Sepogön in the vicinity of the Salween told me the following story.

While still a boy novice, he had accompanied three lamas of his monastery to a house where a man had died. There the lamas were to perform the daily rite for the dead till the day appointed to carry the corpse to the cemetery. At night they had retired to sleep in a corner of the large room where the body was kept, tied up in a seated posture with many scarves and swathed in clothes.

" The charge of reciting the magic formulas had been entrusted to me. In the middle of the night I was overcome with the continuous wearisome repetition and may have dozed a few minutes. A small noise awaked me ! a black cat passed by the corpse and went out of the room. Then I heard a kind of cracking noise like tearing cloth, and to my horror, I saw the dead body moving and freeing himself from his bands. Mad with fright, I ran out of the house, but before I had escaped from the room I saw the ghost stretching out one hand and creeping upon the sleeping men.

" In the morning the three men were found dead ; the corpse had returned to his place but the scarves were torn and the clothes lay on the floor around him."

Tibetans have great faith in such stories.

The touch of the *rolang* is mortal and the mischievous ghost does not fail to lay his hand on all who are within his reach : only the lamas who perform the rites of the dead are said to know magic words and gestures which avert that danger, by controlling the corpse and causing it to sit back if it attempts to move.

We are also told of *rolangs* which escape from the house where they have revived and roam about the country. Again, others are said to disappear without leaving any trace.

One could fill numbers of books with the stories one hears about *rolangs* among the good people of Tibet.

The Enchanted Dagger

It is needless to say that " tongues of the jumping corpse," if they exist at all, are exceptional implements of sorcery. The ritual weapons—called *phurba*—generally used by lamaist magicians are made of bronze, wood or even ivory, shaped to resemble a dagger and often beautifully chiselled or carved.

A true initiate in the Tibetan secret lore, however, would scoff at the sorcerer and his repugnant practices. The power of the magic weapon does not, he thinks, depend on the substance of which it is made but is communicated to it by the magician himself.

Yet, as time goes on, a certain portion of this energy remains attached to the *phurba*. Its strength increases with the repeated use which is made of it in magic rites. The inert object becomes " possessed " just as an animated being could be.

We shall read, in a following chapter, of the process employed by the *ngagspas* who hold this belief.

On the other hand, it is said that the ritual implements which have served in coercion rites should not be kept in the house of a layman or of an uninitiated monk, for fear that the dangerous entities subdued by their means might use them to take revenge upon the possessor, if he does not know how to protect himself.

To that belief I owe a few interesting objects which those who had inherited them begged me to carry away.

One day a windfall of this kind came my way so strangely that the story is worth telling. During a journey in Northern Tibet I met a small caravan of lamas, and talking with them according to the custom along these trails where travellers are scarce, I learned that they were transporting a *phurba* which had become a source of calamity.

This ritualistic implement had belonged to a lama, their master, who had recently died. The dagger had started to work harm in the monastery itself. Two of the three monks who had touched it, had died, and the other one broke his leg by falling from a horse. Then the pole that held the banner of benediction, which was planted in the courtyard of the monastery, broke, and this is considered a very bad omen.

Frightened, yet not daring to destroy the *phurba* for fear of greater misfortunes, the monks had closed it up in a box. Soon after this, strange noises had been heard proceeding from the box.

They had finally decided to place the baleful object in an isolated cavern consecrated to a deity, but the cowherds living in that region threatened armed opposition. They recalled the story of a *phurba* that had moved through the air, wounding and killing numbers of men and animals. No one knew where nor when these wonders had taken place, but such details are of little importance to superstitious minds. The cowherds did not want the *phurba* in their neighbourhood.

The unfortunate *trapas* who carried the enchanted dagger wrapped in many papers printed with charms and sealed in a casket, did not know how to get rid of it. Their dejected countenances prevented me from laughing at their credulity. I was also curious to look at the miraculous weapon.

"Let me see the *phurba*," I said, "perhaps I shall find some way of helping you."

They did not dare to take it out of the box, but after long parleys, they allowed me to do so myself.

The *phurba* was a fine piece of ancient Tibetan art. and I was seized with a desire to possess it, but I knew that the *trapas* would not sell it for anything in the world.

"Camp with us for the night," I said to them, "and leave the *phurba* with me. I will think it over."

My words promised nothing, but the bait of a good supper and of chatting with my men decided the travellers to accept.

At nightfall, I went some distance from the camp ostensibly carrying the dagger which, freed from its box, would have terrified the credulous Tibetans had I left it with them.

When I thought I was far enough away, I stuck the enchanted weapon into the ground and sat down on a blanket to think out a way of persuading the monks to let me have it.

I had been there for several hours when I seemed to see the form of a lama appearing near the spot where I had planted the *phurba*. He moved forward, bending cautiously. From beneath the toga in which his rather indistinct body was wrapped, a hand came out slowly and advanced to seize the magic dagger.

Jumping up, I grabbed it before the thief had been able to touch it.

So, I have not been the only one tempted. This man, less superstitious than his companions, had recognized the value of the *phurba* and very likely hoped to sell it secretly. He thought that I was asleep and

should notice nothing. The next day, the disappearance of the enchanted dagger would be attributed to
some new occult intervention and one more story of
magic would be circulated among the faithful. Too
bad that such a clever scheme had not succeeded,
but I kept the enchanted weapon ; I even grasped it
so tightly that my nerves, excited by the adventure or
by the pressure of the bronze carved handle on my
flesh, gave me the impression that the dagger was
feebly moving in my hand.

And now for the thief !

All around me the barren plain was empty. He
must have made off when I was stooping down to
pull the dagger out of the ground.

I ran to the camp. The man who had just returned
or who came back after me must be the culprit.

I found every one sitting up and reciting religious
texts for protection against the evil powers. I called
Yongden into my tent.

" Which of the monks has been missing ? " I asked
him.

" No one," he answered. " They are half dead
with fright. They did not even dare to go far enough
away from the tents to perform the necessities of nature.
I had to scold them."

Good ! I must have been " seeing things " ; but
perhaps this would stand me in good stead.

" Listen," I said to the *trapas*, " this is what has
happened." And I told them quite frankly about my
illusion and the doubts I had conceived of their honesty.

" Surely that was our Grand Lama ! " they exclaimed.
" He wanted to take back his *phurba* and perhaps he
would have killed you if he had succeeded. Oh !
Jetsunma, you are a true *gomchenma*, although certain
people call you a *phling*.[1] Our *tsawai* lama (spiritual
father) was a powerful magician ; yet he could not

[1] Foreigner.

take his *phurba* away from you. Keep it now, keep it and it will no longer do harm to anyone."

They all spoke together, excited and terrified to think that their lama magician—more to be feared than ever, since he belonged to another world—had passed so close to them, and delighted, at the same time, to get rid of the enchanted dagger.

I shared in their joy but for a different reason : the *phurba* was mine. However, it was only honest not to take advantage of their confused state of mind.

"Think it over," I said. "A shadow may have deceived me. I may have gone to sleep while sitting there and been troubled by a dream."

They would have nothing of this. The lama had come, I had seen him and he had not been able to seize the *phurba* ; so I, by my superior power, became its legitimate owner.

I confess that I allowed myself to be easily convinced. . . .

Practices to acquire Fearlessness—Challenging Demoniacal Beings

There is hardly any country which can vie with Tibet as to the riches, variety and picturesqueness of its folklore regarding ghosts and demons. If we were to rely on popular beliefs, we should conclude that evil spirits greatly outnumber the human population of the " Land of Snow."

Assuming thousands of different shapes, these malignant beings are said to dwell in trees, rocks, valleys, lakes, springs, and many other places. Always bent on mischief they hunt men and animals to steal their vital breath and feed upon it. They wander for pure pleasure across forests and high barren hills and every traveller risks being confronted by one of them at any turning of the road.

Official lamaist magicians undertake to convert, or

to subdue, these dangerous neighbours in order to stop their undesirable activity and transform them into useful obedient servants. Sorcerers compete with them in this art, but, nearly always, practise it with a view to using the power of the malevolent beings which they have tamed for their own, no less evil, purposes.

As for Tibetan mystics, they patronize a certain kind of commerce with demons that is connected with psychic training. This consists in meetings deliberately sought by the disciple, either to challenge demoniac beings or to give them alms. These rites are very different from those which have been described at the beginning of this chapter. Though they, too, may sometimes appear ridiculous or even repugnant, according to our ideas, their purpose is useful or lofty, such as liberating from fear, awakening feelings of boundless practical compassion leading to complete detachment and, finally, to spiritual illumination.

It happens, not infrequently, that credulous men who firmly believe in the strictly objective existence of thousands of demons, betake themselves to a mystic lama and, desirous of leading a religious life, beg to be accepted as his disciples.

All these simpletons are not turned away and sent back to their village with good advice regarding morality and the practice of good will towards every one. Some among them, who appear capable of progressing towards enlightenment, may well be favoured with more extended teaching.

If the lama is a true adept of the " Short Path," his first care will be to provide the new disciple with opportunities of *liberating himself* from his terror of the various demons. Lengthy explanations and demonstrations of truth and error are not part of mystic teachers' methods. They simply place their disciples in the conditions required to experience events and sensations that will awaken their reflection and allow them to acquire knowledge. The extent of the profit derived from such experiences depends on the pupil's intelligence.

A young man of my acquaintance was sent by his master—a lama from Amdo—to a solitary gloomy ravine which was supposed to be haunted by evil non-human beings. There he was told to tie himself to a tree or to a rock and at night, calling on the ferocious *Towos*, which Tibetan painters show eating the brains of men, he was to challenge them.

However terrified he might feel, he was commanded to resist the temptation of untying himself and running away. He must remain, bound to his post, until sunrise.

This is nearly a classic practice. It is enjoined on many Tibetan novices as a first step on the mystic path.

Sometimes the disciples must remain bound for three days and three nights, or for even a longer period, fasting, sleepless, experiencing the conditions of utter weariness and starvation that so easily bring hallucinations.

Such exercises naturally at times have tragic consequences. Yongden was told a story that illustrates this by an old lama of Tsarong, when I was travelling *incognito* to Lhasa. Seated in a corner of the room, the " insignificant mamma " whom I personified at that time did not miss one word of the story.

In their youth, this lama and his younger brother, called Lodö, had left their monastery to follow a wandering ascetic of another region who had established himself for a time as hermit on a hill called Phagri—a well-known place of pilgrimage situated not far from Dayul.

The anchorite commanded the young brother to tie himself by the neck to a tree, in a woody place which was said to be haunted by Thags yang, a demon who generally appears under the shape of a tiger, to whom the ferocious instincts of that animal are ascribed.

Once bound as a victim to the sacrificial post, the man was to imagine that he was a cow which had been led there as a propitiating offering to Thags yang. Keeping his thoughts concentrated on that idea and lowing now and then to identify himself more completely with the beast, he would—if the concentration was strong enough—reach a state of trance in which, having entirely lost the consciousness of his own personality, he would experience the anguish of a cow in danger of being devoured.

The exercise was to last for three consecutive days and nights. Four days went by and the novice did not return to his matter. On the morning of the fifth day, the latter said to the eldest of his disciples :

" I had a strange dream last night. Go and fetch your brother."

The monk obeyed.

An appalling sight awaited him in the forest. The corpse of Lodö, torn and half devoured, remained partly fastened to a tree, while bloody pieces lay scattered among the surrounding bushes.

The terrified man collected the ghastly remains in his monastic toga and hastened back to his *guru*.

When he reached the hut in which the latter lived with his two disciples, he found it empty. The lama had left, taking with him all his belongings, two religious books, a few ritualistic implements and his travelling stick with a trident at the top.

" I felt that I was becoming mad," said the old Tibetan. " That sudden departure frightened me even more than the discovery of my brother's mangled body."

" What had our teacher dreamt ? Did he know the awful fate of his disciple ? Why had he gone ? . . ."

Without actually knowing any better than the afflicted monk what reasons had led the lama to run away, I nevertheless thought that when he saw that his disciple had not returned, he might have feared some accident had befallen the young man in the forest haunted by wild beasts. Perhaps he had really received some kind of mysterious information in a dream about the tragic event, and thought it prudent to escape the anger and revenge of the victim's family.

As for the novice's death, it could be explained quite naturally. Panthers are frequently found in that region, some leopards roam also in the woods. I had met two myself a few days before hearing the story.[1] One of these animals, which the monk himself had perhaps attracted by his lowing, might have killed him before he had time to break his bonds and defend himself.

But a very different interpretation was given to the sad story by the man who told it and those seated around him. According to them the demon-tiger had seized upon the offering imprudently presented to him.

The young disciple, they said, ignored the magic words and gestures which would have protected him. And in this matter the fault of his teacher was very great, for he ought never to have sent him to challenge the demon-tiger without arming him with the teachings and ritualistic formula which are efficacious weapons in such cases.

But in the utmost depth of his soul the monk, wounded in his brotherly love, had a more terrible idea which he expressed in a low and trembling voice.

"Who knows," he said, "if that strange lama was not the demon-tiger himself who had taken on a human form to attract a victim? He could not have killed my poor brother while in human form, but at night

[1] See *My Journey to Lhasa*.

when I was asleep, resuming his tiger shape he ran to the forest and satisfied his ferocious craving."

The last words of the old man met with profound silence. He had probably told this terrifying episode of his long-lost youth many times. But his audience was once more deeply impressed.

Might it not still happen any day? Thags yang and so many other kindred beings continue to prowl around the villages and to follow the travellers, seeking to prey upon those who are unsufficiently protected. Every one there believed it.

In the large kitchen dimly lighted by the flames leaping now and then from the hearth, a woman lifted her eyes instinctively towards the protective charms pasted on the walls, as if she wanted to ascertain that they were still there. The grandfather went into the next room where the evening offering lamps burnt on the family altar, and the sweet fragrance of incense sticks he had lighted floated in to soothe our nerves.

Although one may suppose that a number of accidents, apparently of occult origin, do actually happen during the performance of these rites, yet they can only be exceptional. So it seems only logical that, after spending a certain amount of time sitting in haunted places and challenging evil spirits, the disciple should come to doubt the existence of beings which never appear.

I have questioned several lamas on this subject.

" Incredulity comes sometimes," answered a *Geshes* from Derge.[1] " Indeed, it is one of the ultimate objects of the mystic masters, but if the disciple reaches this state of mind before the proper time he misses something which these exercises are designed to develop, that is fearlessness.

" Moreover, the teachers do not approve of simple incredulity, they deem it contrary to truth. The

[1] A *Geshes* is a graduate, a kind of LL.D. and Ph.D. Derge is a town in the province of Kham, in Eastern Tibet.

disciple must understand that gods and demons do really exist for those who believe in their existence, and that they are possessed with the power of benefiting or harming those who worship or fear them.

" However, very few reach incredulity in the early part of their training. Most novices actually *see* frightful apparitions."

I shall not venture to contradict this latter opinion, a number of instances have proved to me that it is well grounded. Darkness, the peculiarly wild aspect of the places chosen for meeting the dreaded evil beings, the power that Orientals possess to a high degree of visualizing their thoughts, are sufficient to produce hallucinations. But must we classify all phenomena witnessed by the celebrants of these curious rites as hallucination? Tibetans affirm that we must not.

I had the opportunity of talking with a *gomchen* of Ga (Eastern Tibet) called Kushog Wanchen about sudden deaths which occurred while calling up demons.

This lama did not appear inclined towards superstition and I thought he would agree with my opinion on this matter.

" Those who died were killed by fear. Their visions were the creation of their own imagination. He who does not believe in demons would never be killed by them."

I was much astonished when the anchorites replied in a peculiar tone of voice.

" According to that it must also follow that a man who does not believe in the existence of tigers may feel confident that none of them would ever hurt him even if he were confronted by such a beast." . . .

And he continued :

" Visualizing mental formations, either voluntarily or not, is a most mysterious process. What becomes of these creations? May it not be that like children born of our flesh, these children of our mind separate their lives from ours, escape our control, and play parts of their own ? . . .[1]

" Must we not also consider that we are not the only ones capable of creating such formations ? And if such entities exist in the world, are we not liable to come into touch with them, either by the will of their maker or from some other cause ? Could one of these causes not be that, through our mind or through our material deeds, we bring about the conditions in which these entities are capable of manifesting some kind of activity ?

" I will give you an illustration," he continued. " If you are living on a dry spot of ground at some distance from the banks of a river, fishes will never approach you. But cut a channel between the river and your dwelling-place and dig a pond in the dry spot of ground. Then, as the water runs in it, fishes will come from the river and you will see them moving before your eyes.

" It is only prudent to beware of opening channels without due consideration. Few, indeed, suspect what the great store-house of the world which they tap unconsciously, contains." And in lighter vein he concluded : " One must know how to protect oneself against the tigers to which one has given birth, as well as against those that have been begotten by others."

The Dreadful Mystic Banquet

It is these theories and others akin to them which have determined the choice of the places deemed proper as exercise grounds for mental wrestling with occult adversaries, as well as the peculiar form of the rites to be practised on these occasions.

The most fantastic of them is called *chöd*[2] (cutting off). It is a kind of " Mystery " played by one actor

---

[1] See also in Chapter VIII what is said about *tulpas*.
[2] Written *gchod*.

only, the celebrant ; and it has been so cleverly devised to terrify the novices that one hears of men who have suddenly gone mad or died while engaged in its performance.

A cemetery, or any wild site whose physical aspect awakens feelings of terror, is considered to be an appropriate spot. However, the place is thought even more suitable if it is associated with a terrible legend or if a tragic event has actually happened there quite recently.

The reason of this preference is that the effect of *chöd*, or kindred rites, does not depend solely on the feelings aroused in the mind of the celebrant by the stern words of the liturgy, nor upon the awe-inspiring surroundings. It is also designed to stir up the occult forces, or the conscious beings which—according to Tibetans—may exist in such places, having been generated either by actual deeds or by the concentration of many people's thoughts on imaginary events.

It follows that, during the performance of *chöd*, which I have compared to a drama enacted by a single actor, the latter may happen to see himself suddenly surrounded by players of the occult worlds who begin to play unexpected rôles. Whatever part auto-suggestion and visualization may have in the production of these phenomena, they are deemed excellent for the good result of the training ; but the test proves too hard for the nerves of some apprentice *naljorpas* and it is then that the accidents that I have mentioned occur : of madness or death.

Like any other actor, the man who wants to perform *chöd* must first learn his rôle by heart. Then he must practise the ritual dance, his steps forming geometrical figures, and also turning on one foot, stamping and leaping while keeping time with the liturgic recitation. Finally, he must learn to handle, according to rule, the bell, the *dorjee*, and the magic dagger (*phurba*), to beat rhythmically a kind of small drum (*damaru*) and to blow a trumpet made of a human femur (*kangling*).

The task is not easy ; I lost my breath more than once during my apprenticeship.

The lama teacher who directs the drill must be a kind of ballet master. But around him are to be seen no smiling dancing girls in pink tights. The dancers are young ascetics emaciated by austerities, clad in ragged robes, their unwashed faces lighted by ecstatic, hard, resolute eyes. They are preparing themselves, as they think, for a perilous undertaking, and the thought of the dreadful banquet at which they must offer their bodies to be devoured by the hungry demons haunts their minds.

In such conditions this " rehearsal," which might be comical, becomes rather lugubrious.

Lack of place prevents me from giving a translation of the text of *chöd, in extenso*. It includes long mystic preliminaries during which the celebrant *naljorpa* " tramples down " all passions and crucifies his selfishness. However, the essential part of the rite consists in a banquet which may be briefly described as follows.

The celebrant blows his bone trumpet, calling the hungry demons to the feast he intends to lay before them. He imagines that a feminine deity, which esoterically personifies his own will, springs from the top of his head and stands before him, sword in hand.

With one stroke she cuts off the head of the *naljorpa*. Then, while troops of ghouls crowd round for the feast, the goddess severs his limbs, skins him and rips open his belly. The bowels fall out, the blood flows like a river, and the hideous guests bite here and there, masticate noisily, while the celebrant excites and urges them with the liturgic words of unreserved surrender :

" For ages, in the course of renewed births I have

borrowed from countless living beings—at the cost of their welfare and life—food, clothing, all kinds of services to sustain my body, to keep it joyful in comfort and to defend it against death. To-day, I pay my debt, offering for destruction this body which I have held so dear.

" I give my flesh to the hungry, my blood to the thirsty, my skin to clothe those who are naked, my bones as fuel to those who suffer from cold. I give my happiness to the unhappy ones. I give my breath to bring back the dying to life.

" Shame on me if I shrink from giving my *self* ! Shame on you, wretched and demoniac beings,[1] if you do not dare to prey upon it. . . ."

This act of the " Mystery " is called the " red meal." It is followed by the " black meal," whose mystic signification is disclosed only to those disciples who have received an initiation of high degree.

The vision of the demoniacal banquet vanishes, the laughter and cries of the ghouls die away. Utter loneliness in a gloomy landscape succeeds the weird orgy, and the exaltation aroused in the *naljorpa* by his dramatic sacrifice gradually subsides.

Now he must imagine that he has become a small heap of charred human bones that emerges from a lake of black mud—the mud of misery, of moral defile-

[1] Buddhists extend their compassion and brotherly love to all beings, demons included. One must note that according to them, and especially according to lamaists, a demon does not necessarily dwell in the purgatories. The inhabitants of these sorrowful worlds are beings who have been led there by their cruelty or other evil deeds. They may, while in their present sad condition, reject their former bad feelings, and be animated by good will toward others, or with a desire for enlightenment, etc. As for so-called " demons," they are beings who habitually harbour hatred and ill will, who rejoice in unrighteousness and cruelty. And these may—as a result of former deeds—have been born as men, demi-gods or any other kind of beings.

ment, and of harmful deeds to which he has co-operated
during the course of numberless lives, whose origin is
lost in the night of time. He must realize that the
very idea of sacrifice is but an illusion, an offshoot of
blind, groundless pride. In fact, he *has nothing* to give
away, because he *is nothing*. These useless bones,
symbolizing the destruction of his phantom " I," may
sink into the muddy lake, it will not matter.

That silent renunciation of the ascetic who realizes
that he holds nothing that he can renounce, and who
utterly relinquishes the elation springing from the idea
of sacrifice, closes the rite.

Some lamas undertake tours to perform *chöd* near
a hundred and eight lakes, and a hundred and eight
cemeteries. They devote years to this exercise, wandering not only over Tibet, but also in India, Nepal and
China. Others only retire to solitary places for the
daily celebration of *chöd* for a longer or shorter time.

Chöd has a fascinating aspect which cannot be conveyed by a dry account read in surroundings totally
different from those in which this rite is celebrated.
Like many others, I have yielded to the peculiar
attraction of its austere symbolism and been impressed
by the fantastic natural background of the Tibetan
wilds.

The first time that I started alone for one of these
strange peregrinations, I stopped near a clear lake set
between stony shores. The surrounding landscape,
completely barren and impassive, excluded all feelings
of fear or of security, of joy or of sadness. There one
felt oneself sinking into a bottomless abyss of indifference.

Evening darkened the bright mirror of the lake while
I mused on the strange mind of the race that has
invented *chöd* and so many other grim practices.

The fantastic procession of clouds lighted by the
moon marched along the neighbouring summits and
descended towards the valleys surrounding me with a

troop of nebulous phantoms. One of them came forward walking alone over a path of light, suddenly spread out on the dark water, like a carpet before his steps.

The transparent giant, whose eyes were two stars, made a gesture with his long arm emerging from a floating robe. Did he call me? Did he drive me away? . . . I could not tell.

Then he approached still nearer, looking so real, so life-like, that I closed my eyes to dispel the hallucination. I felt myself wrapped in the folds of a soft cold cloak whose subtle substance penetrated me, causing me to shiver. . . .

What strange visions must the sons of these haunted wilds behold, these novices brought up in superstition, sent by their spiritual fathers through the night all alone, their imagination excited by the maddening rites. How many times, in the storm sweeping across the high tablelands, they must hear their challenge answered and shudder with terror in their tiny tent, miles and miles away from all human beings.

I very well understood the fear experienced by some celebrants of *chöd*. Yet I thought there was much exaggeration in the stories circulated about the tragic effects of this rite and I treated them with considerable scepticism. However, as the years went by, I gathered together a few facts which compelled me to have more faith in these tales.

There is one that I will relate.

At that time I was camping in Northern Tibet, in the desert or grassland. I had established myself in the vicinity of three black tents inhabited by herdsmen who spent the summer with their cattle, in a large pasture *thang*.[1]

Chance, which is but an easy word to designate

---

[1] *Thang.* A tableland of level ground between hill ranges or a very wide valley.

unknown causes, had led me there while hunting for butter, of which I had run short. These few cow- herds happened to be good men. My presence near them as a lady-lama and also as a purchaser from whom silver might be obtained, did not displease them in the least. They offered to keep my horses and mules with their own, which would save my servants a good deal of work, and I decided to let men and beasts enjoy a week of rest.

Two hours after my arrival, I already knew all about the neighbouring region. Truly, there was not much to be said about it.

The void immensity of the grassy solitudes extended towards the four quarters, broken only by streams and solitary hill ranges, while over all lay the great sky, luminous and void.

Yet there was an object of interest in that desert; I learnt that a lama, whose seat was somewhere north among Mongolian tribes, had chosen a cave near my camp for practising meditation during the summer months.

With him—the cowherd said—were two *trapas*, his disciples, who lived in a small tent below their master's ascetic lodging. Beside boiling tea, these two had no work to do and they spent most of the time in religious exercises. They often wandered out at night, and no doubt I should sometimes hear the sounds of the *damarus*, *kanglings* and bells accompanying the celebration of nocturnal offices, here or there, on the hills.

As for the lama, whose name was Rabjoms Gyatso, he had not left his cave since his arrival, three months ago.

From this information I guessed that the lama was engaged in the performance of a *dubthab* or some other magic practice.

The following day, at dawn, I started for the lama's cave. I wanted to reach it while the *trapas* were busy in their tent with their morning devotions. I hoped, if I was not seen by them, to be able to approach their master unexpectedly and have a look at what he was doing. This is not at all " etiquette," but being well acquainted with the customs of Tibetan lamas, I feared that Rabjoms Gyatso would refuse to see me if I asked permission to pay him a visit.

Guided by the directions which the cowherds had given me, I easily found the cave on a slope dominating a glen in which flowed a purling brook. A low wall built of stones, sods and turf and a curtain of rough yak hair had been added to the prehistoric dwelling to provide the lama with some sort of comfort and to hide him from passers-by.

My stratagem met with failure. As I climbed towards the cave, I met a sickly looking, matted-haired fellow dressed in ragged ascetic garb who stopped me. I had difficulty in persuading him to go to his master and beg for me the favour of an interview. The answer which he brought was polite but negative. The lama said that he could not see me but that if I would come again in a fortnight he would receive me.

As I had already planned to stay where I was for another week and, indeed, was not in a hurry to continue my journey, there was no special reason against some further delay. But, on the other hand, I did not know whether it was worth while waiting for the lama. I merely told the *trapa* that I might return, but would not engage to do so.

Twice a day, one or the other of the lama's disciples passed by my tent to fetch milk from the cowherds. The lean young man who had stopped me near the lama's cave attracted my attention by his wretched appearance. I thought that I might help him with some medicine and made up my mind to have a talk with him.

At my first words about medical treatment, he denied that he was suffering from any kind of illness, and as I pressed him with questions about the cause of his skeleton-like appearance, an expression of intense terror appeared in his wild eyes. It was impossible to obtain any explanation from him. I told my servants to try and learn something about the matter from his companion, but he too evaded all questions. Unlike the majority of Tibetans, who are rather talkative folk, these men were both uncommonly silent. After my inquiries, they went to the *dokpas's* tents by a roundabout way to avoid my camp, and as it was clear that they did not want me to interfere, even in order to help them, I let them alone.

I had been staying there for seven days, when I was informed that a man had died among a group of herdsmen established about a mile away, in the middle of the *thang*, and this decided me to postpone my departure to witness the rustic funeral.

In great haste, two riders set off for a lama's camp, or as *dokpas* [1] call it, a *banag gompa*—that is to say a monastery composed of an agglomeration of black tents—situated two days' journey from their home. They were to request the service of two monks to perform the rite for the dead. Only the ecclesiastics belonging to the monastery with which a layman is connected, as spiritual son or supporter, are rightly entitled to attend his *post-mortem* needs. But, in the meantime, the disciples of the foreign lama, our neighbour, went each in turn to read religious books over the dead man.

Some friends of the deceased, who had learnt the sad news, arrived from different directions, bringing presents to console the family in its bereavement, and the riders returned with the two monks and a few lay acquaintances. Then the chanting, ringing bells,

---

[1] Cowherds, herdsmen.

beating of drums and cymbals by the *trapas*, and the copious eating and drinking by all concerned, continued as usual in these circumstances in front of the decaying corpse tied in many wrappings and seated in a big cauldron. At last, when all was over, the dead body was carried to a small tableland on the mountains, cut into pieces and abandoned there, as supreme alms to the vultures.

To edify the *dokpas* in complying with a time-honoured custom of their *naljorpas*, whose costume I was wearing, I wrapped myself in a thick " zen " [1] at nightfall and walked to the place where the corpse had been carried, to spend the night there in meditation.

The moon was nearly full and beautifully lit up the immense plain extending from the foot of the hills which I skirted to other distant ranges. Nocturnal tramps in these solitudes have a peculiar charm. I could have walked for joy the whole night, but the cemetery, my goal, was less than an hour's march from my camp.

As I neared it I suddenly heard a strange sound, at the same time hoarse and piercing, that broke the perfect stillness of the desert. It was repeated several times, rending, it seemed, the calm atmosphere in which the sleeping steppes lay. Then the rhythmic beating of a *damaru* followed.

This language was clear enough to me. Some one —no doubt one of the lama's disciples—had gone to the place and performed *chöd* near the corpse.

The configuration of the land allowed me to reach unnoticed a small hillock and to hide myself in a cleft sheltered from the moonlight. From there I could perfectly observe the celebrant of *chöd*. He was the lean, sickly looking *trapa* to whom I had offered medicine. He wore his usual ragged *naljorpa* dress, a garnet-coloured pleated skirt, a yellow chemise with wide

---

[1] *Zen.* The toga worn by Buddhist monks and nuns.

sleeves and a red sleeveless waistcoat of a Chinese shape. But now the monastic toga was thrown over it and though as shabby as the rest of the clothes, its folds imparted a dignified and impressive mien to the tall emaciated monk.

When I arrived, the young ascetic recited the mantra of praise to the Prajñāpāramitā.

"O Wisdom that is gone, gone,
    gone to the beyond, and beyond the beyond : svâhâ ! . . . "

The monotonous *dong, dong* of the deep-voiced drum became slower and finally ceased, the young ascetic seemed sunk in meditation. After a while he wrapped himself more tightly in his *zen*. The *kangling* in his left hand, the *damaru* lifted high in the right and beating an aggressive staccato, the man stood in a challenging attitude, as if defying some invisible enemy.

"I, the fearless *naljorpa*," he exclaimed, "I trample down the *self*, the gods, and the demons."

His voice sounded still louder !

"Ye lamas, spiritual teachers, Heros, Khadomas, by thousands, come join me in the dance ! "

Then he began the ritualistic dance, turning successively towards the four quarters, reciting "I trample down the demon of pride, the demon of anger, the demon of lust, the demon of stupidity."

Each exclamation "I trample down" was accompanied by actual stamping and ritual vociferations of "*tsem shes tsem !* " which grew louder and louder, till the last ones were thundered out in truly deafening tones.

He rearranged his toga, which trailed on the ground, and having put aside his *damaru* and the bone trumpet, he spread the tent, seized a peg in one hand, a stone in the other one, and drove home the pegs while chanting the liturgy.

The tent stood there now, a puny thing made of a thin cotton fabric that had once been white and appeared greyish under the moonlight. It was ornamented with the words *Aum, A, Hum*, cut out in blue and red material and sewn on its three closed sides. Several frills of the five mystic colours—red, blue, green, yellow and white—hung from the little roof. The whole thing was faded and shabby.

Apparently agitated by disturbing thoughts, the lean ascetic looked at the pieces of the corpse scattered on the ground and then turned his head as if inspecting the surroundings. He seemed hesitating and, heaving a deep sigh, he passed his hand twice or thrice over his forehead. Then, shaking himself as if summoning up his courage, he seized his *kangling*, blew loudly a number of times, first slowly, then accelerating the rhythm as if for an exasperated summons, and entered his tent.

The nocturnal landscape that had been animated by the performance recovered its serenity.

What was I to do? The *naljorpa*, I knew, would not leave his tent before daybreak. Nothing more was to be seen. I was not in a meditative mood, I might as well go away. But there was no hurry. I continued to listen.

At intervals, I heard a few words of the ritual, then low indistinct muttering and moaning.

It was useless to remain there any longer. I moved cautiously out of my hiding-place. Then, as I took a few steps forward, I heard a low growl. An animal quickly passed in front of me. It was a wolf. The noise made by the *naljorpa* had kept it away and now, since all was silent, it had ventured to approach the feast laid there for those of its kind.

As I began to round the hillock, and climb down, a sudden exclamation stopped me.

" I pay my debts ! " shouted the *naljorpa*. " As I

have been feeding on you so feed upon me in your
turn !

" Come, ye hungry ones, and you that ungratified
desires torment !

" In this banquet offered by my compassion, my
flesh will transform itself into the very object of your
craving.

" Here, I give you fertile fields, green forests, flowery
gardens, both white and red food, clothes, healing
medicines ! . . . Eat ! eat ! . . ."

The excited ascetic blew furiously his *kangling*,
uttered an awful cry and jumped on his feet so hastily
that his head knocked against the low roof of the tent,
and the latter fell in on him. He struggled a while
under the cloth, and emerged with the grim, distorted
face of a madman, howling convulsively with gestures
betokening intense physical pain.

Now I could understand what *chöd* means for those
who work themselves up until they are absolutely
hypnotized by its ritual. No doubt that the man felt
the teeth of some invisible ghouls in his body.

He looked around him in all directions and addressed
unseen bystanders as if he had been surrounded by
a host of beings from other worlds. Most likely he
beheld some kind of ghastly vision.

The sight was deeply interesting. But I could not
look at it with complete indifference. This poor
fellow would kill himself with his dreadful ritual. I
had discovered the secret of his sickly appearance and
why he had deemed my medicines of no avail in his
case.

I felt most anxious to awaken him from his nightmare. Yet I hesitated because I knew that my intervention would go against the established rule. Those
who have engaged in such training must fight it out
unaided.

As I remained undecided, I heard the wolf growling

again. It had stopped on the top of the hillock. From there, as if petrified, and in an attitude of intense terror, the animal looked fixedly in the direction of the tumble-down tent as if it, too, beheld some appalling sight.

The *naljorpa* continued to groan in agony.

I could not bear it any longer. I rushed towards the poor mad fellow. But, as soon as he caught sight of me, he called to me with a vehement gesture, shouting :

" Come, angry one, feed on my flesh . . . drink my blood ! . . ."

This was too absurd indeed ! He took me for a ghost ! . . . In spite of the pity which I felt, I nearly laughed.

" Do be quiet," I said. " There are no demons here. I am the reverend lady-lama whom you know."

He did not appear even to hear my voice but continued to address me in the words of the ritual.

I thought that the toga in which I was wrapped gave me, perhaps, a somewhat ghost-like aspect. So throwing it on the ground I spoke again.

" Now, do recognize me ! "

It was of no use. The poor novice was utterly out of his mind. He stretched his arms towards my innocent *zen* and addressed it as if it were a new-comer among the troop of phantoms.

Why had I not let him alone and gone away without interfering with his performance ! I had only made things worse. As I pondered over the matter the young man, who was staggering round his tent, stumbled on one of the pegs and fell heavily to the ground. He remained immobile as if he had fainted, and I watched him to see if he would get up, but I did not dare to approach, for fear I should frighten him even more. After a while he moved and I deemed it better to withdraw before he looked at me again.

I decided to inform the lama of what was happening to his disciple. Though I guessed that the latter often went into such a state while performing *chöd*, and probably his teacher did not ignore it, still he might be particularly mad to-night. Rabjoms could send the other *trapa* to fetch him and spare the poor young man several hours of suffering. As I had failed in my attempt to help him directly, I did not see any better way.

I went down to the *thang*. All the way I continued to hear, at intervals, the sound of the *kangling* to which the howling of the wolf sometimes made answer. Then the noise gradually decreased until I heard it no more, and I plunged with delight into the great silent peace of the desert.

The feeble light of a small altar lamp, a tiny star on the slope of the hill, indicated the lama's dwelling-place.

I avoided the tent where his attendant was likely to be asleep and climbed up quickly to the cave.

Rabjoms Gyatso was seated cross-legged, in meditation. Without moving, he only lifted his eyes, when I opened the curtain and addressed him. In a few words, I told him in what condition I had left his disciple.

He smiled faintly.

"You appear to know *chöd*, Jetsunma.[1] Do you really? . . ." he inquired calmly.

"Yes," I said, "I have practised it too."

He did not reply.

After a while, as the lama remained silent, and seemed to have forgotten my presence, I tried again to appeal to his pity.

"Rimpoche," [2] I said, "I warn you seriously. I have some medical knowledge ; your disciple may

---

[1] *Jetsunma*, "reverend lady." A very polite term of address for a nun of high rank. One says also, *Jelsun Kushogs*.

[2] *Rimpoche*, "precious one." A very polite word to address a lama.

gravely injure his health and be driven to madness
by the terror he experiences. He really appeared to
feel himself being eaten alive."

" No doubt he is," answered the lama, with the same
calm, " but he does not understand that he is himself
the eater. May be that he will learn it later on. . . ."

I was about to reply, arguing that the poor novice
might, before that time came, give other candidates
for secret lore the opportunity of performing *chöd*
before his own corpse. Perhaps the lama guessed
what I was about to say, for without allowing me time
to utter a word, he added, slightly raising his voice :

" You seem to imply that you have had some kind
of training in the ' Short Path.' Did your spiritual
teacher not inform you of the risks and did you not
agree that you were ready to run these three : illness,
madness and death ? . . .

" It is hard to free oneself from delusion," he continued, " to blot out the mirage of the imaginary
world and to liberate one's mind from fanciful beliefs.
Enlightenment is a precious gem and must be bought
at a high price. Methods to reach *tharpa* [1] are many.
You may follow another one, less coarse than that
suited to the man whom you pity, but I am certain
that your way must be as hard as that of my disciple.
If it is easy it is a wrong one.

" Now, pray, go back to your camp. You may come
to see me to-morrow in the afternoon if you wish to."

It was useless to add another word. The ideas
expressed by the lama are current among Tibetan
mystics.

I bowed my parting " good night " and returned
to my tent.

The next afternoon, I availed myself of the permission which Rabjoms Gyatso had given me to pay
him a visit, and during the few days that I still spent

[1] *Tharpa.* Supreme liberation.

at that place, I saw him again several times. He was not a great scholar, but had a rather deep insight into a number of subjects and I was glad to have met him.

Inborn tendencies to distrust and incredulity prevent me from granting full faith to the many dreadful stories told by Tibetans regarding the practice of *chöd*. I persist in believing that such a dramatic performance as that which I chanced to witness is exceptional. Yet the feeling of being devoured during the celebration of this rite, and the wasting away of the novices, are not very rare occurrences. I have personally known two or three cases of the kind beside that related above, and like Rabjoms Gyatso, the masters of these unfortunate candidate *naljorpas* also decline to reassure their disciples by disclosing to them the subjective nature of their sensations. Moreover, as I have already mentioned, a number of mystic masters hold that these sensations are not in fact always entirely subjective.

The liturgic text of *chöd* and its scenic part are said to be the work of a certain lama, Padma Rigdzin, head of the Dzogschen sect,[1] who lived about two hundred years ago.

In 1922 I paid a visit to his successor or rather—according to the Tibetan belief—to himself, who, having several times died and been reborn, still occupied the seat of the abbot in the Dzogschen *gompa*.

The wild aspect of the site where the monastery stands, at the border of the immense northern grassy solitudes, is well fitted to incline the mind to fantastic, dismal broodings. Yet the good Padma Rigdzin, who was my host, did not in the least appear to indulge in melancholy musing. Mercantile schemes, together

---

[1] Sect of the " Great accomplissement." The last in date of the " Red hat " sects. Nowadays, it is practically divided in two branches : The Southern, original one, whose head has his seat at Mindoling monastery, near the Brahmaputra's bank ; and the Northern one, with the *tulku* of Padma Rigdzin at its head.

with childish whims, occupied his mind. He questioned me at length on French Indo-China and Burma, inquiring about import and export in these countries. He especially wanted to know if he could get peacocks from there, as he had a great desire to add some of these birds to his little zoological collection of live animals.

However, far away from the sumptuous apartments of the Lama *tulku,* isolated, small dwellings sheltered monks whose grave look and mysterious demeanour matched the surrounding scenery more harmoniously.

Some of these *tsam khangs* [1] were inhabited by strict recluses who had intercourse with nobody. Among them, some aimed at obtaining supernormal psychic faculties or magic powers, while others were absorbed in mystic contemplations which—according to the views held in their sect—should lead them to spiritual enlightenment.

For long, the monastery of Dzogschen has been famous as a centre where secret methods of psychic training are taught and practised.

Those who have obtained the fruit of *chöd* may dispense with the theatrical side of the rite. Its different phases are, then, called to mind only, in the course of silent meditation, and soon even this exercise becomes unnecessary.

Nevertheless, either because they enjoy remembering, through that performance, the exertions of their novitiate days or for other reasons known to themselves alone, certain *gomchens* sometimes meet to celebrate *chöd* together. But, then, the dismal rite changes its character and becomes a mystic feast in which the exulting *naljorpas* rejoice over their utter freedom.

I have had the rare opportunity of beholding some of these ascetics, tall men of Kham, clad in the pictur-

[1] Houses for recluses, see Chapter VII.

esque garb of the hermits, their plaited hair falling to their feet. Under the starry sky, they danced to the strange music of hand-drums and femur-trumpets, in these majestic wilds which lay at the summit of our globe. On their ecstatic faces shone the proud joy of having trampled down the feelings that keep the mind feverish through hopes and fears, through " the burning thirst," " the distressing race towards mirages."

And then they sunk in endless meditations that kept them till late after dawn sitting cross-legged, the body erect, the gaze cast down, motionless, like stone images.

It was a sight never to be forgotten.

CHAPTER V

DISCIPLES OF YORE AND THEIR CONTEMPORARY EMULATORS

THE incidents connected with the admission of a disciple by a mystic teacher, the first years of his novitiate, the tests imposed on him, the peculiar circumstances in which spiritual illumination dawns upon him, might in many cases supply the material for a most curious novel.

Hundreds of such wonderful stories, either ancient or of recent date, handed down by oral tradition, written in the biographies of famous lamas or even told by living witnesses, are circulated all over Tibet.

Translated into a foreign language, read in countries whose customs, thoughts and physical aspect are so different from those of Tibet, the charm of that strange " Golden Legend " largely vanishes. But when told with the pathetic accent of a believer, in the *chiara oscura* of a monastic cell or under the rocky ceiling of a cave-hermitage, the very soul of Tibet reveals itself in all its mystic powerful originality, athirst for occult knowledge and spiritual life.

I shall, first, tell briefly the fantastic and symbolic story of Tilopa's initiation. Though he himself was a native of Bengal and never crossed the border of Tibet, he is considered as the spiritual ancestor of one of the most important of the " Red hat " sects, that of the Kagyudpas.

I may add, by the way, that it is in a monastery of this sect that the lama Yongden began his novitiate at the early age of eight.

Tilopa is seated reading a philosophic treatise when an aged beggar woman appears behind him, reads or makes a pretence of reading a few lines over his shoulder and asks him abruptly : " Do you understand what you are reading ? "

Tilopa feels indignant. What does this witch mean by putting him such an impertinent question ? But the woman does not allow him the time to express his feelings. She spits on the book.

This time, the reader jumps up. How can that diabolical wretch dare to spit on the Holy Scriptures ?

In answer to his vehement reproaches, the woman spits a second time on the book, utters a word that Tilopa cannot understand and disappears.

Strangely enough, that word which was nothing to him but an unintelligible sound, yet suddenly calmed Tilopa's anger. An uncomfortable sensation spreads all over his frame. Distrust, doubt of his knowledge arise in his mind. After all, it may be true that he has not understood the doctrine expounded in that treatise, or any doctrine whatever, and that he is but an utter ignoramus.

What did that strange woman say ?—What word has she pronounced that he has not been able to catch ? He wants to know it. He feels that he *must* know it.

And so Tilopa started in search of the old woman. After much wandering and exertion he found her at night in a solitary wood (others say in a cemetery). She was seated alone, her " red [1] eyes shining like live coals in the darkness."

---

[1] It must be understood that the strange woman is a *dâkinî*. Tibetans call them *Khadoma*, but in mystic terminology they often use the Sanskrit name *dâkinî* or its abbreviation *dâkî*. These are a kind of fairies who play a great part in mystic lamaism, as teachers of secret doctrines, and are styled " mothers." They often appear in the shape of an aged woman and one of their peculiar signs is that they have red or green eyes. There are two kinds of Khadomas : The spiritual ones who do not belong

In the course of the conversation that followed, Tilopa was directed to go to the Dâkinîs's land, in order to meet their queen. On the road, dangers of countless kinds awaited him : abysses, roaring torrents, ferocious animals, delusive mirages, ghastly apparitions, hungry demons. If he allowed himself to be overpowered by fear, or missed the narrow, thread-like path winding across that terrible region, he would fall a prey to the monsters. If, driven by thirst or hunger, he drank at the clear springs or ate the fruits hanging at hand on the trees by the road, if he yielded to the fair maidens inviting him to sport with them in pleasant grooves, he would become bewildered and incapable of finding his way.

For his protection, the woman gave him a magic formula. This he must repeat all along the road, keeping his mind entirely concentrated on it, uttering no word, listening to nothing.

Some believe that Tilopa actually achieved the phantasmagoric journey. Others, better informed regarding the various experiences that may be undergone during certain peculiar states of trance, see in it a form of psychic phenomena.

Anyhow, Tilopa saw the countless frightful or alluring sights, he struggled across steep rocky slopes and foaming rivers, he felt himself freezing amidst snows, scorched on burning sandy steppes, and never departed from his concentration on the magic words.

At last, he reached the castle whose bronze walls were glowing with heat. Monstrous gigantic females opened wide mouths to devour him. Trees, with branches holding weapons, barred his way. Yet he entered the enchanted palace. There innumerable sumptuous rooms formed a labyrinth. Tilopa wended

to our world and are called " Khadomas of wisdom," and the Khadomas who, either incarnated as woman or not, belong to our world.

his way through them and reached the queen's apartment.

There was the beautiful fairy seated on her throne adorned with precious jewels, and she smiled at the daring pilgrim as he crossed the threshold.

But he, unmoved by her loveliness, ascended the steps of the throne and, still repeating the *mantra*, wrenched from her the glittering jewels, trampled under foot the flowery garlands, tore away her precious silk and golden robes, and as she lay naked on her wrecked throne, he violated her.

Such conquests of a *dâkinî*, either by sheer violence or by magic devices, are a current theme in Tibetan mystic literature. They are an allegory referring to the realization of truth and to some psychic process of self-spiritual development.

Tilopa handed down his doctrine to Narota, a learned Kashmiri, and a Tibetan pupil of the latter—the lama Marpa—brought it to his own country. The foremost disciple of Marpa, the famous anchorite poet Milarespa, in his turn, communicated it to his disciple Dagpo Lhajee. And the lineal succession still continues nowadays under the name of the Kagyudpa sect.

We find in the biography of Narota an amusing description—not as fantastic as might be supposed—of the tests devised by a master of the " Short Path " to train and direct his disciple.

A brief summary will give an idea of it.

Narota—or Naropa, as Tibetans call him—was a Brahmin of Kashmir who lived in the tenth century A.D. Deeply learned in philosophy, he was also believed to be an adept in magic.

Having been greatly offended by a rajah to whom he was chaplain, he resolved to kill the prince by an occult process. For this purpose, he shut himself up in an isolated house and began a *dragpoi dubthab*.[1]

---

[1] A magic rite to bring about death or injury.

As he was performing the rite, a mother fairy appeared at a corner of the magic diagram and asked Naropa if he deemed himself capable of sending the spirit of the rajah towards a happy place in another world, or of bringing it back into the body which it had left and resuscitating it. The magician could only confess that his science did not extend so far.

Then the mother fairy assumed a stern mien and reproached him for his heinous undertaking. She told him that no one had the right to destroy who could not build up again the being destroyed or establish it in a better condition. The consequence of his criminal thought, she added, would be his own rebirth in one of the purgatories.

Terror-stricken, Naropa inquired how he could escape that terrible fate. The Khadoma advised him to seek the Sage named Tilopa and to beg, from him, initiation into the secret doctrine of " *tsi chig lus chig sangyais.*" That is to say the mystic doctrine of the " Short Path " which frees a man from the consequences of his actions, whatever they may be, by the revelation of their true nature, and ensures the attainment of buddhahood " in one single life." [1] If he succeeded in grasping the meaning of that teaching and realizing it, he would not be reborn again and, consequently, would escape a life of torment in the purgatories.

Naropa stopped the performance of the rite, and hastened towards Bengal, where Tilopa lived.

Tilopa, whose fantastic initiation by a *dâkinî* I have just related, enjoyed a great reputation when Naropa started to meet him. He belonged to a tantric sect

---

[1] That is to say that buddhahood is attained in a short time, during the very life in which one has begun the training, instead of the usual course which requires many centuries, during which death and re-birth take place several times.

and was one of those *avadhutas*,[1] of whom it is said that " they like nothing, hate nothing, are ashamed of nothing, do not glorify in anything, are utterly detached from all things, having cut off all family, social and religious bonds." [2]

As for Naropa, history shows him to have been a man of refinement, deeply convinced of his superiority as a member of the Brahmin caste and a learned doctor. The meeting of these two different characters brought about a series of incidents which may well appear to us rather like rough practical jokes, but must have been a heart-breaking drama for Naropa.

The first meeting of Naropa with Tilopa occurred in the courtyard of a Buddhist monastery. The cynic ascetic, naked, or nearly so, was seated on the ground, eating fish. As the meal went on, he put down beside him the fishes' backbones. In order not to defile his caste purity, Naropa was on the point of passing by at some little distance from the eater, when a monk started to reproach Tilopa for parading his lack of compassion for the animals [3] in the very premises of a Buddhist monastery. And so saying, he ordered him to depart at once.

Tilopa did not even condescend to answer. He muttered some magic words,[4] snapped his fingers and

---

[1] An ascetic who has cut himself entirely off from the world and has renounced all social and moral rules and laws, believing that he has reached a state of enlightenment where the distinction between good and evil does not exist any more.

[2] *Mahânirvâna tantra.* It is a current description of the Sage which is found in countless texts.

[3] Because the food he ate had been obtained by killing the fish.

[4] Such resurrections are a favourite theme in Oriental stories. We read in Milarespa's biography that the lama Chösrdor of Gnog resuscitated, in the same way, a number of birds and field mice which had been killed during a hailstorm. A still queerer story was told me by a Korean. A holy monk, so runs the story, met on his way a man who was boiling, near a river, a broth made

behold ! . . . The fish bones were again covered with flesh, the fishes moved as if living, they went up in the air for a while and vanished. No vestige remained of the cruel meal on the ground.

Naropa was petrified, but suddenly an idea flashed through his mind. This strange wonder-worker, no doubt, was the very Tilopa whom he was seeking. He hurriedly inquired about him, and the information given by the monks agreeing with his own intuition, he ran after the yogin, but the latter was nowhere to be found.

Then, in his eagerness to learn the doctrine that could save him from the purgatories, Naropa wanders from town to town, with the only result that each time he reaches a place where Tilopa is said to be staying, the latter has, invariably, just left it a little before his arrival.

It is quite probable that Naropa's biographers have lengthened and exaggerated his peregrinations, but their account is certainly grounded on actual facts.

Sometimes—so goes the story—Naropa met, as if by chance on his way, singular beings who were phantoms created by Tilopa. Once, knocking at the door of a house, to beg food, a man comes out who offers him wine. Naropa feels deeply offended and indignantly refuses the impure beverage.[1] The house and its master vanish immediately. The proud Brahmin

with the fishes he had just caught. The monk, without uttering a word, took the pot and swallowed the boiling broth. The man was astonished to see how he could bear the touch of the boiling liquid, but yet scoffed at him, reproaching him for his sinful gluttony. (Chinese and Korean Buddhist monks never eat animal food.) But the monk, still keeping silent, entered the river and micturated. And, then, with his water the fishes came out living and went away swimming in the river.

[1] Orthodox Brahmins are not allowed to drink strong drink. To offer wine or spirit to them is to treat them like a low-caste man and is, consequently, an insult.

is left alone on the solitary road, while a mocking
voice laughs—" That man was I : Tilopa."

Another day, a villager asks Naropa to help him to
skin a dead animal. Such work, in India, is only done
by untouchable outcastes. The mere approach of such
men makes a Hindu, belonging to one of the pure
castes, unclean. Naropa flees, utterly disgusted, and
the invisible Tilopa scoffs at him : " That man was
myself."

Again, the traveller sees a brutal husband who drags
his wife by her hair, and when he interferes, the cruel
fellow tells him : " You had better help me, I want
to kill her. At least, pass your way and let me do it."
Naropa can hear nothing more. He knocks the man
down on the ground, sets free the woman . . . and
lo ! once more the phantasmagoria disappears while
the same voice repeats scornfully : " I was there, I :
Tilopa."

The adventures continue in this same vein.

Proficient magician though he may be, Naropa has
never even conceived the idea of such display of supernormal powers : he stands on the brink of madness,
but his desire to become Tilopa's disciple grows still
stronger. He roams at random across the country,
calling Tilopa aloud and, knowing by experience that
the *guru* is capable of assuming any form, he bows down
at the feet of any passer-by and even before any animal
he happens to see on the road.[1]

One evening, after a long tramp, he reaches a ceme-

[1] In one of the deceitful apparitions, Tilopa had taken the
shape of a hare. To be able to show oneself under various shapes
is one of the supernormal powers with which Tibetans credit
their great *naljorpas*. It is related that Milarespa showed himself
as a snow leopard and as a crow to people who visited him in his
snow-buried hermitage of Lachi Kangs. The legend of Gesar
of Link contains numbers of such prodigies. Suggestion, no
doubt, plays an important part in visions of this kind which are
not all mere tales. I have been able to see something of them myself.

tery. A crumbled-down pyre is smouldering in a corner. At times, a dark reddish flame leaps from it, showing shrivelled-up carbonized remains. The glimmer allows Naropa to vaguely discern a man lying beside the pyre. He looks at him . . . a mocking laugh answers his inspection. He has understood, he falls prostrate on the ground, holding Tilopa's feet and placing them on his head. This time the yogin does not disappear.

During several years, Naropa follows Tilopa without being treated as of any importance. His master teaches him nothing, but by way of compensation, he tests his faith in him by means of twelve great and twelve small ordeals.

Space is lacking to describe each of the twenty-four tests which, in fact, often repeat the same details. I shall confine myself to a few.

According to the custom of Indian ascetics Naropa went on a begging round. Coming back to his master he offered him the rice and curry which he had received as alms. The rule is that a disciple eats only after his *guru* is satisfied, but far from leaving something for his follower, Tilopa ate up the whole contents of the bowl, and even declared that the food was so much to his taste that he could have eaten another bowlful with pleasure.

Without waiting for a more direct command, Naropa took the bowl and started again for the house where generous householders bestowed such tasty alms. Unfortunately, when he arrived there, he found the door closed. Burning with zeal, the devoted disciple did not let himself be stopped for so little. He kicked the door open, discovered some rice and various stews keeping warm on the stove in the kitchen, and helped himself to more of what Tilopa had so much enjoyed. The masters of the house came back as he was plunging a spoon in their pots and gave him a first-rate thrashing.

Bruised from head to feet, Naropa returned to his *guru*, who showed no compassion whatever for his suffering.

" What an adventure has befallen you on my account ! " he said with mocking calm. " Do you not regret having become my disciple ? "

With all the strength that his pitiful condition left at his disposal, Naropa protested that far from regretting having followed such a *guru*, he deemed the privilege of being his disciple could never be paid for too dearly, even if one was to purchase it at the cost of one's life.

Another day Tilopa, passing by an open drain, asked the disciples who walked with him : " Which of you would drink of that drain water if I ordered him to ? "

It must be understood that it was not here only a question of overcoming natural disgust for the filthy liquid, but of being defiled according to the religious Hindu Law.[1] Nevertheless, while his companions hesitated, the Brahmin Naropa ran forward and drank the foul beverage.

Another test was still more cruel.

Master and disciple lived at that time in a hut, near a forest. Once, returning from the village with Tilopa's meal, Naropa saw that during his absence, the latter had fabricated a number of long wooden needles and hardened them in the fire. Greatly astonished, he inquired about the use Tilopa meant to make of these implements.

The yogin smiled queerly.

" Could you," he asked, "bear some pain if it pleased me ? "

Naropa answered that he belonged entirely to him and that he could do whatever he liked with him.

---

[1] At that time, tenth century A.D., Buddhism had already greatly degenerated, reverting to a number of Hindu superstitions strongly condemned by the Buddha.

" Well," replied Tilopa, " stretch out your hand."
And when Naropa had obeyed, he thrust one of the
needles under each of the nails of one hand, did the
same to the other, and finished with the toes.   Then
he pushed the tortured Naropa into the hut, commanded him to wait there till he returned, closed the
door, and went away.

Several days elapsed before he came back.   He found
Naropa seated on the ground, the needles still in his flesh.

" What did you think while alone ? " inquired Tilopa.
" Have you not come to believe that I am a cruel
master and that you had better leave me ? "

" I have been thinking of the dreadful life of torments
which will be mine in the purgatories if I do not succeed,
by your grace, in becoming enlightened in the mystic
doctrine, and so escaping a new rebirth," answered
Naropa.

As years went by, Naropa threw himself down from
the roof of a house, crossed a blazing fire and performed
a number of other fantastic feats which often put his
life in jeopardy.

To conclude, I shall relate one more of these curious
tests, the story being rather amusing.

Master and disciple were strolling in the streets
when they happened to meet a wedding procession
accompanying a bride to her husband's house.

" I desire that woman," said Tilopa to Naropa.
" Go, bring her to me."

He had scarcely finished speaking before Naropa
joined the cortège.

Seeing that he was a Brahmin, the men of the wedding
party allowed him to approach the bride, thinking that
he meant to bless her.   But when they saw that he took
her in his arms and intended to carry her away, they
seized on everything they could find—the palanquin's
sticks, the torches that lighted the way of the procession
and other implements—to belabour poor Naropa.   So

soundly was he cudgelled that he fainted and was left for dead on the spot.

Tilopa had not waited for the end of the performance to pass quietly on his way.

When he came to his senses again and had painfully dragged himself along until he overtook his whimsical *guru*, the latter, as welcome, asked him once more the usual question, " Do you not regret . . ." And, as usual also, Naropa protested that a thousand deaths seemed to him but a trifle to purchase the privilege of being his disciple.

At last, Naropa got the reward of his long tribulations. But not in the form of regular teaching and initiation.

If we trust the tradition, Tilopa seems to have used, on that occasion, a queer method somewhat akin to that patronized by the Chinese teachers of the Ts'an sect. There is no doubt that, though left apparently untaught, Naropa had been able to grasp a number of points in the " Short Path's doctrine," during his lively period of probation. However, the manner of his full enlightening is related as follows :

Naropa was seated near a fire in the open with his master. Quite unexpectedly, the latter took off one of his shoes and soundly slapped the disciple's face with it. Naropa saw all the stars of heaven, and at the same time the inner meaning of the " Short Path's doctrine " flashed into his mind.

Naropa had, later on, a large number of disciples, and, according to the tradition, was a most kind master, sparing his pupils the painful ordeals which he had himself so bitterly experienced.

Already advanced in age, he left the monastery of which he was a reputed doctor and, retiring in solitude, devoted twelve consecutive years to uninterrupted contemplation. He is said to have finally reached " the excellent success," [1] that is to say Buddhahood.

[1] *Mchog gi dnos grub.*

Naropa is especially known in Tibet as the spiritual teacher of the lama Marpa, who was himself the master of the famous ascetic poet Milarespa whose religious songs are most popular all over Tibet.

If Naropa showed himself a mild spiritual father, such was not the case with Marpa, who tortured the poor Milarespa for years, commanding him to build a house unaided and then ordering him several times to pull it down when nearly finished, and rebuild it again.

Milarespa was to dig out the stones alone and to carry them on his back. The repeated rubbing of these hard loads caused sores which became infected on account of the earth and dirt that entered them. Marpa pretended to ignore the martyrdom which his disciple endured. When, at last, yielding to the supplications of his wife Dagmedma,[1] the lama condescended to look at the bleeding back of Milarespa, he coldly advised him to place a piece of felt on it with holes to isolate the sores. This is a process commonly used in Tibet for the sore backs of pack animals.

The house built by Milarespa still exists in Lhobrag, Southern Tibet.

Tibetans do not entertain the least doubt regarding the complete authenticity of such stories. If we cannot vie in faith with them, we must, however, beware of considering all traditional accounts of the novice *naljorpas'* exertions as mere fictions. It would be also an error to believe that such facts belong to a remote past and cannot occur again nowadays. The Tibetan mind has not changed since the time of Marpa. In the house of many lamas I have recognized the very picture of his home and customs, as they are depicted in Tibetan literature, while Marpa himself appeared to me personified by the master of the house.

[1] Marpa, who lived before the reform of Tsong Khapa, was a married lama.

The young monk in quest of a spiritual guide has also remained the image of his predecessors. If not quite equal in zeal to Naropa and Milarespa, who have been, in all times, exceptional characters, he is still ready to bear uncommon hardship, make a number of sacrifices and see many prodigies. And so the fantastic adventures of yore are lived over again every day at the four corners of the " Land of Snows."

However barbarous the physical ordeals with which the hermits think useful to test the quality of their disciples may appear, these are, nevertheless, the lightest part of the training. The really dreadful trial is the purely mental one.

This begins when the first idea arises in the candidate for initiation of begging the guidance of a mystic anchorite. So many things are rumoured about these *gomchens*, their life is so mysterious, their appearance and the rare words they utter are so exceedingly strange that, for Tibetans already inclined to superstitious terror, they seem a thousand times more to be feared than gods and demons. Indeed, they must be so, for they are credited with the power of enslaving gods and demons. Lost travellers or hunters have more than once related that while wandering across solitary hills they have had a glimpse of non-human beings attending on some of these hermits.

To betake oneself to such a master, to put one's present life and one's fate hereafter in his hands is a hazardous step. It is easy to imagine the hesitations, the conflicting feelings, and the anguish which prey on the mind of the aspirant to secret lore.

The long distances which the candidate generally has to travel through desert regions to reach the hermitage of the master whom he has chosen, the wild majesty of the site in which such hermitages are generally situated, all these again contribute to deeply impress the young monk.

Psychic training undertaken in such a disposition, in such surroundings, and under such a master cannot help being fantastic. Around the disciple abandoned to prolonged solitary meditations, heaven and earth quake and whirl so that he can nowhere find a firm footing. Gods and demons mock him with visions at first appalling, then ironical and disconcerting when he has conquered fear. The maddening succession of impossible occurrences may continue ten or twenty years. It may torture the disciple until his death, unless, one day, he awakes from the nightmare, having understood *that which was to be understood*, and, bowing at the feet of his impassive master, takes leave of him without asking for any more teaching.

Among several stories which I have heard from anchorites and *naljorpas*, regarding their initiation, the following is typically Tibetan.

When he betook himself to a lama *gomchen*, Yeshes Gyatso was not quite a novice in mystic training. He had spent several fairly long periods in strict seclusion, endeavouring to find an answer to a question which puzzled him painfully.

What is the mind? he asked himself. And he tried to catch his mind in order to examine and analyse it. But the fugitive thing—" as the water that a child endeavours to keep in its closed hand "—always escaped.

His *guru*, a lama from the monastery to which Yeshes belonged, seeing him tortured by his unsuccessful efforts, directed him to an anchorite whom he knew.

The journey was not very long. Only about three weeks—which is reckoned a short time in Tibet—but the track went across desert regions and passes 18,000 feet high. Yeshes started, carrying on his back a few books, a blanket and the usual provisions : roast barley flour, butter and tea. It was in the second

month of the Tibetan year.¹ Deep snow covered the
ground and all along his way the traveller could behold
those awe-inspiring frozen landscapes of the high
summits which seem to belong to another world.

One evening, at sunset, he reached the *gomchen*
hermitage, a vast cave, in front of which extended a
small natural terrace that had been enclosed by a wall.

Some distance below, a few huts sheltered those
disciples who, for a short time, were allowed to stay
near the lama. The anchorites' dwellings stood on
the upper heights of a mountain formed by blackish
rocks, commanding a view of the emerald-green water
of a small rippleless lake.

I arrived there once, at dusk, as Yeshes had done
many years before, and looking at the desolate scenery
lighted by the dim twilight, I could understand how
strong an impression it had made on him.

Yeshes asked one of the lama's disciples to beg for
him the permission to be admitted to his master.

The *gomchen* did not allow him to climb to his cave.
This is habitual and did not astonish Yeshes, who had
never expected to be received immediately. He shared
the cell of a novice and waited.

After a week had elapsed he timidly ventured to have
the hermit reminded of his request. The answer came
at once. He was ordered to leave the place immediately
and to return to his monastery.

He cried out his despair to the eyrie of the teacher,
and prostrated himself at the foot of the rocky slope.
But no compassionate answer broke the dead silence
of the desert. Yeshes had to go.

The same evening, a hail-storm swept across a barren
tableland which he had to cross. He distinctly saw
giant threatening phantoms, lost his way in the darkness
and was wandering about all the night. The following days brought nothing but trouble. The weather

¹ In March. The Tibetan New Year fell early in February.

remained awful, the traveller had exhausted his provisions, he was nearly drowned in crossing a mountain stream and reached his *gompa*, at last a victim of disease and despair.

Yet, the faith which he had intuitively put in the stern *gomchen* remained unshaken. Three months later he started again. As during his previous journey, he met terrible storms on the high passes. The credulous Yeshes did not fail to ascribe them to supernormal cause. Either, he thought, the lama had let the winds loose to test his steadiness of purpose, or evil spirits had stirred them up to prevent him from reaching the *gomchen's* hermitage and being initiated by him in the mystic doctrine.

That second journey did not prove more successful than the first one. Yeshes was not even allowed to bow at the feet of the hermit, but was sent back immediately.

He made two more journeys to the anchorite during the next year and the second time he was at last admitted before him.

" You are mad, my son," the *gomchen* told him. " Why are are you so obstinate? I do not accept new disciples. I have also got some information about you; you have already pursued philosophic study and spent a long time in meditation. What do you hope for, from an old, ignorant man ?

" If you really wish to learn the secret mystic lore, go to the lama N . . . at Lhasa. He is conversant with all works of the more learned authors and is fully initiated in the esoteric traditions. Such a master is just what a young well-read man like you needs."

Yeshes knew that this way of speaking is usual with *gurus*. It is a way of testing the degree of confidence and esteem in which the candidate disciples hold them. Moreover he was full of faith.

So, he remained obstinate, testified in various manners

of his sincere devotion and earnestness, and was finally accepted by the lama.

Another monk whom I have known had sought an anchorite teacher for reasons that had nothing to do with philosophic or mystic pursuits. If I relate his case it is because it contrasts with that of Yeshes and shows another aspect of the Tibetan mind.

Karma Dorjee was low born. As a little boy, in the monastery where he was a geyok,[1] he had been the butt of ridicule and contempt of the young novices of his age who belonged to a higher social class. These vexations had embittered his young mind and he confessed to me that he was but a little over his tenth year when he had sworn that he would rise above those who humiliated him.

When he was grown up, his companions had at last to refrain from too open manifestations of their scorn, but they revealed it clearly enough by their silence and their aloofness. Karma Dorjee was proud and possessed a strong will, he still dreamed of keeping the oath taken in his early youth. His low birth and his monastic condition left him only one way of reaching his aim. He must become a famous naljorpa, a magician, one of those who coerce the demons and make them their retainers. In this way he could revenge himself on his tormentors and make them tremble before him.

In this not very pious frame of mind, Karma Dorjee applied to the head of his monastery for a two years' leave, being desirous, he said, to retire to the forest for meditation. Permission he knew is never refused to such requests.

Karma climbed high up on the hills, found a convenient place near a spring and built a hut there with branches and mud. Immediately, in order to imitate

---

[1] A young novice of poor parentage whose family cannot maintain him, and who does menial work at a lama's house for his living. See Chapter III.

the *reskyangpas*,[1] he discarded all clothes and let his hair grow. Those who brought him supplies of food at long intervals found him seated cross-legged and naked even in the heart of winter, apparently sunk in a deep trance.

People began to talk about him, but he was still far from the fame he desired. He realized that his hermitage in the forest and his nakedness were not sufficient to obtain it for him. So he went down to his monastery, and this time asked permission to leave the country in search of a spiritual teacher. No one endeavoured to detain him.

Karma's peregrinations were much more fertile in incidents than those of Yeshes, for the latter at least knew where he was going and under which lama he wished to practise the mystic life, while Karma had no idea of either and tramped at random.

After a time, as he did not succeed in discovering a magician whom he thought capable of leading him to the topmost heights of the secret lore, he resolved to seek one by an occult process.

Karma was a staunch believer in gods and demons. He knew by heart the story of Milarespa who, with their help, had caused a house to fall down on his enemies, and remembered many other tales of terrible deities who brought the bloody heads which he had claimed into the middle of the *kyilkhor* (magic diagram) constructed by the magician. He had acquired himself a certain knowledge regarding *kyilkhors*. So he drew one with stones in a narrow gorge and began his conjurations in hopes that the mighty wrathful Lords Towos would direct him to one of the masters whom they serve.

In the course of the seventh night a mountain stream

---

[1] The *naljorpas* who have acquired the power of developing *tumo*, the internal heat, and wear but a single cotton dress (*reskyang*) or even remain naked   See Chapter VI.

that flowed in the gorge suddenly rose with startling rapidity. An enormous quantity of water—probably due to the breaking of a natural dam or to a cloud-burst higher up the hill—suddenly swept across the defile and the young monk was swept away with his *kyilkhor* and his small luggage. Whirled along amongst the rocks, Karma was lucky enough to escape being drowned and came aground at the end of the gorge in an immense valley. When day broke he saw at a distance, a *ritöd* (hermitage) that stood sheltered by a rocky wall on the spur of a mountain range.

The sun rose bright as it does on the tableland of Central Asia, and the little white-washed house appeared rosy and luminous under its first touch. Karma could clearly discern the rays of light that flashed from it and rested on his head.

Certainly his long-sought-for master lived there. The help of the deities answering his summons was not to be doubted. He had intended to walk up the gorge and to cross the mountain range, but they had brought him down to the *ritöd*. The intervention had mani-fested itself in a somewhat rough way, Karma admitted, but he ascribed this to a cause that could not but flatter his vanity. The *Towos*, he thought, have not been able to resist the strength of my conjuration, but fore-seeing what a powerful magician I shall become, after I have received proper teaching, felt angered at the idea of eventually becoming my slaves.

Rejoicing in his glorious future, Karma did not give a thought to the loss of the provisions and clothes that had been carried away by the flood. And as he had stripped himself of all garments, to resemble Heruka [1] when officiating before his *kyilkhor*, he now confidently marched toward the hermitage in a state of nature.

As he neared it, a disciple of the anchorite came down to fetch water at a stream. The *trapa* almost let fall

[1] A deity represented as a naked ascetic.

the bucket he carried when he caught sight of the strange apparition.

Tibetan climate greatly differs from that of India, and if unclad ascetics, or pseudo-ascetics, are legion in the latter country, it is not so on the heights of the " Land of Snows." There, only a very few *naljorpas* adopt that simple fashion, and as they live far away from all tracks, in the recesses of wild mountains, one has few opportunities of catching a glimpse of them.

" Who lives in that *ritöd* ? " inquired Karma.

" My master, the *geshes* [1] Tobsgyais," answered the *trapa*.

The aspirant magician did not put a second question. What information did he now require ? He knew all that he needed to know. The deities had led him to his very *tsawai lama*.[2]

" Tell the lama that the *Chöskyongs* [3] have brought him a disciple," said the naked traveller.

Quite bewildered, the water-carrier reported his words to the hermit, who commanded him to show in the strange visitor.

Lama Tobsgyais was a well-read man, the grandson of a Chinese official and of his Tibetan wife. According to Karma's account he appears to me to have been a gentle agnostic, who had perhaps adopted a hermit's life by the desire to study without being disturbed by troublesome people and by an aristocratic taste for solitude. This is rather frequent in Tibet. In fact, Karma really knew very little about his *guru*. As we shall learn, by his own story, he did not see much of him, and the few particulars he could tell me about his parentage and character he had learnt from two disciples of the lama, who were inmates of the *ritöd*.

In situation Kushog Tobsgyais' hermitage followed

---

[1] A high graduate monk scholar.   [2] The spiritual guide.
[3] According to Lamaists, deities who have taken an oath to protect the Buddhist doctrine and its followers.

the rule set down in Buddhist Scriptures : " Not too near to a village. Not too far from a village." From his small window the anchorite saw a wide uninhabited valley, while crossing the hill on which his dwelling was built, was a hamlet, at a distance of half a day's march.

The hermitage was furnished with an ascetic simplicity ; but a large library and some beautiful scrolls of painting on the walls showed that the hermit was neither poor nor ignorant of art.

As Karma Dorjee, a tall athletic fellow, clad only in his long plaited hair, stood before the thin refined scholar he has described to me, they must have formed a curious picture.

After having prostrated himself with the utmost fervour before the lama, he once more announced himself as a disciple brought by the deities to the very feet of the master.

The lama allowed him to relate the story of the *kyilkhor*, the " miraculous " flood and so on without interruption. Then, as Karma once more repeated that he had been brought " to his feet," Kushog Tobsgyais remarked simply that the place where the water had carried him was rather far from them. Then he inquired the reason of his wearing no clothes.

When Karma, full of his own importance, had mentioned Heruka and the two years which he had spent naked in the forest, the hermit looked at him silently for a while, then, calling one of his attendants, he said calmly :

" Take that poor man into the kitchen that he may sit near the fire and drink very hot tea. Find him also an old fur robe and give it to him. He has been shivering for two years."

And with these words he bid him leave.

Karma put on the shabby *pagtsa* [1] with pleasure.

---

[1] Sheep skin.

The flaming fire, the generously buttered hot tea refreshed him agreeably after his nocturnal bath. Yet his physical comfort was diminished by the mortification of his pride.

The lama, he thought, had not welcomed him as he ought to have welcomed a disciple brought to him " miraculously." However, he intended, after having satisfied his hunger and taken a little rest, to make the *gomchen* understand who he was and what he expected from a teacher. But Kushog Tobsgyais did not give him the opportunity of further explanations. He seemed even to have entirely forgotten his presence in the *ritöd*, though no doubt he had given instructions about him, for the two disciples continued to feed him well and the very same place, next the fire, was always put at his disposal.

Days and weeks went and Karma grew impatient. The kitchen, however comfortable it was, now seemed to him a prison. He wanted to work, to go out to fetch water or fuel, but the lama's disciples did not allow him to leave the hermitage. The lama's orders were positive : He had to eat and warm himself, that was all his duty.

Karma felt more and more ashamed at being treated like a pet animal that is not expected to do anything in return for its food. At the beginning of his stay he had repeatedly asked his companions to remind the lama that he expected an audience, but the latter had always declined to take any message, saying that they would not dare to trouble their lama, and that when *Rimpoche* [1] wanted to see him he would send for him.

After a time, Karma gave up asking useless questions. His only comfort was to watch for the lama's appearance on a small balcony where he sometimes sat, or to listen when, at long intervals, he explained a philo-

---

[1] *Rimpoche,* " precious one." The most reverential title of address for a lama.

sophical treatise to his disciples or to an occasional
visitor. Beside these rare gleams, the empty hours
dragged on while he revolved the various circumstances
which had led him where he was again and again, in
his mind.

A little more than one year passed in this way.
Karma became a prey to despair. He would gladly
have borne the most cruel ordeals the lama could have
had devised, but this complete forgetfulness amazed
him.

Though during his first and only interview with
the hermit, he had carefully avoided telling him anything regarding his low birth, he now suspected that
the latter, through his supernormal powers, had discovered it. Thus he explained the way in which he
had been treated. Probably the master despised him,
did not consider him worthy to be taught, and fed
him only out of pity. Every day this idea took
firmer footing in his mind, and cruelly tortured the
proud Karma.

Still convinced that a miracle had brought him to
lama Tobsgyais and that no other *guru* existed for him
in the world, he did not think of undertaking a new
journey to find another master, but the thought of
committing suicide sometimes came into his mind.

Tibetans believe that in order to progress on the
mystic path, one must meet one's true *tsawai lama*,
that is to say the spiritual teacher of whom one has
already been the disciple during previous lives, or if
this cannot be contrived, the lama of whom one has been
the loving relative, supporter or faithful servant. The
tie formed in that way is that of the " past deeds " [1]
as Tibetans call it.

Karma was sinking in despondency when a nephew
of the anchorite arrived at the *ritöd*. The visitor was
a lama *tulku*, head of a monastery and travelled with

[1] *Sngon las.*

a large retinue. Clad in shining robes of yellow brocade, wearing a gilt glittering hat shaped like a pagoda, the lama and his attendants stopped in the plain at the foot of the hermitage. Beautiful tents were pitched and after having refreshed himself with tea that the hermit had sent in an enormous silver teapot, the *tulku* went up to his uncle's dwelling.

During the following days, the *tulku* noticed the strange figure of Karma with his ragged sheep skin robe and his hair which reached to the floor. He asked him why he was always seated next the fire, doing nothing.

The aspirant magician took time by the forelock. He had at last found favour with the deities. There could be no doubt that they had aroused this interest in the *tulku's* mind.

He introduced himself with all his titles, told about his long retreat naked in the forest, the conjuration and the *kyilkhor* in the gorge, the flood, the rays of light which, springing from the hermitage, rested on his head. He ended by relating the forgetfulness of Kushog Tobsgyais and entreating the *tulku* to plead on his behalf.

From the account which I have heard, it appears probable that the lama to whom Karma now told his story was of the same stamp as his uncle. He does not appear to have been in the least moved by pity and merely inquired about the kind of teaching which his interlocutor craved from the hermit.

The question gladdened Karma. Now he had found somebody who would speak to him about the matter he had so much at heart. He boldly declared that he wished to acquire magic powers, such as that of flying in the air, of causing the earth to quake. . . . But he prudently avoided confessing why he wanted to work wonders.

The *tulku*—Karma realized later on—was only amused

by such childish ambitions, but he promised to convey his request to Kushog Tobsgyais. Then during the two weeks of his visit he did not even look in the young man's direction again.

The day came when the *tulku* took leave of his uncle. Karma looked sadly at the *trapas* attendants at the foot of the hill, who were holding by the bridle the richly caparisoned horses ready to start. The man whom he had considered as a Heaven-sent protector was to depart without having obtained any answer to his request. Most likely Kushog Tobsgyais had not granted it. Despair again overwhelmed him. . . .

The *tulku* passed the hermitage's door and Karma was about to salute him with the usual triple bowing down, when the latter gave him this laconic order :

" Follow me."

Karma Dorjee felt rather astonished. He had never been asked to do any service. What could the lama want ?

When he reached the foot of the hill the *tulku* turned toward him :

" I conveyed to *Kushog rimpoche* your desire of acquiring the various magic powers which you mentioned," he said. " *Rimpoche's* reply was that he has not got the books which you must study in his *ritöd*. A full collection of them exists in the library of my monastery, so *Rimpoche* has desired me to take you there, in order that you may begin work. There is a horse for you, you will travel with my *trapas*."

Then he left Karma and joined the small group of the dignitaries of his *gompa* who had accompanied him in his journey. All turned towards the hermitage, respectfully bowed their farewell to the invisible anchorite, vaulted into the saddle, and started at full trot.

Karma remained motionless, lost in amazement. A *trapa* gave him a push and put the bridle of a horse in his hand. . . . He found himself on the back of the beast trotting fast with the lama's attendants before he had realized what happened.

The fourth day after his arrival at the *gompa*, a *trapa* informed Karma that, according to the *tulku's* order, the collection of books mentioned by Kushog Tobsgyais had been carried in to a *tsham khang*. He could begin his study at once. Food would be sent regularly to him from the monastery.

Karma followed his guide and was led up hill to a tiny pleasantly situated whitewashed house. From the window he could look down on the monastery with its gilded roofs and beyond it a valley enclosed by woody slopes. Inside the cell, next a small altar, thirty big *potis*,[1] carefully wrapped in their " robes "[2] and tied between carved boards, were placed on several shelves.

A wave of joyful pride swept across Karma's mind. At last, some one had begun to treat him with proper respect.

The *trapa* informed him that the *tulku* did not wish him to remain in strict seclusion. He was at liberty to live as he liked, to fetch his water at the stream near by, and to walk outside wherever and whenever he wished. Left alone, Karma buried himself in the books. He learnt by heart a large number of magic formulas, built scores of *kyilkhors*, using more *tsampa* and butter to make the *tormas* than for his meals. He also practised the many various meditations described in the treatises.

For about eighteen months, his zeal did not slacken. He went out only to fetch water, did not speak a single word to the *trapas* who twice a month brought him his

---

[1] *Poti*, a volume.
[2] Tibetan books are made of detached oblong sheets of paper and usually wrapped in a piece of cloth—cotton or often silk—which is called their robe : " *namza* " spelt *nabzah*.

food and fuel supply, and never so much as glanced through his window at the world outside.

Then, slowly, thoughts that had never occurred to him crept into his mind during his meditations. Certain words of the books, certain figures of the mystic diagrams appeared to him as pregnant with significations formerly unsuspected. He often stood long in front of his window, watching the monks going in and out of the monastery. Finally, he walked across the hills, examining the plants and pebbles, looking attentively at the clouds travelling in the sky, observing the ever-flowing water of the stream, the play of the lights and shadows. He also spent hours watching the villages scattered in the valleys below, the peasants working in the fields, the animals passing loaded on the roads and those who roamed free across the pasture grounds.

Every evening after lighting the altar lamp, Karma Dorjee sat in meditation, but he gave up trying to follow the practices taught in the books. Late in the night, and sometimes till dawn, he remained sunk in a trance, dead to all sensations, to all cogitations, seeing himself as on a shore, watching the slowly mounting tide of a white luminous ocean ready to submerge him.

Several months elapsed and then one day or one night, he did not know which, Karma Dorjee felt that his body was being lifted from the cushion on which he was seated. Without changing his usual cross-legged attitude of meditation, he passed through the door and, floating in the air, travelled a long time. At last he arrived in his country, in his monastery. It was morning, the monks were coming out of the assembly hall. He recognized a number of them : officials, *tulkus*, certain of his old mates. They appeared tired, painfully preoccupied, with dull, joyless faces and heavy gait. Karma examined them with curiosity. How puny and insignificant they seemed from the height

where he now stood. How astonished, how awe-
struck they would be when in a moment he would
appear to them enthroned in mid-air ! And how
those who had treated the low-born monk with contempt would prostrate themselves, trembling before the
triumphant *dubtob*, the magician who baffled the
apparent laws of nature ! . . .

Then, as he dwelt on these ideas of victory, scorn
awakened in the inmost depth of his mind and his
elation subsided. He smiled in derision at the mean-
ness of a revenge on such paltry puppets. They did
not interest him any longer. . . . His thoughts went
out to the bliss of watching the flowing tide of the
strange rippleless, white, luminous ocean.

No, he would not show himself to the monks. That
Karma Dorjee who had suffered in the monastery
was as contemptible as those who had wickedly humiliated him. He rejected them all together. . . .

Thus thinking, he started to leave the place.

Then, suddenly, the monastery buildings were shaken
and cracked. The neighbouring mountains pitched
and tossed in confusion, their summits tumbled on
each other, while new ones arose. The sun crossed the
sky like a thunderbolt and fell on the earth, another
sun sprang out, piercing the heavens, and the rhythm
of the phantasmagoria went on with increasing speed
till Karma discerned nothing but a kind of furious
torrent whose foaming waves were made of all beings
and things of the world.

Visions of this kind are not very rare among Tibetan
mystics. They must not be mistaken for dreams.
The visionary is not asleep. Often, in spite of his
imaginary peregrinations, the sensations he experiences
and the scenery he perceives, he remains quite clearly
conscious of his actual surroundings and of his own
personality. Often, also, when going into a trance
where they are liable to be interrupted, they quite

consciously hope that none come by, or speak to them and trouble them in any other manner. Though they may be themselves incapable of speaking or moving, they hear and understand what is going on around them ; but they do not feel connected with any material objects, all their interest being absorbed in the events and sensations of the trance. If that state of trance is abruptly broken by any exterior agent, or if he who experiences it has to break it himself by a strong effort, the shock that ensues is peculiarly painful and leaves a prolonged feeling of discomfort.

It is to avoid these unpleasant effects and the consequences which they may have on the general health of those who suffer them, that rules have been devised for coming out of a period of ecstatic meditation, or even of ordinary meditation, if it has lasted for any length of time.

As an instance, one is advised to turn the head slowly from one side to another, to massage the forehead and the crown of the head, to stretch the arms while clasping the hands behind the back and bending the body backward. There are numbers of similar exercises, and each one may choose whichever suits him best.

The followers of the Zen sect in Japan, who meditate together in a common hall, appoint a kind of superintendent who is skilled in detecting when a monk is overcome by fatigue. He refreshes the fainting and revives their energy by striking them on one shoulder with a heavy stick. Those who have experienced it agree that the ensuing sensation is a most pleasant relaxation of the nerves.

When he returned from his strange journey, Karma Dorjee found himself seated at his usual place in his cell. He curiously inspected the objects around him. His small room, with the books on the shelves, the altar, the hearth, was the same that he had seen the day before ; nothing had changed during the years that he lived in the *tshams khang*.

He got up, looked through the window. The monastery, the valley, the woods wore their usual appearance. Nothing had changed, yet everything was different.

Karma calmly lighted the fire and when the wood burnt brightly he cut his long hair and threw it into the flames. Then he made tea, drank and ate without haste, put some provisions in a bag and went out, carefully closing the *tshams khang's* door behind him.

In the monastery he walked straight to the *tulku's* mansion, and meeting a servant in the courtyard, he told him to inform his master that he was leaving and to convey him his gratitude for his kind hospitality. Then he left the *gompa*.

He had already gone some way when he heard somebody calling him. One of the young monks belonging to the *tulku* household ran after him.

" *Kushog rimpoche* wishes to see you," he said.

Karma Dorjee returned with him.

" You leave us ? " asked the lama politely. " Where are you going to ? "

" To bow down at the feet of my *guru* and thank him," answered Karma.

The *tulku* remained silent for a while and then said sadly :

" My worshipful uncle is ' gone beyond sorrow ' [1] six months ago."

Karma Dorjee did not utter a single word.

" If you wish to go to his *ritöd*," continued the lama, " I will give you a horse, it shall be my parting gift. You will find one of Kushog Tobsgyais' disciples living in the hermitage."

Karma thanked his host but accepted nothing.

A few days later, he again beheld the white little

[1] A reverential expression to say that a lama is dead.

house from which he had seen the light springing and coming towards him.

He entered the lama's small private room where he had been admitted but once, remained long prostrated before the seat of the departed anchorite and spent the night in meditation.

In the morning he took leave of his master's successor. The latter handed him a monastic toga that had belonged to the late hermit. Before he died Kushog Tobsgyais had expressly commanded that it should be given to him when he came out of his *tshams khang*.

From that time on Karma Dorjee led the life of an itinerant ascetic, somewhat like that of the famous Milarespa whom he deeply venerated. When I happened to meet him he was already old, but he did not appear to be thinking of settling anywhere.

Few are the anchorites or other *naljorpas* whose novitiate has proved so strange as that of Karma. It is because it is, indeed, quite peculiar that I have ventured to give so long an account of it. Nevertheless, the spiritual training of a disciple always includes a number of curious incidents. Many strange descriptions which I have heard, and my own experiences as a " disciple " on the heights of the " Land of Snows," incline me to believe that most of them are perfectly authentic.

CHAPTER VI

PSYCHIC SPORTS

The Lung-gom-pas Runners

UNDER the collective term of *lung-gom* Tibetans include a large number of practices which combine mental concentration with various breathing gymnastics and aim at different results either spiritual or physical.

If we accept the belief current among the Lamaists we ought to find the key to thaumaturgy in that curious training. Keen investigations do not, however, lead to extraordinary enthusiasm for the result obtained by those who have practised it, seeking to acquire occult powers. Nevertheless, it would also be an error to deny that some genuine phenomena are produced by the adepts of *lung-gom*.

Though the effects ascribed to *lung-gom* training vary considerably, the term *lung-gom* is especially used for a kind of training which is said to develop uncommon nimbleness and especially enables its adepts to take extraordinarily long tramps with amazing rapidity.

Belief in such a training and its efficacy has existed for many years in Tibet, and men who travelled with supernormal rapidity are mentioned in many traditions.

We read in Milarespa's biography that at the house of the lama who taught him black magic there lived a *trapa* who was fleeter than a horse. Milarespa boasts of similar powers and says that he once crossed in a few days, a distance which, before his training, had taken him more than a month. He ascribes his gift to the clever control of " internal air."

However, it should be explained that the feat expected from the *lung-gom-pa* is one of wonderful endurance rather than of momentary extreme fleetness. In this case, the performance does not consist in racing at full speed over a short distance as is done in our sporting matches, but of tramping at a rapid pace and without stopping during several successive days and nights.

Beside having gathered information about the methods used in training *lung-gom-pas*, I have been lucky enough to catch a glimpse of three adepts. In this I was extremely fortunate as, though a rather large number of monks endeavour to practise some kind of *lung-gom* exercises, there is no doubt that very few acquire the desired result, and in fact true *lung-gom-pas* must be very rare.

I met the first *lung-gom-pa* in the Chang thang [1] of Northern Tibet.

Towards the end of the afternoon, Yongden, our servants and I were riding leisurely across a wide tableland, when I noticed, far away in front of us, a moving black spot which my field-glasses showed to be a man. I felt astonished. Meetings are not frequent in that region, for the last ten days we had not seen a human being. Moreover, men on foot and alone do not, as a rule, wander in these immense solitudes. Who could the strange traveller be ?

One of my servants suggested that he might belong to a trader's caravan which had been attacked by robbers and disbanded. Perhaps, having fled for life at night or otherwise escaped, he was now lost in the desert. That seemed possible. If such was really the

---

[1] An immense wild grassy region at a high level, inhabited only by a few tribes of nomad herdsmen living in tents. Literally, *chang thang* means " northern plain," but this term is used to designate any large track of wild land, similar to the solitudes of Northern Tibet.

case, I would take the lone man with us to some cow-herds encampment or wherever he might wish to go if not far out of our route.

But as I continued to observe him through the glasses, I noticed that the man proceeded at an unusual gait and, especially, with an extraordinary swiftness. Though, with the naked eyes, my men could hardly see anything but a black speck moving over the grassy ground, they too were not long in remarking the quickness of its advance. I handed them the glasses and one of them, having observed the traveller for a while, muttered :

" *Lama lung-gom-pa chig da.*" [1] (It looks like a lama *lung-gom-pa.*)

These words " *lama lung-gom-pa* " at once awakened my interest. I had heard a great deal about the feats performed by such men and was acquainted with the theory of the training. I had, even, a certain experience of the practice, but I had never seen an adept of *lung-gom* actually accomplishing one of these prodigious tramps which are so much talked about in Tibet. Was I to be lucky enough to witness such a sight ?

The man continued to advance towards us and his curious speed became more and more evident. What was to be done if he really was a *lung-gom-pa* ? I wanted to observe him at close quarters, I also wished to have a talk with him, to put him some questions, to photograph him. . . . I wanted many things. But at the very first words I said about it, the man who had recognized him as a lama *lung-gom-pa* exclaimed :

" Your Reverence will not stop the lama, nor speak to him. This would certainly kill him. These lamas when travelling must not break their meditation. The god who is in them escapes if they cease to repeat

---

[1] Written : *blama rlung sgom pa chig hdrah.* (It is like a lama *lung-gom-pa.*)

the *ngags*, and when thus leaving them before the proper time, he shakes them so hard that they die."

Put in that way, the warning seemed to express pure superstition. Nevertheless it was not to be altogether disregarded. From what I knew of the " technique " of the phenomena, the man walked in a kind of trance. Consequently, a sudden awakening, though I doubt if it could cause death, would certainly painfully disturb the nerves of the runner. To what extent that shock would harm him I could not guess and I did not want to make the lama the object of a more or less cruel experiment. Other reasons also forbade me to gratify my curiosity. Tibetans had accepted me as a lady-lama, they knew that I was a professed Buddhist and could not guess the difference existing between my philosophic conception of the Buddha's doctrine and lamaist Buddhism. Common Tibetan folk completely ignore the fact that the term Buddhism includes a number of sects and views. So, in order to enjoy the confidence, respect and intimacy which my religious garb brought me, I was compelled to behave in close accordance with Tibetan customs, especially with religious ones. This was a serious hindrance, and often deprived my observations of a great part of their scientific interest, but it was the unavoidable price I had to pay for being admitted on ground still much more jealously guarded than the material territory of Tibet. This time, again, I had to repress my desire for full investigation and remain satisfied with the sight of the uncommon traveller.

By that time he had nearly reached us ; I could clearly see his perfectly calm impassive face and wide-open eyes with their gaze fixed on some invisible far-distant object situated somewhere high up in space. The man did not run. He seemed to lift himself from the ground, proceeding by leaps. It looked as if he had been endowed with the elasticity of a ball and rebounded each time his feet touched the ground. His steps had the regularity of a pendulum. He wore the usual monastic robe and toga, both rather ragged. His left hand gripped a fold of the toga and was half hidden under the cloth. The right held a *phurba* (magic dagger). His right arm moved slightly at each step as if leaning on a stick, just as though the *phurba*, whose pointed extremity was far above the ground, had touched it and were actually a support.

My servants dismounted and bowed their heads to the ground as the lama passed before us, but he went his way apparently unaware of our presence.

I thought I had done enough to comply with local customs by suppressing my desire to stop the traveller. I already began to vaguely regret it and thought that at any rate I would see some more of the affair. I ordered the servants to remount their beasts at once and follow the lama. He had already covered a good distance ; but without trying to overtake him, we did not let that distance increase and, with the glasses as well as with our naked eyes, my son and I looked continually at the *lung-gom-pa*.

It was no longer possible to distinguish his face, but we could still see the amazing regularity of his springy steps. We followed him for about two miles and then he left the track, climbed a steep slope and disappeared in the mountain range that edged the steppe. Riders could not follow that way and our observations came to an end. We could only turn back and continue our journey.

I wondered if the lama had, or had not, noticed that we were following him. Of course, though we were a good distance behind him, anyone in a normal state would have been aware of the presence of a troop of six riders. But, as I said, the traveller seemed to be in a trance and I could not therefore tell whether he was only pretending not to have seen us and climbed the hill to escape our inquisitive looks, or if he really did not know that he was being followed, and merely went in that direction because it was his way.

On the morning of the fourth day after we had met the *lung-gom-pa*, we reached the territory called Thebgyai, where there are a number of scattered *dokpas* [1] encampments. I did not fail to relate to the herdsmen how we had approached a *lama lung-gom-pa* as we joined the track that led to their pasture ground. Now some of the men had seen the traveller when gathering their cattle together at sunset the day before we had met him ourselves. From that information I made a rough reckoning. Taking into account the approximate number of hours we had actually travelled each day at the usual speed of our beasts—leaving out the time spent camping and resting—I came to the conclusion that in order to reach the place where we met him, the man, after he had passed near the *dokpas*, must have tramped the whole night and next day, without stopping, at about the same speed as he was going when we saw him.

To walk for twenty-four hours consecutively cannot be considered as a record by the hillmen of Tibet who are wonderful walkers. Lama Yongden and I, during our journey from China to Lhasa, have sometimes tramped for fully nineteen hours, without stopping or refreshing ourselves in any way. One of these marches included the crossing of the high Deo pass, knee deep in the snow. However, our slow pace could not in any way be compared to that of the leaping *lung-gom-pa*, who seemed as if carried on wings.

And the latter had not started from Thebgyai. Whence had he come and how far was he still going when we lost sight of him? Both were a mystery to me. The *dokpas* thought that he might have come from Tsang, some monasteries of that province having

---

[1] *Dokpas*, literally " men of the solitudes," herdsmen.

a reputation as colleges for *lung-gom* training in swiftness. Yet they had not spoken to him, and tracks
coming from various directions join up on the Thebgyai
territory.

Methodical investigations were impossible in these
immense solitudes, or would have required several
months of research without any certainty of obtaining
a satisfactory result. To undertake them was out of
the question.

I have just mentioned that monasteries in the Tsang
province are renowned for training in swiftness. There
is a legend which recounts the circumstances by which
the most important of them—*Shalu gompa*—was led to
undertake the instruction and exercise of *lung-gom-pas*
runners.

The heroes of that legend are two prominent lamas :
Yungtön Dorje Pal and the historian Bustön. The
former was famous as a powerful magician who speci-
alized in the coercion of terrible deities. Born about
A.D. 1284 he is said to be the seventh of the successive
reincarnations of Subhuti (a disciple of the historical
Buddha) the line of whose reincarnations was continued,
later on, by the Tashi Lamas, the present being the
sixteenth reincarnation. Yungtön Dorje Pal lived for
a time at the court of the Emperor of the Mongol
dynasty which then ruled in China. His *guru* is said
to have been a mystic lama whose name was *Zurwang
Senge* [1] of whom nothing seems to be known except
through legends and rather fantastic traditions. Yungtön Dorje Pal died at the age of 92 years.

Bustön was born at Tho phug in the vicinity of
Shigatze in 1288. He wrote several books on history
and arranged the Buddhist Scriptures, translated from
Sanskrit, into the present collection called *Kahgyur*.

Now the magician Yungtön had decided to perform
a solemn *dubthabs* to coerce Shinjed [2] the Lord of

---

[1] Spelt *Zur dwang byampa sengge*.   [2] Spelt *gshin rje*.

Death. This rite had to be accomplished every twelve years, or the deity would slay a sentient being every day to satisfy his hunger. The effect of the *dubthabs* is to bring Shinjed under the control of the Lama magician and to extort from him a promise, on his oath, to give up the slaughter of human beings for the twelve years. Some offerings are presented to him during the rite, and daily worship is instituted as a substitute for the lives which he has sworn to spare.

Bustön heard of Yungtön's intention and wishing to ascertain if his friend really possessed the power of coercing the terrible deity, he proceeded to the latter's temple accompanied by three other learned lamas. There he found that Shinjed had already answered Yungtön's summons. His fearful form was " as large as the sky," says the story.

The magician told the lamas that they had just come in time to prove the extent of their love and compassion. He had, he said, coerced the god for the sake of humanity, now it was necessary to feed him so that he might be propitiated, and he suggested that one of the lamas should offer himself as victim. The three companions of Bustön declined the invitation under various pretexts and took hasty leave. Bustön remained alone with Yungtön and declared that if the success of the rite really required the sacrifice of a human life which would prevent the daily slaughter of a being for twelve years, he was ready to walk into the wide-open mouth of Shinjed.

To this generous proposal the magician replied that he could manage to secure the purpose of the *dubthabs* without his friend sacrificing his life. But he would entrust to him and his lineal successors, the charge of performing the prescribed rite every twelve years. Bustön having accepted the responsibility, Yungtön, by his magic power, created countless phantom doves and threw them into Shinjed's mouth.

Since then, the successive incarnations of Lama Bustön who ruled over *Shalu gompa*, have kept up the celebration of the propitiating ceremony. It seems that, as time went on, Shinjed acquired some companions, for the Shalu lamas now speak of *many* demons who are evoked upon that occasion.

A runner is required to gather these demons from various parts. This runner is called *Maheketang*. The name "mahe" is taken from the buffalo on which Shinjed rides. This animal is said to be fearless and consequently dares to call the evil spirits. At least, such is the explanation given at Shalu.

The elected runner is alternatively a monk from Nyang töd kyïd phug or one from Samding.

Those who aspire to play the part of *Maheketang* undertake a preliminary training in either of the above-mentioned monasteries. The training consists in breathing exercises practised during a strict seclusion in complete darkness, which lasts three years and three months.

Amongst these exercises the following one enjoys the greatest favour amongst those many Tibetan ascetics who are not of an especially intellectual type.

The student sits cross-legged on a large and thick cushion. He inhales slowly and for a long time, just as if he wanted to fill his body with air. Then, holding his breath, he jumps up with legs crossed, without using his hands and falls back on his cushion, still remaining in the same position. He repeats that exercise a number of times during each period of practice. Some lamas succeed in jumping very high in that way. Some women train themselves in the same manner.

As one can easily believe the object of this exercise is not acrobatic jumping. According to Tibetans, the body of those who drill themselves for years, by that method, become exceedingly light; nearly without

weight. These men, they say, are able to sit on an
ear of barley without bending its stalk or to stand
on the top of a heap of grain without displacing any
of it. In fact the aim is levitation.

A curious test has been devised, and the student
who passes it with success is believed capable of performing the feats here above mentioned or, at least, of
approaching proficiency.

A pit is dug in the ground, its depth being equal to the
height of the candidate. Over the pit is built a kind of
cupola whose height from the ground level to its highest
point again equals that of the candidate. A small aperture is left at the top of the cupola. Now between the
man seated cross-legged at the bottom of the pit and
that opening, the distance is twice the height of his
body. For instance, if the man's height is 5 feet 5
inches, the top hole will be at 10 feet 10 inches from
the pit's bottom.

The test consists in jumping cross-legged, as during
the training exercises which I have described, and
coming out through the small opening at the top of
the cupola.

I have heard Khampas declare that this feat has
been performed in their country, but I have not myself
witnessed anything like it.

According to information which I have gathered
on the spot, the final test that consecrates the success
of candidate " Calling buffalos " (*Maheketang*) is accomplished somewhat differently.

After their seclusion in darkness for three years,
those monks who deem themselves capable of going
successfully through the test, proceed to Shalu where
they are immured in one of the grave-like huts which
I have already described. But, at Shalu, the opening
is in the side of the cell. The candidate does not have
to leap through the roof. A stool is left him, so that he
can climb out of the pit where he has remained for

seven days. He must crawl out through the square
hole in the side of the cell. The size of this hole is
calculated in proportion to the span between the second
finger and thumb of the candidate's hand.

He who succeeds is qualified to become *Maheketang*.
It is difficult to understand that a training which
compels a man to remain motionless for years can
result in the acquisition of peculiar swiftness. However, this is the special training of Shalu, and in other
places we meet with different and apparently more
rational methods, including the actual practice of
marching. Moreover, it must be understood that the
lung-gom method does not aim at training the disciple
by strengthening his muscles, but by developing in
him psychic states that make these extraordinary
marches possible.

The *Maheketang* starts on the eleventh day of the
tenth month of the Tibetan year (corresponding to
November) ; after visiting Lhasa, Samye, and several
other places, he is back at Shalu on the 25th of the
same month. He immediately sets out again, goes
to Shigatze, makes an extended tour in the highlands
of Tsang (Tsang töd) and returns to Shalu after one
month's time. Then the lineal successor of Bustön
performs the propitiation rites, as *Maheketang's* invita-
tions to the demons are, apparently, always accepted
without demur.

I, by chance, caught a glimpse of another *lung-
gom-pa* in the region inhabited by some independent
tribes of Tibetan origin in the Szetchuanese Far West.
But this time I had not the opportunity of watching
him tramp.

We were travelling in a forest, Yongden and I walking
ahead of our servants and beasts, when at the turning
of the path, we came upon a naked man with iron
chains rolled all round his body.

He was seated on a rock and seemed so deeply buried in thoughts that he had not heard us coming. We stopped, astonished, but he must have suddenly become aware of our presence, for after gazing at us a moment, he jumped up and threw himself into the thickets more quickly than a deer. For a while we heard the noise of the chains jingling on his body growing rapidly fainter and fainter, then all was silence again.

"That man is a *lung-gom-pa*," said Yongden to me. "I have already seen one like him. They wear these chains to make themselves heavy, for through the practice of *lung-gom*, their bodies have become so light that they are always in danger of floating in the air."

My third meeting with a *lung-gom-pa* happened in Ga, a region of Kham, in Eastern Tibet. I was again travelling with my small caravan. The man appeared under the familiar and commonplace figure of an *arjopa*, that is to say a poor pilgrim carrying his luggage on his back. Thousands of such fellows may be seen on all the tracks of Tibet, so we did not pay much attention to a member of such a large tribe.

These needy, solitary pedestrians have the habit of attaching themselves to any trader's caravan or to any rich traveller whom they happen to meet on their way and following them. They walk beside the pack animals, or if these are few and lightly loaded, so that they trot together with the riders, the beggars who, of course, fall behind, tramp on till they join the party at the evening camping. This is not generally difficult, for during long journeys Tibetans start at daybreak and stop at about midday in order that their beasts may rest and graze during the whole afternoon.

The trouble that the *arjopa* gives himself to hurry after the horsemen, or any odd help he is always ready to give the servants, are rewarded by a daily evening meal and occasional buttered tea and *tsampa* from the travellers themselves.

According to this custom, the man whom we had met attached himself to our party. We learnt from him that he had been staying at the Pabong monastery in Kham, and was going to the Tsang province. A pretty long journey which, done on foot and begging on the way, would take three or four months. However, such tramps are undertaken by thousands of Tibetan pilgrims.

Our companion had already spent a few days with us when, in consequence of a slight break-down, it was nearly noon before we started. Thinking that the pack-mules would be late in crossing a ridge that lay ahead of us, I rode on with my son and a servant, to look for water and a grassy place where we could camp before dusk.

When the master travels ahead, the man who accompanies him always carries a vessel to make tea and some provisions, so that the gentleman or the lama may have a meal while waiting for the arrival of the luggage and tents. My servant had not failed to comply with this habit, and it was this point so trivial in itself which caused the display of the *lung-gom-pa's* abilities.

The way to the pass was longer than I had suspected, and I soon realized that the pack-mules would not reach the top of the ridge before nightfall. It was out of the question to let them attempt going down the other side of the range in the dark, so having reached a grassy spot near a brooklet, I stopped there. We had already drank tea and were collecting dry cow-dung to feed the fire [1] when I saw the *arjopa* climbing the slope at some distance below us, progressing with

[1] With the exception of woody regions, the cattle dung is the only fuel used in Tibet. In the parts of the country inhabited by *dokpas*, travellers collect what is left by the animals on the pasture grounds to light their camp fire.

extraordinary rapidity. As he came nearer, I could see that he was walking with the same peculiar nimble springing gait which I had noticed in the lama *lung-gom-pa* of Thebgyai.

When he reached us, the man stood quite still for a while staring straight before him. He was not at all out of breath, but appeared only half conscious and incapable of speaking or moving. However, the trance gradually subsided and the *arjopa* came back to his normal state. Answering my questions, he told me that he had begun the *lung-gom* training for acquiring fleetness with a *gomchen* who lived near the Pabong monastery. His master having left the country, he intended to go to *Shalu gompa* in Tsang.

He did not tell me any more and looked sad the whole evening. On the morrow, he confessed to Yongden that the trance had come on him involuntarily and had been produced by a most vulgar thought.

As he was walking along with the servants who led my mules, he had begun to feel impatient. They were going so slowly, he thought, and during that time we were, no doubt, grilling on the fire the meat he had seen my servant carry with him. When the three other servants and he himself would have overtaken us they would have to pitch the tents, to look after the beasts, and so there would only be time to drink tea and eat *tsampa* before retiring to sleep.

He visualized our little party. He saw the fire, the meat on the red embers, and sunk in contemplation gradually became unconscious of his surroundings. Then, prompted by the desire of sharing our meal, he accelerated his pace and in so doing mechanically fell into the special gait which he was learning. The habitual association of that peculiar gait with the mystic words his master had taught him, caused the mental recitation of the proper formula. The latter led to the regulation of the breath in the prescribed rhythm, and the trance followed. Nevertheless, the concentration of his thoughts on the grilled meat dominated everything.

The novice regarded himself as a sinner. The mixture of gluttony, holy mystic words and *lung-gom* exercises seemed to him sacrilegious.

My lama-son did not fail to report the confidences he had received. I felt interested and put different questions to the novice. He was most unwilling to answer, but I managed to obtain some information which confirmed what I knew already. He had been told that sunset and clear nights were favourable conditions for the walker. He had also been advised to train himself by looking fixedly at the starry sky.

I suppose that, like most Tibetan mystics, he had taken an oath not to divulge the teaching imparted by his master and that my questions troubled him.

The third day after his racing performance, when we awoke, at daybreak, he was no longer in the tents. He had fled at night, perhaps using his power of *lung-gom* and, this time, for a more worthy purpose than that of sharing a " bonne bouche."

The information which I obtained from different sources regarding the peculiar practice of *lung-gom* may be summarized as follows :

The first step before undertaking the training is, as usual, to acquire power by the *angkur* rite. One must then, under the guidance of an experienced teacher, drill oneself for several years in various kinds of breathing exercises. It is only when the disciple has acquired a sufficient degree of proficiency that he is permitted to attempt the racing performance itself.

A new *angkur* is conferred at this stage and a mystic formula [1] imparted by the master to the novice. The

[1] The formula differs according to the tradition of the mystic school to which the lama belongs.

latter is advised to concentrate his thoughts on the cadenced mental recitation of that formula with which, during his walk, the *in and out breathing* must be in rhythm, the steps keeping time with the breath and the syllables of the formula. The walker must neither speak, nor look from side to side. He must keep his eyes fixed on a single distant object and never allow his attention to be attracted by anything else.

When the trance has been reached, though normal consciousness is for the greater part suppressed, it remains sufficiently alive to keep the man aware of the obstacles in his way, and mindful of his direction and goal.

Wide desert spaces, flat ground, and especially evening twilight are said to be favourable conditions. Even if one has already made a long tramp during the day and feels tired, the trance is often easily attained at sunset. Fatigue is then no longer felt and the traveller can continue walking for miles.

The first hours of the day are also favourable, but in a lesser degree.

Noon and early afternoon, narrow valleys, woodlands, uneven ground are considered unfavourable conditions and only adepts in *lung-gom* are deemed capable of overcoming the adverse influences which emanate from them.

These explanations seem to imply that uniformity in the landscape and absence of near-by conspicuous objects are helpful in attaining the trance. It is certain that a wide, desert plain offers fewer occasions of distracting attention from the formula and the movement of the breath, than a ravine half obstructed with rocks and bushes, noisy mountain streams, etc. As for the regularity of the pace it cannot be easily kept up on a rough uneven path.

From my own superficial experience of the practice, though desert tablelands are choice ground, I feel convinced that a forest of tall straight trees, devoid of undergrowth and crossed by tolerably even paths, may be quite favourable to the trance, perhaps also on account of the uniformity of the landscape. However, this is my own idea and is based on a single personal observation which I made in the primeval forests of Poyul.

Any clear night is deemed good for the training of beginners, but strong starlight is especially favourable. One is often advised to keep the eyes fixed on a particular star. This appears connected with hypnotic effects, and I have been told that among novices who train themselves in that way, some stop walking when "their" star sinks below the skyline or rises above their head. Others, on the contrary, do not notice its disappearance because by the time that the star has passed out of sight, they have formed a subjective image of it which remains fixed before them.

Some initiates in the secret lore also assert that, as a result of long years of practice, after he has travelled over a certain distance, the feet of the *lung-gom-pa* no longer touch the ground and that he glides on the air with an extreme celerity.[1]

Setting aside exaggeration, I am convinced from my limited experiences and what I have heard from trustworthy lamas, that one reaches a condition in which one does not feel the weight of one's body. A kind of anæsthesia deadens the sensations that would be produced by knocking against the stones or other obstacles on the way, and one walks for hours at an unaccustomed speed, enjoying that kind of light agreeable dizziness well known to motorists at high speed.

Tibetans distinguish between the regular prolonged

[1] Mentions of such accomplishment are repeatedly found in the *Padma bkah thang* and in various other books. It is styled *rkang mgyogs ngo sgrubs*, pronounced *kang gyog ngo dub*, " success in swiftness of foot."

tramps accomplished by the *lung-gom-pas* and those of the *pawos*, possessed *mediums*, who go into trances involuntarily and walk with no definite goal in view.

Intellectual lamas do not deny the reality of the phenomena brought about, in the long run, by *lung-gom* practices, but they care little for them.

Their attitude reminds us of that ascribed to the Buddha, in an old story.

It is said that the Buddha was once journeying with some of his disciples and met an emaciated Yogin, all alone in a hut in the middle of a forest.

The Master stopped and inquired how long the man had been living there, practising austerities. " Twenty-five years," answered the Yogin. " And what power have you acquired by such long and arduous exertion ? " asked the Buddha. " I am able to cross a river by walking on the water," proudly replied the anchorite.

" My poor fellow ! " said the Buddha with commiseration. " Have you really wasted so many years for such trifling result ? Why, the ferry man will take you to the opposite bank for a small coin."

The Art of Warming Oneself Without Fire up in the Snows

To spend the winter in a cave amidst the snows, at an altitude that varies between 11,000 and 18,000 feet, clad in a thin garment or even naked, and escape freezing, is a somewhat difficult achievement. Yet numbers of Tibetan hermits go safely each year through this ordeal. Their endurance is ascribed to the power which they have acquired to generate *tumo*.[1]

The word *tumo* signifies heat, warmth, but is not used in Tibetan language to express ordinary heat or warmth. It is a technical term of mystic terminology, and the effects of that mysterious heat are not confined to warming the anchorites who can produce it.

[1] Written *gtumo*.

Tibetan adepts of the secret lore distinguish various kinds of *tumo* : exoteric *tumo*, which arises spontaneously in the course of peculiar raptures and, gradually, folds the mystic in the " soft, warm mantle of the gods " ; esoteric *tumo*, that keeps the hermits comfortable on the snowy hills ; mystic *tumo*, which can only claim a distant and quite figurative connection with the term " warmth," for it is the experience of " paradisiac bliss " in this world.

In the secret teaching, *tumo* is also the subtle fire which warms the generative fluid and drives the energy in it, till it runs all over the body along the tiny channels of the *tsas*.[1]

Superstition and odd physiological ideas have contributed to give birth to many extraordinary stories on this subject, one of which I will venture to briefly relate.

The famous ascetic, Reschungpa, anxious to become an erudite, left his master Milarespa, against the latter's advice, to study the philosophic literature at Lhasa. Lacking his spiritual father's blessing, things turned badly for him—at least from a religious point of view. A rich man became quite enthusiastic about the young lama's learning and mastery of occult lore and, in order to attach him to his house, he gave him his only child as wife. This happened before the reform of Tsong Khapa at a time when all lamas were allowed to marry. The girl did not in the least share her father's admiration for Reschungpa, but she was obliged to obey him, and in revenge made life rather hard for her poor husband, who might well regret having yielded to the attraction of wealth.

His meekness in bearing ill-treatment did not soften his wife's heart. She went so far as to stab him with a knife. And lo ! instead of blood, generative fluid ran out of the wound. By the practice of *tumo*—so said the lama who told me the story with absolute

[1] Written *rtsa*, which means at once vein, artery and nerve.

conviction—the body of Reschungpa had been filled
with the seed of life.

To do justice to Tibetans, I must add that another
lama scoffed at the tale and thus explained it. Truly,
through *tumo* practices one may fill one's body with
generative force which allows psychic creations, but
this is subtle, invisible energy (*shugs*) and not gross
material substance.

However, only a few, even in mystic circles, are
thoroughly acquainted with these several kinds of
tumo, while the wonderful effects of the *tumo* that warms
and keeps alive the hermits in the snowy wilds are
known to every Tibetan. It does not follow that the
process by which that mysterious heat is produced
is equally familiar to all of them. On the contrary,
It is kept secret by the lamas who teach it, and they do
not fail to declare that information gathered by hear-
say or by reading is without any practical result if one has
not been personally taught and trained by a master
who is himself an adept.

Moreover, only those who are qualified to undertake
the training may hope to enjoy its fruit. The most
important qualifications required are : to be already
skilled in the various practices connected with breathing ;
to be capable of a perfect concentration of mind, going
as far as the trance in which thoughts become visualized ;
and to have received the proper *angkur* from a lama
possessed with the power of conferring it.

Tumo initiation [1] is preceded by a long period of
probation.

Among other objects, I think probation aims at
testing the robustness of the candidates. As great as
may be my confidence in the *tumo* method, I still
doubt whether it could be safely practised by people

---

[1] Or more exactly and literally " empowerment," *angkur* : the
rite by which a peculiar power is communicated by the master
to his disciple.

of weak constitution. It is probable, however, that *tumo's* teachers, wisely, endeavour to avoid failures that might prove harmful to presumptuous disciples and lower their own repute.

I do not know whether, when yielding to my pressing requests and shortening my time of probation, the venerable lama who " empowered " me only wanted to get rid of me or not. He simply told me to go to a lonely spot, to bathe there in an icy mountain stream, and then, without drying my body or putting on my clothes, to spend the night motionless in meditation. Winter had not yet begun, but the level of the place, about 10,000 feet high, made the night rather chilly, and I felt very proud of not catching cold.

Later on I took another bath of the same kind, this time involuntarily, when I lost footing as I was fording the Mekong River, near Rakshi in Northern Tibet. When I reached the shore, in a few minutes my clothes froze on me. . . . I had no spare ones.

One may easily understand that Tibetans, who are frequently exposed to accidents caused by a hard climate, hold a method that protects them against the cold in high esteem.

Once initiated, one must renounce all fur or woollen clothing and never approach the fire to warm oneself.

After a short period, during which he exerts himself under the close supervision of his master, the novice must retire to a very remote, absolutely solitary place situated high up on the hills. In Tibet " high up " means generally an altitude well above 10,000 feet. According to *tumo* teachers and adepts, one must never practise the training exercises inside a house, or near inhabited places. They believe that foul air produced by smoke and smells, together with various occult causes, impede the success of the student and may even harm him. Once conveniently settled, the disciple must see nobody besides his lama, who may visit him occasionally, or to whose hermitage he may repair at long intervals.

The novice must begin his training each day before dawn and finish the special exercise relating to *tumo* before sunrise, because as a rule he has to perform one or another meditation at that time. The practice must be done in the open, and one must be either naked or clothed in a single cotton garment.

Beginners may sit on a straw mat, if they own one, or on a piece of hard sackcloth or a wooden stool. More advanced disciples sit on the bare ground, and at a still higher degree of proficiency, on the snow or the ice of a frozen pond or stream. They must not breakfast or even drink anything, especially any hot drink, before practising.

Two postures are allowed. Either the usual meditation posture cross-legged or seated in Western fashion, each hand placed on the corresponding knee, the thumb, the forefinger and the little finger being extended, and the middle and fourth fingers bent under the palm.

Various breathing drills are first performed which aim at clearing the passage of the air in the nostrils.

Then pride, anger, hatred, covetousness, sloth, stupidity are mentally rejected with the rhythmic breathing out. All blessings from saintly beings, the Buddha's spirit, the five wisdoms, all that is good and lofty in the world are attracted and assimilated while drawing in the breath.

Now, composing oneself for a while one dismisses all cares and cogitations. Having become perfectly calm, one imagines that a golden lotus exists, in one's body on a level with the navel. In this lotus, shining like the sun, stands the syllable *ram*. Above *ram* is the syllable *ma*. From *ma*, Dorjee Naljorma (a feminine deity) issues.

These mystic syllables, which are called " seed," must not be regarded as mere written characters, or symbolic representations of things, but as living beings standing erect and endowed with motive power. For instance *ram* is not the mystic name of the fire, it is the *seed* of fire. Hindus attach great importance to the right pronunciation of these " seed formulas " (*bija* mantras). They think that their power resides in the sound which they believe to be creative. Certain Tibetan mystics agree that *ram* correctly pronounced, may produce fire, yet these mystic syllables are not generally used in Tibet as *sound,* but rather as representations of elements, deities, etc. Tibetans identifying *ram* with the fire, think that he who knows how to make mental use of the subjective image of that word, can set anything ablaze or even produce flames without apparent fuel.

As soon as one has imagined Dorjee Naljorma springing from the syllable *ma,* one must identify oneself with her.

When one has " become " the deity, one imagines the letter *A* placed in the navel and the letter *Ha* [1] at the top of one's head.

Slow, deep inspirations act as bellows and wake up a smouldering fire, the size and shape of a minute ball.[2] This fire exists in *A.* Each inspiration produces the sensation of a breath of wind penetrating the abdomen at the height of the navel and increasing the force of the flames.[3]

Then, each deep inspiration is followed by a retention of the breath. Gradually the time spent holding in the breath is increased more and more.

One's thoughts continue to follow the waking up of fire which ascends along the *uma* vein arising in the middle of the body.

[1] A letter of the Tibetan alphabet.
[2] Tibetan literal similitude is, " the size and shape of goat dung."
[3] In other *tumo* exercises, drops of oil must be imagined as oozing from *Ha* and falling into the fire situated in *A,* to feed it.

Tibetans have borrowed from India the three mystic *nadi* (arteries, veins) which play an important part in the various yoga psychic trainings. In Tibetan, *nadis* are called *tsas* and respectively named *roma kyangma* and *uma*.

These so-called "arteries" are not supposed to be true arteries containing blood, but exceedingly thin nerves that distribute currents of psychic energy. The three *tsas* just mentioned are the most important, but there exist countless others.

However, enlightened mystics consider the *tsa* system as devoid of any physical reality. According to their opinion it is but symbolical imagery.

The exercises goes on, through ten stages, but one must understand that there exists no pause between them. The different subjective visions, as well as the sensations which accompany them, succeed each other in a series of gradual modifications. Inhalations, retentions of the breath and expirations continue rhythmically, and a mystic formula is continually repeated. The mind must remain perfectly concentrated and "one pointed" on the vision of the fire and the sensation of warmth which ensues.

The ten stages may be briefly described as follows :

1. The central artery *uma* is imagined—and subjectively seen—as thin as the thinnest thread or as a hair, yet filled with the ascending flame and crossed by the current of air produced by the breath.

2. The artery has increased in size and become as large as the little finger.

3. It continues to increase and appears to be the size of an arm.

4. The artery fills the whole body, or rather the body has become the *tsa* itself, a kind of tube filled with blazing fire and air.

5. The bodily form ceases to be perceived. Enlarged beyond all measure, the artery engulfs the whole w~~~~

and the *naljorpa* feels himself to be a storm-beaten flame among the glowing waves of an ocean of fire.

Beginners whose mind has not yet acquired the habit of very protracted meditation go more quickly through these five stages than more advanced disciples, who progress slowly from one to another, sunk in deep contemplation. Yet, even the quickest ones take about an hour to reach the fifth stage.

Now the subjective visions repeat themselves in reverse order.

6. The stormy wind abates, the fiery waves sink lower and are less agitated, the blazing ocean narrows and is absorbed in the body.

7. The artery, which is reduced to the size of an arm, is seen again with the fire enclosed in it.

8. The artery decreases to the size of the little finger.

9. It becomes as thin as a hair.

10. It entirely disappears : the fire ceases utterly to be perceived, as well as all forms, all representations whatsoever. All ideas of any kind of objects vanish likewise. The mind sinks into the great " Emptiness " where the duality of the knower and the object perceived does not exist any longer.

It is a trance which, according to the spiritual and psychic development of the *naljorpa*, is more or less deep and more or less prolonged.

The exercise, either with or without the five last stages, may be repeated during the day or whenever one is suffering from cold. But the training, properly speaking, is done during the early practice before dawn.

It is probable that Milarespa resorted to it when he happened to be unexpectedly surrounded by the snow in a cave of the Lachi Kang (near the mount Everest) and found himself compelled to stay there till the next spring. He made his adventure the subject of a poem, part of which is freely translated below.

Disgusted with the worldly life
I sought solitude on the slopes of Lachi Kang.
Heavens and earth having held a council,
Sent me the tempest as their messenger
The airy and watery elements
Associated with the Southern dark clouds.
They imprisoned the sun and the moon,
Blew the small stars away from the sky
And shrouded the large ones in the mist.
Then, it snowed continually for nine days and nights,
The biggest flakes were as big as the fleece of wool,
They came down flying like birds.
The small ones were the size of peas and mustard seeds,
They came down rolling and whirling.
The greatness of the snowfall was beyond all expression,
High up it covered the crest of the glacier ranges,
Low down it buried, up to their tops, the trees of the forest.
The black hills appeared to be whitewashed.
The frost flattened the billowy lakes
And the blue running streams were hidden under the ice.
The mountains and the valleys were levelled and looked like a plain.
Men were prisoners in the villages,
Domestic animals suffered from famine,
Birds and wild beasts fasted,
Mice and rats were sealed under ground like a treasure
During that time of calamity.
The snow, the wintry blast and my thin cotton garment fought
    against each other on the white mountain.
The snow as it fell on me, melted into a stream,
The roaring blast was broken against the thin cotton robe which
    enclosed fiery warmth,
The life and death struggle of the fighter could there be seen
And I, having won the victory, left a landmark for the hermits
Demonstrating the great virtue of *tumo*.

Milarespa describes his impressions as a poet, but
excepting the fact that he was shut up *unexpectedly* in
the snows, without sufficient provisions and a proper
shelter, there is nothing exceptional in his experience.
Many Tibetan hermits spend the winter in surroundings
resembling those that he depicts.

I am not so presumptuous as to compare my wintry

" villegiatures " on the Tibetan hills with the exertions of anchorites of Milarespa ilk, yet scenery like that of which he tells is familiar to me.

I, too, have lived in caves and huts on high altitudes. Though I did not lack provisions, and had fuel enough to light a fire whenever I wished it, I yet know the hardships of that life. But I also remember the perfect silence, the delightful aloofness and the wonderful peace in which my hermitage was bathed, and I do not think that those who spend their days in such wise need to be pitied. I would rather say they are to be envied.

Beside the exercises which I have outlined, there exist a few others aiming at producing *tumo*. However, they are all more or less alike. The process always combine prolonged retention of the breath and visualization of fire. This, in fact, amounts to auto-suggestion.

One of the six occult doctrines taught by Narota [1] is said to have included *tumo*.

Here is an abridged account of Narota's method. One must bear in mind that—as it has already been stated—such exercises were devised for the use of disciples who had already thoroughly drilled themselves for years in preparatory breathing and other gymnastics.

The posture of the body is described as follows :

Squatting with the legs crossed, the hands passing under the thighs and then clasped together.

In that posture, one must (1) turn the stomach from right to left thrice, and from left to right thrice ; (2) churn the stomach as hard as possible ; (3) shake the body in the way " a restive horse shakes himself," and perform a short leap while keeping the legs in the same crossed position. These three exercises must be repeated thrice successively and concluded with a leap, jumping as high as possible.

It does not seem to me very wonderful that a man should feel warm after performing this feat. The

[1] About Narota, see Chapter V

exercise is borrowed from Indian *hatha yoga* practices, but in *hatha yoga* treatises it is not connected with the kind of *tumo* known to Tibetans.

The process continues by holding in the breath, until the abdomen becomes " the shape of a pot." [1]

Next comes the visualization of Dorjee Naljorma as in the exercise previously described. Then a sun is imagined in the palm of each hand, on the sole of each foot and below the navel.

By rubbing together the suns placed in the hands and in the feet, fire flares up and strikes the sun below the navel, which flares up in its turn and fills the whole body with fire.

With each expiration of the breath, the world is visualized as being filled with fire.

The exercise ends by twenty-one big leaps. [2]

Though there are certain resemblances in the images visualized in these two methods, the difference between them is nevertheless considerable, for while the second includes leaps and gesticulations, the former requires complete immobility.

It is not impossible that here, as in many other cases, certain elements of the training have been borrowed from the autochthonous Bönpos occultists. One of the latter once told me that it is the visualization of the fire, rather than the motion of the breath, which produces warmth during the trance. As I did not agree, he added : " A man may be killed by suggestion, he may kill himself by auto-suggestion. [3] If death can be produced in that way, so much more easily may heat be generated."

---

[1] That very expression I have also heard from Tibetan anchorites.

[2] From *Chös drug bsdus pahi zin bris*, " Treatise of the six doctrines," ascribed to Narota.

[3] I need not to say that the terms *suggestion* and *auto-suggestion* are mine. The Tibetan used the words, " killed by the power of mind " ; kill himself " by his own imagination."

Inhalations, retentions and expirations of the breath are accomplished mechanically, in the prescribed order, by those who are already well trained in the *tumo* practice. They do not break the concentration of the mind on the mirage of the fire, nor the repetition of the mystic formula which must accompany the contemplation. These advanced students do not need to make any effort of imagination to see the growing intensity of the fire. In their case, the process goes on by itself as a result of habit which they have acquired, and a pleasant feeling of warmth spreads gradually all over the body, which is the aim of the practice.

Sometimes, a kind of examination concludes the training of the *tumo* students.

Upon a frosty winter night, those who think themselves capable of victoriously enduring the test are led to the shore of a river or a lake. If all the streams are frozen in the region, a hole is made in the ice. A moonlight night, with a hard wind blowing, is chosen. Such nights are not rare in Tibet during the winter months.

The neophytes sit on the ground, cross-legged and naked. Sheets are dipped in the icy water, each man wraps himself in one of them and must dry it on his body. As soon as the sheet has become dry, it is again dipped in the water and placed on the novice's body to be dried as before. The operation goes on in that way until daybreak. Then he who has dried the largest number of sheets is acknowledged the winner of the competition.

It is said that some dry as many as forty sheets in one night. One should perhaps make large allowances for exaggeration, or perhaps for the *size* of the sheets which in some cases may have become so small as to be almost symbolical. Yet I have seen some *respas* dry a number of pieces of cloth the size of a large shawl.

According to the old rule, one must have dried at

least three sheets to be a true *respa* entitled to wear the white cotton skirt, insignia of proficiency in *tumo*. But I doubt if the rule is strictly observed nowadays.

Respa means one who wears but a single cotton garment in all seasons and at any height. Yet *respas* who slip warm clothes on under their cotton robes are not lacking in Tibet. They are either complete frauds or monks who have really gone through *tumo* training, but have not pursued it long enough to obtain its full benefits.

Nevertheless, though there are frauds and mediocrities, some *tumo* adepts go beyond the *respa* and, rejecting even their cotton garment, live entirely naked in the recesses of the high mountain ranges for long periods, sometimes it is said even for life.

Tibetans feel rather proud of such feats and do not fail to scoff at the naked Indian yogins whom they meet when going on a pilgrimage to India. They do not understand that, with Indians, nakedness is the symbol of absolute renunciation and not a display of extraordinary physical endurance.

One of these super-*respas* who had trained himself in *tumo* near Kang Tise,[1] while journeying over the plains of India with another *respa* and a lay servant, from Nepal to Gaya, happened to see a pretentious-looking *sadhu* lying naked and sunbaked on a mat.

" Old chap, you should go naked like that and lie on tso Mophang's shore,[2] then you will surely pull another face," said the Tibetan anchorite mockingly to the Indian who, of course, did not understand his language, nor why the three travellers irreverently burst out laughing at him.

This was related to me by the hermit himself who, in his old age, still enjoyed this little joke of his younger days.

[1] Tibetan name of Kailas mountain, in Western Tibet.
[2] A sacred lake near Kailas mountain, about 15,000 feet high.

In fact, when one begins the training, the phenomenon of increasing heat, or perhaps in some cases, the
subjective sensation of warmth, only lasts while practising the exercise. When the concentration of mind
and the breathing gymnastics cease, cold is again
gradually felt. On the contrary, it is said that, with
those students who have persevered in the training
practice for many years, the production of heat becomes
a natural function of the organism, which works all
by itself, as soon as the weather grows cold.

Beside drying wet sheets on one's body, there exist
various other tests to ascertain the degree of heat
which the neophyte is able to radiate. One of these
tests consists in sitting in the snow. The quantity
of snow melted under the man and the distance at
which it melts around him are taken as measures of
his ability.

It is difficult for us to get a perfectly correct idea about
the extent of the results obtained through *tumo* training,
but some of these feats are genuine. Hermits really
do live naked, or wearing one single thin garment
during the whole winter in the high regions I have
mentioned. I am not the only one who has seen some
of them. It has been said that some members of the
Mount Everest expedition had an occasional glimpse of
one of these naked anchorites.

In conclusion I may say that I have myself obtained
remarkable results from my small experience of *tumo*.

Messages Sent " On the Wind "

Tibetan mystics are not talkative ; those of them who
accept disciples teach them according to methods in
which discourses have but little place. The disciples of
the contemplative hermits seldom see their master and
only at intervals determined by the spiritual attainment
and needs of the novice.

A few months or a few years may elapse between

these meetings. But in spite of their seeming aloofness, master and disciples—especially advanced disciples—do not lack means of communication when they deem it necessary.

Telepathy is a branch of the Tibetan secret lore and seems, in the "Land of Snows," to play the part that wireless telegraphy has recently taken in the West. Yet, while apparatus for wireless transmissions are, in Occidental countries, at the public's disposal, the subtler ways of sending messages "on the wind" remain the privilege of a small minority of adepts in that art in Tibet.

Telepathy is not altogether a novelty to Westerners, psychic research societies have, more than once, called attention to telepathic phenomena. These, however, usually seem to have occurred by chance. The author of the phenomenon was not aware of his part in it. Under some peculiar circumstances, he had sent forth the mysterious waves that had reached, at a greater or lesser distance, a human receiver, but he had not done this knowingly and on purpose. On the other hand, the experiments made to transmit volitional telepathic messages have given doubtful results, for they could not be repeated successfully as often as desired.

Things are different among Tibetans. They assert that telepathy is a science, which can be learnt like any other science, by those who have proper teaching and are fit instruments to put the theory into practice.

Various ways are mentioned for the acquisition of telepathic power, though Tibetan adepts of secret lore are unanimous in ascribing the cause of the phenomena to an intense concentration of thought.

One may remark that as far as telepathy has been observed and studied in Western countries, its cause has seemed identical with that discovered by Tibetans. Mystic teachers declare that mastery in telepathy requires a perfect command over the mind, in order to produce, at will, the powerful " one-pointedness of thought " on which the phenomenon depends.

The part of conscious " receiver," always ready to vibrate at the subtle shock of the telepathic waves, is considered almost as difficult as that of the sender. To begin with, the intended receiver must have been " tuned " with him from whom he especially expects messages.

Now, volitional perfect concentration of mind on one single object, until every other object vanishes from the field of consciousness, is the basis of the lamaist spiritual training, and this training also includes psychic exercises that aim at developing the power of detecting the various " currents of energy " that are crossing each other in every direction.

So some affirm that telepathy, as well as *tumo* and other kindred accomplishments, is a natural by-product of the spiritual training and, consequently, need not be studied separately. This also explains the power with which all great *gomchens* and *dubchens* [1] are credited, of communicating with their disciples, whatever may be the distance that separates them

However, some see the matter in another light. Though they agree that proficiency in the spiritual training brings in its train proficiency in minor accomplishments, such as telepathy, they think that those who are not able to reach the high stages of the mystic path may rightly cultivate telepathy or other by-products separately.

Mystic masters agree to this to a certain extent and, in fact, a number of them train their disciples in telepathy.

A number of Tibetan anchorites have become able,

[1] Literally " a great successful one." This must be understood as " one who is possessed with supernormal powers." The equivalent of our term magician.

without having undergone any special training, to catch the telepathic messages of their *guru*. This is commonly considered as proof of their great devotion to him. A few have spontaneously acquired the power to emit messages.

As for those who cultivate telepathy, the main lines of the training may be sketched as follows.

First, it is necessary to go through all the practices devised to produce the trance of " one-pointedness," the concentration of thought on one single object and complete oblivion of all other things.

The complementary practice which consists in " emptying " the mind from all cogitations, establishing in it complete silence and blankness, must also be mastered.

Then comes the analysis and discrimination of the various influences which cause sudden, apparently inexplicable, psychic or even physical sensations or moods of the mind, such as abrupt feelings of joy, of melancholy, of fear, and also sudden memories of persons, things or events apparently unconnected with anything going on around one.

When the pupil has exercised alone for a time, he may sit in meditation with his master in a silent and darkened room, the thoughts of both being concentrated on the same object. At the end of a given period, the student tells his teacher the phases of his meditation and these are compared with those of the master ; concordances and discrepancies are noted.

Now, stopping, as far as he can, the activity of his mind, emptying it of all ideas, reflections and mental representations, the novice watches the thoughts which arise involuntarily and unexpectedly in him withou⁺ being apparently linked with any of his present pre-occupations or feelings. He notes the subjective images which appear. And, again, at the end of the meditation, thoughts and images are made known to the lama teacher who sees whether or not they correspond to those he mentally suggested to his disciple.

Then, the master sends mental orders to his disciple, while the latter is at a short distance from him. If these are duly received and the student answers by acting accordingly, the exercise continues, the distance between master and disciple being gradually increased.

It is believed in Tibet that *dubchens* are capable of reading the thoughts of others at will. The master being credited with such a power, it would be absurd to train anyone to send him telepathic messages. The very intention of sending them would be detected by him before the messages had actually been sent. Whether this power is real or not, the master is compelled to act as if he possessed it. Consequently, his disciples practise the exchange of telepathic messages among themselves. Two novices or a number of them associate for that purpose under their teacher's supervision and the training is very much like that described above.

Novices test their progress in dispatching unexpected telepathic messages to one another at a time when the person designated is likely to be busy and not thinking about receiving communications.

They also try to convey messages to people with whom they have never been connected through training in common, and who know nothing about telepathy. Some make experiments with animals.

Years are devoted to these practices. It is impossible to guess how many of the students who pursue this study really obtain results from it.

Whatever may be the fruits they reap, the most worshipful among mystic teachers do not encourage this kind of exertion. The efforts made to acquire supernormal powers are considered by these masters as uninteresting childish sports.

It seems proved that great contemplative anchorites

are able to communicate by telepathy with their
disciples, and some even say, with any sentient being,
but that power—as already stated—is considered as a
mere by-product of deep insight into psychic laws,
and of spiritual perfection.

It is said that, when on account of the enlightenment
acquired through various contemplative meditations,
one has ceased to consider " one's self " and " others "
as entirely distinct entities, devoid of points of contact,
then telepathy is easily practised.

The discovery—during prolonged introspections—of
these " points of contact " leads to a sphere in which
delimited beings vanish and only continual exchanges
are perceived.

These are psychic and mystic experiences which
words cannot describe. Whatever may be the share
of truth or fancy in such theories, I prefer to avoid
discussing them.

One thing I may say, however, is that communications from mystic masters to their disciples through
gross material means, such as letters falling from the
ceiling or epistles one finds under one's pillow, are
unknown in lamaist mystic circles. When questions
regarding such facts are put to contemplative hermits,
erudite lamas or high lamaist dignitaries, they can
hardly believe that the inquirer is in earnest and not
an irreverent joker.

I remember the amusing reflection of a lama from
Tashilhunpo when I told him that some " Philings " [1]
believed in such ways of communicating with departed
ones or even with Tibetan mystic teachers : " And
these are the men who have conquered India ! " he
exclaimed, utterly amazed at such simplicity in these
otherwise redoubtable Englishmen.

[1] *Philing* means a foreigner in general, but Tibetans apply the
term specially to Englishmen, the only white foreigners they know
excepting Russians. The latter they call *Urusso* and not *Philing*.

Relying on observations which extend over a large number of years, I shall venture to say that Tibet seems to offer peculiarly favourable conditions for telepathy—as well as for psychic phenomena in general. What are, exactly, these " conditions " ?

It would be presumptuous to attempt defining them while the very nature of psychic phenomena is still so mysterious.

Maybe the very high level of the country is helpful. Perhaps we may, also, take into account the great silence in which the country is bathed, that extra-ordinary silence of which—if I dared to use so strange an expression—I would say that it is *heard* above the loudest voices of the most furiously roaring torrents.

Again, solitude might be reckoned with : the absence of big crowds whose mental activity creates many whirlpools of psychic energy which trouble the ether. And perhaps the placidity of Tibetans whose minds are not filled, like ours, with cares and cogitations is another of these favourable conditions.

Whatever may be the causes at work, telepathic transmissions, either conscious or unconscious, seem to occur rather frequently in Tibet.

Regarding my own experience, I am certain that I did receive on several occasions telepathic messages from lamas under whom I had practised mental or psychic training. It may even be that the number of these messages has been larger than I suspect. How-ever, I have only retained a few cases in which the lama afterwards inquired if I had understood what he meant to tell at a given time.

Beside communications regarding spiritual matters, which may not be entirely due to telepathy, but to a certain identity in the trend of thoughts between a master and his pupil, I may relate two incidents of an entirely different kind.

One of them happened in the Dainshin River valley,

during my journey to Lhasa. The lama, who produced what seemed to me a characteristic telepathic transmission, belonged to the monastery of Chösdzong.

Yongden and I had spent the night in the open, sleeping in a ditch dug by the waters during successive rainy seasons, but for the moment dry and hardened by the frost. The lack of fuel had compelled us to start our daily tramp without drinking our usual hot buttered tea. So, hungry and thirsty, we walked till about noon when we saw, seated on his saddle carpet,[1] near the road, a lama of respectable appearance who was finishing his midday meal. With him were three young *trapas* of distinguished mien, who looked more like disciples accompanying their master than common servants. Four fettered horses were trying to graze on some dry grass near the group.

The travellers had carried a bundle of wood with them and kindled a fire, a teapot was still steaming on the embers.

As befitted our assumed condition of beggarly pilgrims,[2] we respectfully saluted the lama. Most likely, the desire that the sight of the teapot awakened in us could be read in our faces. The lama muttered : " *ñingje !* " [3] and, aloud, told us to sit down and bring out our bowls [4] for tea and *tsampa*.

A *trapa* poured the remaining tea in our bowls, placed a bag of *tsampa* near us and went to help his companions who had begun to saddle the beasts and make ready to start. Then, one of the horses suddenly took fright

---

[1] Tibetans ride on a padded saddle with a carpet over it. When a traveller alights to rest on the road, this carpet is often spread on the ground for him to sit on.

[2] See *My Journey to Lhasa*. This journey was effected in disguise.

[3] A current exclamation which expresses compassionate feelings and may be rendered as : " How sad ! " " The poor things ! " etc.

[4] Tibetan travellers always carry a wooden bowl in the breast pocket formed by their dress tied with a belt. Wealthy travellers keep the bowl in a case which is carried by an attendant.

and ran away. This is a common occurrence, and a man went after the animal with a rope.

The lama was not talkative, he looked at the horse that ran in the direction of a hamlet and said nothing. We continued to eat silently. Then, I noticed an empty wooden pot besmeared with curd and guessed that the lama had got the curd from a farm which I could see at some distance away from the road.

The diet of daily *tsampa* without any vegetables proved rather trying for the stomach and I availed myself of all opportunities to get milk food. I whispered in Yongden's ear : " When the Lama is gone, you shall go to the farm and ask for a little curd."

Though I had spoken very low and we were not seated very near to the lama, he appeared to have heard my words. He cast a searching glance at me and again uttered *sotto voce* : " ñingjed ! "

Then he turned his head in the direction where the horse had run away. The animal had not gone far, but was apparently in a playful mood and did not permit the *trapa* to capture it easily. At last it let him throw the rope round its neck and followed him quietly.

The lama remained motionless, gazing fixedly at the man who advanced toward us. Suddenly, the latter stopped, looked around and went to a boulder near by, where he tied his horse. Then he retraced his steps a little way and leaving the road, walked to the farm. After a while I saw him come back to his horse carrying something. When he reached us the " something " turned out to be a wooden pot full of curd. He did not give it to the lama, but held it in his hand, looking interrogatively at his master as if saying " Was that what you wanted ? What am I to do with this curd ? "

To his unspoken question the lama answered by an affirmative nod, and told the *trapa* to give me the curd.

The second incident which I will relate did not occur

in Tibet itself, but on the borderland territory that has been annexed to the Chinese provinces of Szetchuan and Kansu.

At the skirt of the immense primeval forest that extends from Tagan to the Kunka pass, six travellers had joined my small party. The region is known as being haunted by daring Tibetan robbers, and those who must cross it look for opportunities of forming as large and as well armed a company as possible. Five of my new companions were Chinese traders, the sixth was a Bönpo *ngagspa*, a tall man whose long hair, wrapped in a piece of red material, formed a voluminous turban.

Anxious to glean anything that I could, regarding the religion of the country, I invited the man to share our meals in order to find an opportunity of chatting with him. I learned that he was going to join his master, a Bönpo magician, who was performing a great *dubthab* on a neighbouring hill. The object of this rite was to coerce a malignant demon who habitually harmed one of the small tribes which live in that region. After diplomatic preambles I expressed my desire of paying a visit to the magician, but his disciple declared the thing utterly impossible. His master must not be disturbed during the full lunar month necessary to perform the rite.

I understood that it was useless to argue with him, but I planned to follow him when he parted with us, after crossing the pass. If I succeeded in coming unexpectedly upon the magician, I might perhaps have a glimpse at him and at his magic circle. Consequently, I ordered my servants to keep good watch on the *ngagspa* so that he could not leave us unnoticed.

Probably they spake too loudly among themselves about the matter. The *ngagspa* saw through the trick I intended playing upon his *guru* and told me that it was no use attempting it.

I replied that I did not harbour any evil intention

against his master and only wanted to have a talk with him for the sake of enlightenment. I also commanded my servants to keep a still closer watch on our companion. The *ngagspa* could not but be aware that he had become a prisoner. But as he also understood that no harm would be done to him and that he was well fed—a thing to which Tibetans are keenly alive—he took his adventure good humouredly.

"Do not fear that I shall run away," he said to me. "You may bind me with ropes if it pleases you. I need not go ahead to inform my master of your coming. He already knows all about it. *Ngais lung gi teng la len tang tsar*"[1] (I have sent a message on the wind).

Ngagspas are in the habit of boasting of so many and such various miraculous powers that I did not pay any more attention to his words than to those of his colleagues in the black art.

This time, I was wrong.

When we had crossed the pass, we entered a region of pasture land. Robbers were not much to be feared on these wide tablelands. The Chinese traders, who had clung to us day and night while in the forest, recovered their assurance and took leave. I still intended to follow the *ngagspa*, when a troup numbering half a dozen riders emerged from an undulation of the ground. They rode at full speed toward me, then dismounted, saluted, offered "*kha-tags*" (complimentary scarves) and a present of butter. After the polite demonstrations were ended, an elderly man told me that the great Bönpo *ngagspa* had sent them and begged me to renounce my intention of visiting him, for no one but an initiated disciple ought to approach the place where he had built his secret magic *kyilkhor*.

I had to give up my plan. The *ngagspa*, it seemed, had really informed his master by "sending a message on the wind." To persist would have been useless.

[1] Spelt *ngas rlung gi steng la len btang tsar*.

Even if, in spite of the proof of his strange ability the disciple had given me, I still doubted that the master's occult power was strong enough to prevent my progress, I could not ignore the sturdy armed hillmen that surrounded me. They were most respectful and certainly meant to be as pleasant as they could be, but their attitude might change if my obstinacy should jeopardize the success of a rite that interested a whole tribe. So, I gave a complimentary scarf and some silver to the *ngagspa* to be presented to his master. I congratulated the Tibetans on their good luck in having secured the service of a first-rate magician and we parted on friendly terms.

Visual telepathy seems also to be known in Tibet. If we could rely on the stories told about famous lamas by Tibetans, we should find in them many examples of such phenomena. But truth and fiction mingle freely in these tales, and one feels inclined rather to doubt than give credence to any specially unusual event.

However, there exist men to-day who affirm they have beheld visions transmitted to them by a kind of telepathic process. These are quite different from the images seen in dreams. Sometimes the vision appears during the period of meditation, but at other times it is seen while the observer is busy about his ordinary affairs.

A lama *tsipa* [1] told me that once when taking his meal he saw a *gyud* [2] lama, a friend of his whom he had not met for several years. The *gyud* lama stood at the door of his house side by side with a young *trapa*, who carried a small load on his back, as if ready to start on a journey. The traveller bowed his farewell at the feet of the lama and then the latter smilingly spoke a few words and pointed with his hand towards the north. The *trapa* turned in that direction and bowed down again thrice.

[1] Astrologer.   [2] A fellow of a college of magic ritual.

As he got up, he arranged his monastic toga more tidily and the *tsipa* noticed that it was badly torn at one end. After this, the vision vanished.

A few weeks later, the same young man whom he had seen, arrived from the *gyud* lama, who wished him to be taught some astrological calculations.

The *trapa* related that, when taking leave of his former teacher, after he bowed to him, the latter said " As you are now going to your new master you had better bow down to him also. And he had pointed towards the north, the *tsipa's* dwelling being situated in that direction.

The lama also noticed the large rent in his pupil's toga, which he had already seen in his vision.

I inquired if the *gyud* lama had meant to convey to his friend the news that he was sending him the young *trapa*. No answer could be given to my question, because the event was recent, and since it happened, the *tsipa* had had no opportunities of despatching a message to the *gyud* lama.

I may add that average Tibetans are much less eager than we are to investigate psychic phenomena. They take them as certainly uncommon, but not altogether extraordinary occurrences. They have no fixed ideas about the laws of Nature or what is possible and impossible, to be disturbed by such phenomena. Educated or ignorant, all implicitly admit that everything is possible to him who knows the way of doing it, and consequently supernormal feats do not, as a rule, awaken any special emotion beyond admiration for the competent wonder worker.

CHAPTER VII

MYSTIC THEORIES AND SPIRITUAL TRAINING

THE religious world in Tibet, generally speaking, is divided into two sections. The first includes those who advocate the strict observance of moral precepts and monastic rules as the means of salvation, the second is formed of those who prefer an intellectual method which frees its followers from all laws whatsoever.

Nevertheless there exists no rigid division between these two categories. Though their respective theories are always a favourite subject of controversy between the followers of the two schools, it seldom happens that one stands in the position of a harsh, pugnacious adversary towards those in the opposite camp.

Even the monks attached to morality acknowledge that a virtuous life and the monastic discipline, though of great value and advisable for the many, are but a mere preparation to a higher path. As for the adepts of the second system, they all believe in the beneficial results of a faithful adherence to the moral laws and the rules laid down for members of the religious Order.

Moreover, all are unanimous in declaring the first method the safer of the two. A pure life, the performance of good deeds, righteousness, compassion, detachment from worldly cares, selflessness and quietness of mind act—they say—as a cleansing process which gradually removes the " impure dust that covers the mental eyes," [1] therefore leading to enlightenment which is salvation itself.

As for the method which mystics call the " Short Path," the " Direct Path," [2] it is considered as most hazardous. It is—according to the masters who teach it—as if instead of following the road which goes round a mountain ascending gradually towards its summit, one attempted to reach it in straight line, climbing perpendicular rocks and crossing chasms on a rope. Only first-rate equilibrists, exceptional athletes, completely free from giddiness, can hope to succeed in such a task. Even the fittest may fear sudden exhaustion or dizziness. And there inevitably follows a dreadful fall in which the too presumptuous alpinist breaks his bones.

By this illustration Tibetan mystics mean a spiritual fall leading to the lowest and worst degree of aberration and perversity to the condition of a demon.

I have heard a learned lama maintain that the bold theories regarding complete intellectual freedom and the enfranchisement from all rules whatever, which are expounded by the most advanced adepts of the " Short Path," are the faint echo of teachings that existed from time immemorial in Central and Northern Asia.

The lama was convinced that these doctrines agree completely with the Buddha's highest teaching as it was made evident in various passages of his discourses. However, said the lama, the Buddha was well aware that the majority do better to abide by rules devised to

---

[1] A favourite Buddhist illustration. We read in the Mahāvagga (I, 10) : " Bhagavan, looking over the world with his eyes of a Buddha, saw beings whose mental eyes were darkened by scarcely any dust and beings whose eyes were covered by much dust, beings sharp of sense and blunt of sense, of good disposition and bad disposition, easy to instruct and difficult to instruct. . . ."

[2] Technically, in mystic parlance : *tse gchig, lus gchig sang rgyais*, to attain Buddhahood in one life, one body. That is to say, in the very life in which one has begun one's spiritual training. Tibetans say also : *lam chung* (" the short road ").

avert the baleful effects of their ignorance and guide
them along paths where no disasters are to be feared.
For that very reason, the all-wise Master has established
rules for the laity and monks of average intelligence.

The same lama entertained serious doubts as to the
Aryan origin of the Buddha. He rather believed that
his ancestors belonged to the Yellow race and was convinced that his expected successor, the future Buddha
Maitreya, would appear in Northern Asia.

Where did he get these ideas ?—I have not been able
to find out. Discussion is hardly possible with Oriental
mystics. When once they have answered : " I have
seen this in my meditations," little hope is left to the
inquirer of obtaining further explanations.

I have also heard similar ideas expressed by Newars
from Nepal. Their argument was that the native land
of the Buddha was their own country. " The great
Sage of India," they said, " belonged to the same stock
as ourselves. And as for us, we are of the same race
as the Chinese."

It is, of course, only the learned lamas and mystics
who hold the theories just mentioned, regarding the
" Path of the Rules " and the " Short Path." Now, in
Tibet, as elsewhere, scholars and thinkers are few. So
while amongst the partisans of the " rules " the many
merely vegetate in the monasteries, the doctrine of
" complete freedom " affords a *raison d'être* to countless
people scarcely capable of haunting any summit, but
whose originality cannot be denied.

Most magicians shelter themselves under the flag of
the latter party. Not that many of them seek rapid
spiritual achievement. That which appeals to them in
the " Short Path " is freedom from the bondage of
discipline and the permission thus granted to proceed
with whatever experiments may be useful for their own
advancement. The formula is vague enough to allow
interpretations that fit all kinds of characters.

A broad classification of Tibetan professed magicians and students of the magic art divides them into two categories.

The first includes all those who do not seek direct mastery over nature, but only the power of coercing certain gods and demons to secure their help. The men who practises that method believe in the real existence of the beings of the other worlds as entities completely distinct from them. They also think that their own ability and power are much inferior to those of the personalities whom they endeavour to enslave, and that they would be incapable of obtaining the results which they expect from the latter's help by their own efforts.

Again, whatever other means they use : spells, charms, etc., they also implicitly recognize that their active power, though put into motion by the man who uses them, does not emanate from him.

In the second category only a small number of adepts are to be reckoned.

These employ, at times, the very same means as their less enlightened colleagues, but they do it for different reasons. They hold the view that the various phenomena which the vulgar consider as miracles, are produced by an energy arising in the magician himself and depend on his knowledge of the true inner essence of things. Most of them are men of retired habits, even hermits, who do not exhibit any singularity in their ways and appearance. They make no attempt to exhibit their powers and often remain entirely unknown. On the contrary, the magicians of the first group are fond of indulging in many kinds of showy and bewildering eccentricities. Sorcerers, soothsayers, necromancers, occultists from the meanest beggarly class to those of high social standing, can be met with among them. A lover of odd discourses and deeds may enjoy himself listening to the theories regarding " integral freedom " and its practice that are current in such society. But behind these absurd extravagances there are elements of knowledge regarding old traditions, forgotten history and the handling of psychic forces to be gleaned. But in these circles, as elsewhere in Tibet, the great difficulty is to gain a footing.

It is unnecessary to be an ordained monk to enter the " Short Path to Deliverance." According to its adepts, only initiations are of value. So any layman, if recognized as fit to undertake the spiritual climbing, may be accepted by a mystic master and in due time initiated by him. The same rule applies to students of magic. Nevertheless, most mystics and magicians have begun their career as youths in the religious Order.

The choice of the master who is to guide him along the mystic path, arduous and fraught with deceitful mirages, is a momentous decision for the candidate to initiation. The course which his life will follow depends to a great extent upon the character of the lama he elects.

For having asked admittance at a door from which they ought to have turned away, some have met with fantastic adventures. Yet, if the young monk is satisfied with begging the spiritual guidance of a lama who is neither an anchorite nor an " extremist " of the " Short Path," his novitiate will probably not include any tragic incidents.

During a probation period of undetermined length the master will test the character of his new disciple. Then he may simply explain some philosophical treatises and the meaning of a few symbolic diagrams (*kyilkhors*), teaching him the methodic meditations for which they are used.

If the lama thinks his pupil capable of proceeding farther, he will expound him the programme of the mystic training.

The latter includes three stages, namely :

Tawa—to look, examine.

Gompa—to think, meditate.

Chyöd pa—to practise, realize. This is the fruit of accomplishment through the two former stages.

Another less current enumeration makes use of four terms to convey the same meaning, as follows :

FIRST STAGE

> *Tön*—" meaning," " reason." That is to say investigation of the nature of things, their origin, their end, the causes upon which they depend.
>
> *Lob*—" study " of various doctrines.

SECOND STAGE : *Gom*—thinking or meditating on that which one has discovered and learnt. Practising introspective meditation.

THIRD STAGE : *Togs*—Understanding.

In order that the novice may practise in perfect quietness the various exercises which that programme requires, it is nearly certain that the lama will command him to shut himself in *tsams*.[1]

The word *tsams* signifies a barrier, the border of a territory. In religious parlance, to " stay in tsams " means to live in seclusion, to retire beyond a barrier which must not be passed.

That " barrier " may be of different kinds. With advanced mystics it becomes purely psychic and it is said that the latter need no material contrivances to isolate themselves while meditating.

There exist several categories of *tsams*, each one being subdivided into a number of varieties.

Proceeding from the less austere towards the most severe forms, we find the following ones :

A lama or a lay devotee shuts himself in his room or private apartment. He does not go out or only does so at fixed time, to perform some devotional practices, such as walking around religious edifices making repeated prostrations before sacred objects, or the like.

According to the rule which he has adopted, the

[1] Written *mtshams* and pronounced *tsam*.

tsamspa [1] either may be seen or must remain invisible. In the first case, he is generally permitted to talk briefly with the members of the household, his relatives or servants, and even to receive a few visitors. In the second case, he may only be seen by those who attend him. If a visitor is admitted, he must remain within hearing *outside* the *tsamspa's* room. A curtain screens the entrance and the interlocutors remain invisible to each other as in some Roman Catholic contemplative Orders of nuns.

A number of Tibetans resort occasionally to one or another of these mild forms of seclusion for non-religious motives, seeking merely to avoid disturbance while engaged in the study of any branch of Tibetan learning : grammar, philosophy, astrology, medicine, etc.

Next come the recluse who sees but one attendant.

He who renounces speaking and makes known his needs by writing.

He who partly covers his window, so that he cannot see the surrounding landscape, nor any outside object except the sky.

He who renounces the sight of the sky, covering his window entirely or, living in a windowless room which, nevertheless, admits the daylight indirectly.

He who sees no one at all.

In this case, if the *tsamspa* enjoys the use of a suite of rooms, his meals are brought into one of them, while he retires into another. When he lives in a single room, food is placed next the entrance. Someone knocks at the door to inform the recluse that what he needs is ready, and then the inmates of the house leave the adjacent room or corridors for a moment to allow the *tsamspa* to come out without being seen. Any object is returned in the same way, the *tsamspa* calling attention by knocking at the door or ringing a bell.

[1] He who practises *tsams*. Not to be mistaken for *tsampa* : flour of roast barley, written *rtsampa*.

Among those who practise this particular kind of *tsams*, some ask by writing for the things which they require, but others renounce this facility. Consequently, whatever may be their needs, they cannot make them known. Even if those who attend on them forgot to give them their meal, they ought to fast in silence.

Generally *tsams* in one's own house do not last long, especially of the strict kind. One year seems to be an exceptional period. One usually hears of people who live in seclusion for three months, one month and even a few days only. Laymen rarely shut themselves in their apartment for more than one month.

It is easy to understand that prolonged and severe *tsams* cannot be practised in an ordinary residence. There, whatever care is taken, the moving about of people busy with worldly affairs and the noise inevitably reach the *tsamspa*, through the thin barrier of his closed door.

The silence and quiet surroundings which may be enjoyed to a high degree in the monasteries are not even deemed sufficient by some, and many *gompas* own special small houses built for the use of their members who wish to live in strict seclusion.

These houses are called *tsams khang*.[1] They are sometimes situated in an out-of-the-way spot, inside the monastery's walls, but more frequently stand aloof on some hill, at a little distance outside the walled enclosure. It is not unusual to find groups of these meditation houses standing in the solitude, at a few days' march from their parent monastery.

The plans of the *tsams khangs* correspond to the various rules and requirements here above mentioned.

From the windows of some of them, the recluse may enjoy the sight of beautiful landscapes, while others

[1] From *mtshams* and *khang*, house : "a house where to live in seclusion."

are surrounded by walls that cut off the view on all sides. In that case, the enclosure often forms a small courtyard or terrace where the *tsamspa* may sit or walk in the open, without being seen, or himself seeing anything of the outside world.

Most *tsams khangs* are divided into two rooms. In one of them, the recluse sits and sleeps, the other one is the kitchen in which an attendant may live.

When the *tsamspa* must see no one and keep the rule of silence, his attendant lives in a separate hut. A double wicket is then built in the wall or the door of the recluse's room, and through it meals are given to him.

Solid food is generally served only once a day, but buttered tea is brought several times. If the lama belongs to one or another of the " Red cap " sects, beer [1] alternates with the tea. Tibetans having the custom of keeping a small bag of barley flour at hand, the recluse is at liberty to eat some with his tea or beer, whenever he likes.

Only members of the religious Order retire in the cottages specially built to be used as meditation houses. Some remain in seclusion during several consecutive years. A canonic period is three years three months three weeks and three days. Some repeat that long

[1] Though drinking fermented beverages is strictly prohibited by Buddhism, Tibetan " Red caps " declare that Padmasambhava, their founder, allowed it. Nevertheless, some of them seem to know better. Padmasambhava, they say, allowed the drinking of alcohol when performing certain rites, and then the quantity to be drunk was that which fills the hollow of the palm. Padmasambhava, who was a Western Indian and an adept of Tantrism, taught his Tibetan converts the form of worship of his sect and, as with many *tantrikas*, the two drops of wine to be drunk in sacramental fashion led to habitual drinking. An Indian saying goes : " Some drink to perform the rite, and some perform the rite in order to drink." But Tibetans addicted to drinking do not seek a religious excuse any more than their Western brethren in drunkenness.

retreat twice or thrice in the course of their life, and a few shut themselves in *tsams* for life.

There exists a still more austere form of *tsams* : that of dwelling in complete darkness.

Meditation in darkness is not a practice peculiar to Lamaism. It is known in all Buddhist countries. I have seen different kinds of room in Burma, specially built for the purpose, and made use of them myself during my stay on the Sagain hills. But while Burmese and other Buddhist monks only spend a few hours at a time there, certain Tibetan ascetics bury themselves for years, and even till death, in such grave-like dwellings. However, these extreme cases are rare.

When complete night is desired and the sojourn in the *tsams khang* is to be long, the latter is often established in a grotto or a partly underground building, ventilated by chimneys constructed in such a way that they do not allow the light to penetrate into the recluse's cell. This, however, is very seldom done. Usually the dark hermitage is aerated in a natural—and, indeed, very imperfect—way, through fissures and the like. Though these must, perforce, admit some light together with air, that light seems often of a purely theoretical kind, for in some of these obscure abodes it is impossible to distinguish any object. Yet, after a time, the eyes of the *tsamspas* get accustomed to dark, and succeed in vaguely seeing their surroundings.

According to what I have heard from men who have spent long periods of seclusion in darkness, these hermits enjoy, at times, wonderful illuminations. Their cell becomes bright with light or, in the darkness, every object is drawn with luminous outlines ; or again, a phantasmagoria of shining flowers, landscapes and personages arises before them.

Optic phenomena of that kind are certainly common, for they have also been described to me in Burma, by *bhikkhus* who practised meditation in darkness, and I suppose that everybody has seen something of the kind at night.

Tibetans see in this a way of testing the degree of fixity attained by the mind. The kaleidoscopic mirage is considered by them as entirely subjective. It is, they think, caused by the uncontrolled agitation of the mind. When the latter is brought near stillness, the phantasmagoria vanishes. There remains only a spot (*thigle*) which may be either dark coloured or like a diminutive globe of light. At first that spot moves and the aim of the practice is to fix it.

The stage in which the spot remains motionless, without undergoing any change in size, colour, etc., is the moment when the mystic is able to concentrate his thoughts on any object he chooses without any other ideas breaking his " one-pointedness " of mind. The next stage is marked by the disappearance of the spot which sinks in utter darkness. This however is not always attained ; many continue to proudly enjoy the fairy-scene thinking that they have obtained a glimpse of paradise.

Beside recreations of this kind, a number of subtler enchantments await the *tsamspa* in his hermitage. These, according to religious teachers, are traps which catch the unintelligent disciple who ventures on the mystic path.

When the *tsamspa*, who has spent a long time in darkness, is nearing the end of his retreat, he gradually accustoms his eyes to see the daylight again. For that purpose, a hole, the size of a pin's head, is pierced in a mud part of the wall and is enlarged each day till the aperture forms a small window. This operation may take several months and is either done by the recluse himself or by another person : his *guru* or a friend. The longer the time spent in obscurity the slower is the admission of light into the cell.

Novices who shut themselves up entirely for the first

time, either in light or dark *tsams khangs*, generally receive instructions from their *guru* during their seclusion.

The lama speaks to them from outside, through the double wicket which is used to pass in the recluse's meal. The *guru* of a *tsamspa* who must see nobody, often shuts the entrance of the latter's cell with his own seal. A religious ceremony is performed on that occasion and another one when the master breaks the seal and the recluse steps out.

If the *tsams* is not of the severe kind, a flag may be placed at the recluse's door, on which are written the names of the persons who are allowed to enter his rooms : attendants or visitors allowed by the *tsamspa's* teacher.

A dry branch is sometimes driven in the earth or stuck in a pot, near the hermitage of a *tsamspas* who shuts himself up for life.

The term *tsams khang* is more generally applied to meditation—cottages built in the vicinity of a monastery. Those standing in more remote places are called *ritöd*.[1]

Ritöds are never built at the bottom of a valley, they are always perched on a dominating spot, and the choice of the site is made in accordance with special rules. Two well-known Tibetan verses depict the main conditions required.

> *Gyab rii tag*
> *Dun rii tso* [2]
> The mountain rock, behind.
> The mountain lake in front.

That is to say that the hermitage should be built on the hillside with a background of rocks, or better still against the rock itself, looking down on a lake or, at least, a stream.

Various other regulations have been laid down, in

---

[1] Written *Ri khrod*.
[2] Spelt *rgyab rihi brag, mdun rihi mtsho*.

accordance with the requirements of peculiar spiritual and psychic trainings. Thus, some dwellings must permit an extended view so that the anchorite can see the sun rising and setting. The noises produced by running water or wind must be muffled as far as possible. The vicinity of woodland is advised or a barren landscape deemed more suitable, etc.

Ritödpas do not remain continually shut in their houses. Outside the periods of strict *tsams*, most of them go out between the hours which they devote to meditation or other practices. According to the rule imposed by their *guru*, or self-imposed, they are either allowed, or forbidden, to talk with their neighbours while fetching water, collecting fuel or taking a walk around their cabin. Meditation in the open is sometimes advised by the *ritödpa's* spiritual guide or some practise it from their own inclination.

Though the term *ritöd*, properly speaking, means a " group of hermitages," current usage applies it to all single isolated anchorite abodes : huts or caves.

It is to such primitive dwellings, far away from inhabited regions, that staunch *naljorpas* who aim at climbing the rugged rocks of spiritual heights, retire.

Those who are still at the novice stage, tramp at long intervals to their *guru's* place to tell him about their psychic experiences, the ideas to which their meditation have given birth, and also to receive his advice and communication of spiritual power (*angkur rite*). Several years may elapse between such meetings.

As for the hermits who are teachers, some of them allow a few promising beginners to live in their vicinity. " Vicinity " is, however, a wide term. The disciple may stay on the same hill as his master at a spot situated lower down than the latter's dwelling, or at one or two days' march.

One can well imagine that all of the many *tsams khangs* and *ritöds'* dwellers are not saints or sages.

False pretence and sham mysticism have long ago crept into the world of Tibetan anchorites. Even on the shining snowy ranges, one can meet the hypocrite. Under the guise of *gomchens*, boasting of secret knowledge and supernormal powers, they deceive simple-minded peasantry or tent-dwelling herdsmen. It may appear to a Westerner that they pay dearly for the material advantages or the fame they enjoy, by purchasing them at the cost of the hardships of hermit life. But one must appreciate the bargain from a Tibetan, and not from a Western point of view.

Tibetans are a strong and sturdy people ; the cold, sleeping on the ground in the open, solitude, and many other things from which the average Westerners would shrink, do not frighten them in the least. There are but a few of them, even among the upper classes, who have not experienced something of the kind whilst travelling or on other occasions. Adventurous clerical charlatans, often illiterate and of poor parentage, who cannot expect any standing in their monastery, enjoy a much more agreeable life in a *ritöd* than they could hope for elsewhere.

The more ambitious among them may, indeed, submit to uncommon austerities, in order to gain repute, but they give up all these after a few years, when their fame is sufficiently well established. Then, they may settle in some private abode, relying on the gifts of the laity to enable them to spend their days in comfort.

Others make no attempt at calling attention to themselves. They merely settle down in a cabin or a cave conveniently situated at a few miles from a prosperous village or herdsmen tribal ground. Things may be a little hard at first and food not always plentiful, for Tibetans are not hasty in giving their confidence and faith to " uncommissioned " lamas. But if the man is clever and knows " the ways " he will gradually succeed. He must play the soothsayer of course and drive away

the demons which cause illness. If chance favours
him, a few of the oracles he delivers may prove true,
man or beast recover after he has exorcised the evil
one. Nothing more is needed to secure quite brilliant
prospects.

I suppose that few Westerners would enjoy the life
of a pseudo-ascetic in the Tibetan wilds, but Tibetans
do. Frauds of this kind always end by being caught
at their own tricks. Of course, they do not attain the
bliss which awaits true mystics ; but they live free,
respected, without any occasion for working ; and they
receive enough tea, butter, and *tsampa* for all their daily
wants. Beyond this any cabin or cave roughly fitted
up as a dwelling-place satisfies the unsophisticated
craving of these ingenious, yet simple, rogues. Many
of them are far from being bad characters and altogether
unsympathetic. They nearly always struck me as
practical jokers, and the fun I derived from their naive
cunning inclined me to kindly judgment.

The current idea in the West is that a man cannot
maintain seclusion or absolute solitude for a considerable
length of time. It is believed that these unavoidably
bring in their train, brain disorders, finally leading to
stupidity and madness.

This is perhaps true about the individuals on whom
the effects of isolation have been studied : light-
house guards, travellers thrown on to desert island after
a shipwreck, explorers lost in uninhabited regions,
prisoners in solitary confinement, etc. But such observations do not apply to Tibetan hermits. The latter
after ten or twenty years, or even a longer time, in
the wilderness or in *tsams khangs*, are far from being
insane. One may dispute the theories which they have
conceived during their protracted meditations, but it
is impossible to question their sanity.

There is nothing really remarkable about this. These
men are prepared for loneliness. Before shutting them-

selves in their *tsams khang* or settling in a *ritöd*, they have accumulated in their mind a store of ideas which keep them company. Moreover, they are not inactive during their retreat, long as it may be. Their days are occupied by methodical exercises in spiritual training, the search for occult knowledge or meditations on philosophic problems. And so, often passionately interested in these manifold investigations and introspections, they are actually very busy and hardly notice their solitude.

I have never heard a Tibetan hermit say that, even at the beginning of his retreat, he had suffered from lack of associations with men. Generally, those who have tasted the anchorite life find it difficult, if not impossible to resume life among other people or to enjoy regular social intercourse.

Whatever those unacquainted with it may think, solitude and utter loneliness are far from being devoid of charm.

Words cannot convey the almost voluptuous sweetness of the feelings experienced when one closes the door of one's *tsams khang*, or when one looks down from the heights at the first wintry snow heaping up in the lower valleys, creating for months around the hermitage an impassable white and cold rampart.

But, most likely, only those who have lived through it themselves can understand the irresistible attraction that hermit life exerts on many Orientals.

The practices to which Tibetan recluses apply themselves while shut in their *tsams khang* or *ritöds* are many and of a various nature. Any attempt to compile a complete list of them would be vain, for most probably nobody in the world knows them all.

One finds in the Tibetan mystic literature more or less exhaustive descriptions of a few practices, but, as a rule, they are reticent on the points which interest us most, that is to say the purpose of the practices. Reliable

information can only be obtained from those who are
acquainted with traditional oral teaching for each
particular exercise. One must, especially, beware of
remaining satisfied with interpretations obtained of only
one initiate, for they vary not only among different sects,
but among individual teachers.

It would be a mistake to fancy that all Tibetans who
live in seclusion in a *tsams khang* or betake themselves
to solitude, are endowed with uncommon intelligence
and ponder over transcendental problems.

I have already spoken of the sham *gomchens* who have
taken to religious life as to a profession. There also
exists a very large number of well-meaning simpletons
and men of average mental power who bring the
superstitions of popular lamaism to their retreat.

Amongst those, many devote the time of their seclusion
repeating thousands and even millions of times one
single formula : generally a Sanskrit *mantra* which is
unintelligible to them. Others recite a Tibetan text,
but often they understand no more of its meaning than
if they were uttering words in a foreign language.

The most ordinary formula is the well-known *Aum
mani padme hum !* I say, well known as far as the words
are concerned, because foreigners have read it in many
books. It does not follow that its meaning has been
made clear to them.

Lay travellers and even Orientalists are sometimes a
little too quick to declare that meaningless which they
do not at once understand. Erudite authors, even
to-day, translate the first word of the formula, *aum*,
by our commonplace exclamation *ah !* and *hum*, the
last word, by *amen*.

There exists an immense literature in India devoted
to the explanation of the mystic word *Aum*. The latter
has exoteric, esoteric and mystic meanings. It may
signify the three persons of the Hindu Trinity : Brahma,
Vishnou, Shiva. It may signify the Brahman, the " One

without a second " of the adwaita philosophy. It stands as a symbol of the Inexpressible Absolute, the last word to be uttered in mysticism, after which there follows only silence. It is, according to Shri Sankarâcharya,[1] " the support of the meditation," or, as declared in the Mundakopanishad's text itself, " it is the bow by the means of which the individual self attains the universal self." [2]

Again, *Aum* is the creative sound whose vibrations build the worlds. When the mystic is capable of hearing all in one the countless voices, cries, songs, and noises of all beings and things that exist and move, it is the unique sound *Aum* which reaches him. That same *Aum* vibrates also in the utmost depth of his inner self. He who can pronounce it with the right tone, is able to work wonders, and he who knows how to utter it silently, attains supreme emancipation.

Tibetans who have received the word *Aum* from India together with the *mantras* with which it is associated, do not appear to have been acquainted with its many meanings among their Southern neighbours, nor do they know the very prominent place it occupies in their religions and philosophies.

Aum is repeated by lamaists along with other Sanskrit formulas, without having a special importance by itself, while other mystic syllables as *hum !* and especially *phat !* are supposed to possess great power and are much used in magic and mystic rites.

So much for the first word of the formula.

Mani padme are Sanskrit terms that mean " jewel in the lotus." Here we come, it seems, to an immediately intelligible meaning, yet the current interpretation does not take any account of that plain meaning.

---

[1] In his commentary on *Mundakopanishad*.
[2] " The *Pranava* (that is the name of the sacred syllable *Aum*) is the bow, the *Atman* (the individual self) is the arrow and the Brahman (universal self: the Absolute) is said to be the mark."

Common folk believe that the recitation of *Aum mani padme hum !* will assure them a happy rebirth in *Nub Dewa chen,* the Western Paradise of the Great Bliss.

The more " learned " have been told that the six syllables of the formula are connected with the six classes of sentient beings and are related to one of the mystic colours as follows :

Aum is white and connected with gods (lha).

Ma is blue and connected with non-gods (lhamayin).[1]

Ni is yellow and connected with men (mi).

Pad is green and connected with animals (tudo).

Me is red and connected with non-men (Yidag [2] or other mi-ma-yin[3]).

Hum is black and connected with dwellers in purgatories.

There are several opinions regarding the effect of the recitation of these six syllables. Popular tradition declares that those who frequently repeat the formula will be reborn in the Western Paradise of the Great Bliss. Others who deem themselves more enlightened declare that the recitation of *Aum mani padme hum !* may liberate from a rebirth in any of the six realms.

Aum mani padme hum ! is used as a support for a special meditation which may, approximately, be described as follows :

One identifies the six kinds of beings with the six syllables which are pictured in their respective colours, as mentioned above. They form a kind of chain without

[1] A kind of Titans always at war with the gods.

[2] The bodies of *Yidags* are as big as a hill, their necks are as thin as a thread. These miserable beings are perpetually tortured by hunger and thirst. When they approach water to drink it transforms itself into flame. Every morning the lamas offer consecrated water to the *Yidags* to relieve their sufferings. This consecrated water does not turn into flame at their approach.

[3] In the *mi ma yin* class are included demi-gods, genii; spirits of various kind, either friendly or malevolent.

end that circulates through the body, carried on by the breath, entering through one nostril and going out through the other.

As the concentration of mind becomes more perfect, one sees mentally the length of the chain increasing. Now when they go out with the expiration, the mystic syllables are carried far away, before being absorbed again with the next inspiration. Yet, the chain is not broken, it rather elongates like a rubber strap and always remains in touch with the man who meditates.

Gradually, also, the shape of the Tibetan letters vanishes and those who " obtain the fruit " of the practice perceive the six syllables as six realms in which arise, move, enjoy, suffer, and pass away the innumerable beings, belonging to the six species.

And now it remains for the meditator to realize that the six realms (the whole phenomenal world) are subjective : a mere creation of the mind which imagines them and into which they sink.

Advanced mystics reach, by the way of this practice, a trance in which the letters of the formula, as well as the beings and their activity, all merge into *That* which, for lack of a better term, Mahâyânist Buddhists have called " Emptiness."

Then, having realized the " Void," they become emancipated from the illusion of the world and, as a consequence, liberated from rebirths which are but the fruit of that creative delusion.

Another of the many interpretations of *Aum mani padme hum !* ignores the division in six syllables and takes the formula according to its meaning : " a jewel in a lotus." These words are considered as symbolic.

The simplest interpretation is : In the lotus (which is the world) exists the precious jewel of Buddha's teaching.

Another explanation takes the lotus as the mind. In the depth of it, by introspective meditation, one is able to find the jewel of knowledge, truth, reality, liberation, nirvāna, these various terms being different denominations of one same thing.

Now we come to a meaning related to certain doctrines of the Mahâyânist Buddhists.

According to them *nirvāna*, the supreme salvation, is not separated from *samsāra*, the phenomenal world, but the mystic finds the first in the heart of the second, just as the " jewel " may be found in the " lotus." Nirvâna, the " jewel," exists when enlightenment exists. Samsâra, the " lotus," exists when delusion exists, which veils nirvâna, just as the many petals of the " lotus " conceal the " jewel " nestling among them.

Hum ! at the end of the formula, is a mystic expression of wrath used in coercing fierce deities and subduing demons. How has it become affixed to the " jewel in the lotus " and the Indian *Aum* ?—This again is explained in various ways.

Hum ! is a kind of mystic war cry ; uttering it, is challenging an enemy. Who is the enemy ? Each one imagines him in his own way : either as powerful fiends, or as the trinity of bad propensities that bind us to the round of rebirth, namely lust, hatred and stupidity. More subtle thinkers see him as the " I." *Hum !* is also said to mean the mind devoid of objective content, etc., etc.

Another syllable is added to conclude the repetition of *Aum mani padne hum !* one hundred and eight times on the beads of a rosary. It is the syllable *hri !* Some understand it as signifying an inner reality hidden under the appearances, the basic essence of things.

Beside *Aum mani padme hum hri !* other formulas are also repeated as *Aum vajra sattva !* That is to say, " Aum most excellent (diamond) being." It is understood that the excellent One meant is the Buddha. The followers of the Red cap sects often repeat : *Aum vajra guru padma siddhi hum !* as praise of their founder Padmasambhava.

These words mean *Aum*, most excellent powerful guru Padma, miracle worker, *hum!*

Amongst longer formulas one of the most popular is that called " Kyabdo." [1] It is Tibetan without admixture of Sanskrit and its significance is plain, yet far from crude. The text runs as follows :

" I take refuge in all holy refuges. Ye fathers and mothers (ancestors) who are wandering in the round of rebirths under the shapes of the six kinds of sentient beings. In order to attain Buddhahood, the state devoid of fear and sorrow, let your thoughts be directed towards enlightenment."

Often this formula is given to beginners for their first period of *tsams*. Its words are well known and anyone can repeat them without being shut in *tsams*. They are held as meritorious and efficacious under any circumstance. For this reason, I had chosen them during my journey to Lhasa, to break the monotonous repetition of *Aum mani padme hum!* when I deemed it prudent to appear absorbed in a pious exercise to avoid annoying talks and embarrassing questions that might have put my incognito in jeopardy.

The common " *kyabdo—tsams* " consists in remaining in seclusion in a hut or in one's own room and repeating the above-mentioned formula one hundred thousand times, while prostrating oneself the same number of times. Any formula may be repeated in the same way, with one hundred thousand prostrations.

Tibetans perform prostrations in two ways. One is very much like the Chinese *kowtow*. The difference is that before kneeling, one lifts the arms above the head, joining the palms and, then, brings the folded hands successively in front of the forehead, the mouth and the heart.

Obeisances of that kind are repeated three times when saluting the images in the temples, the lamas

[1] " Going to the refuge."

of rank, one's own *guru*, and the sacred books or edifices.

The second kind of prostration is called *kyang chag*. It is made in Indian fashion, the body lying flat on the ground, and is only performed in a few special very devotional exercises such as the *kyabdo* practice.

Tsamspas, who aspire to the title of *chagbum*, repeat one hundred thousand times a *kyabdo* formula while prostrating themselves as many times, their foreheads actually touching the ground or the floor of the room at each prostration. This repeated contact of the flesh with a hard surface produces a bump or even a sore. The latter must show certain peculiarities understood by experts in the matter, which indicate whether the object of the rite has, or has not, been obtained.

Tsamspas, who consider themselves far above the practice of *kyabdo*, perform breathing exercises. These consist in taking different, often extraordinary, postures while one trains oneself to inhale, exhale, hold the breath in and keep it out [1] in various ways.

Often the *tsamspas* drill themselves naked, and the shape of the belly during the exercises is a sign that shows the degree of proficiency attained by the disciple.

Beside physical results, some of which have been described in a preceding chapter, Tibetans affirm that through mastery over breath one may conquer all passion and anger as well as carnal desires, acquire serenity, prepare the mind for meditation and awake spiritual energy.

" Breath is the courser and mind is the rider," say the Tibetan mystics. So it is essential that the courser must be well trained. But breath, in its turn, influences bodily and mental activity. Consequently, two methods have been devised · the most easy one which quiets

---

[1] That is to say after having breathed out, one remains for a while without breathing in. In technical terms, this is called : *to stay void.*

the mind by controlling the breath and the more difficult way which consists in regulating the breath by controlling the mind.

To the breathing drill repeated several times each day, the recluse often adds the contemplative meditation practised with *kyilkhors*.[1] The latter are, also, most important and conspicuous in the magic rites called *dubthabs* (method of success).

Kyilkhors are diagrams drawn on paper or material, or engraved on stone, metal or wood. Others are constructed with small flags, altar lamps, incense sticks and vases containing various things such as grain, water, etc. The personalities who are supposed to dwell in the *kyilkhor* and their requisites are represented by pyramidal cakes named *torma*.

Kyilkhors are also drawn with coloured powders on the temple floor or on boards. I have seen some which measured about seven feet in diameter.

The word *kyilkhor* means a circle, nevertheless, amongst the numberless kinds of *kyilkhors*, there exist square and quadrangular forms, while those used in black magic or for the coercion or destruction of malignant entities are triangular.

The monks who wish to become proficient in this kind of art spend years studying its rules. One of the four high colleges which exist in all large monasteries teaches the art of drawing the *kyilkhors* that are parts of the official lamaist magic rites. As for secret ones connected with mystic training or black magic, each student must learn them privately from his own teacher.

The least mistake in the drawing of a *kyilkhor* or the place given to the *tormas* in its construction, may have most terrible consequences, for the *kyilkhor* is a magic instrument which hurts him who handles it unskilfully.

Moreover, no one should construct or draw a *kyilkhor* if he has not been empowered to do so, by a proper

[1] Written *dkyilkhor*.

initiation, and each variety of *kyilkhor* requires the corresponding initiation. That which is the work of a non-initiated cannot be animated and remains powerless.

As for the true understanding of the symbolic meaning of the *kyilkhors*, and the theories which support their use in psychic training, very few are aware of them.

Needless to say that elaborate and large-sized *kyilkhors* cannot find room in the *tsams khangs*. Their form, there, is very much simplified.

At the beginning of his spiritual education the novice is likely to be taught by his teacher the way of constructing a diagram which is to be used as support (*rten*) to fix the attention during meditation.

One of the exercises most generally practised—either with or without a *kyilkhor*—at that stage of the training, is the following :

A deity is imagined ; it is first contemplated alone, then from its body spring out other forms sometimes like its own, sometimes different. There are often four of them, but in some meditations they become hundreds or even innumerable.

When all these personages have appeared quite clearly around the central figure, they are one after another reabsorbed in it. Now the original deity remains again alone and gradually begins to disappear. The feet vanish first and then slowly the whole body and finally the head. Only a dot remains. This may be dark, coloured or purely luminous. Mystic masters interpret this as a sign which shows the degree of spiritual progress attained by their disciples.

Then, the dot moves towards the man who beholds it and sinks into him. One must note the part of the body in which it seems to disappear. A period of meditation follows that exercise, which may be done again and again as many times as desired.

One may also imagine a lotus. It opens slowly and

on each of its petals stands a Bodhisatva, one of them being enthroned in the heart of the flower. After a while, as the lotus begins to fold its petals again each one emits a ray of light that sinks into the centre of the flower, and when it closes entirely, light escapes from its heart and penetrates the man in meditation.

There exist many kinds of similar practices.

Many novices do not proceed farther. Thus dryly described, such visions cannot but appear absurd, yet they constitute a somewhat fascinating puzzle on account of the multifarious unexpected aspects they assume after a certain time of training.

They provide the recluse with spectacles which rival the most beautiful fairy-plays that can be seen on the stage. Even those who are well aware of their illusive nature may enjoy them, and as for those who believe in the reality of the divine players, it is not surprising that they are bewitched.

However, it is not to amuse the hermits that these exercises have been invented. Their true aim is to lead the disciple to understand that the worlds and all phenomena which we perceive are but mirages born from our imagination.

> " They emanate from the mind
> And into the mind they sink."

In fact this is the fundamental teaching of Tibetan mystics.

If we now consider the case of a monk (who instead of placing himself under the spiritual guidance of a lama who is a regular member of a monastery) ventures to solicit the teaching of a contemplative anchorite *naljorpa* the training takes another aspect. Methods become strange, sometimes even cruel ; we have seen it in a previous chapter.

The trilogy : *Examination, Meditation, Understanding,* takes a peculiar importance among the followers of the

" Short Path " and the intellectual activity of the disciple is exclusively directed towards these results.
Sometimes the means that are used seem extravagant,
yet when closely investigated one sees that the object
aimed at is quite reasonable. It is also clear that the
inventors of these curious methods perfectly understand
the mind of their brethren in religion and have devised
them accordingly.

Padmasambhava is said to have described the stages
of the mystic path in the following way.

1. To read a large number of books on the various
religions and philosophies. To listen to many learned
doctors professing different doctrines. To experiment
oneself with a number of methods.

2. To choose a doctrine among the many one has
studied and discard the other ones, as the eagle carries
off only one sheep from the flock.

3. To remain in a lowly condition, humble in one's
demeanour, not seeking to be conspicuous or important
in the eyes of the world, but behind apparent insignifi-
cance, to let one's mind soar high above all worldly
power and glory.

4. To be indifferent to all. Behaving like the dog
or the pig that eat what chance brings them. Not
making any choice among the things which one meets.
Abstaining from any effort to acquire or avoid anything.
Accepting with an equal indifference whatever comes :
riches or poverty, praise or contempt, giving up the
distinction between virtue and vice, honourable and
shameful, good and evil. Being neither afflicted, nor
repenting whatever one may have done and, on the
other hand, never being elated nor proud on account
of what one has accomplished.

5. To consider with perfect equanimity and detachment the conflicting opinions and the various manifestations of the activity of beings. To understand
that such is the nature of things, the inevitable mode

of action of each entity and to remain always serene. To look at the world as a man standing on the highest mountain of the country looks at the valleys and the lesser summits spread out below him.[1]

6. It is said that the sixth stage cannot be described in words. It corresponds to the realization of the " Void " [2] which, in Lamaist terminology, means the Inexpressible reality.

In spite of these programmes, it is impossible to establish a regular gradation of the multifarious training exercises devised by Tibetan mystic anchorites. In practice, these various exercises are combined. Moreover each lama adopts a peculiar method, and it is even rare to see two disciples of the same master following exactly the same path.

We must make up our minds to accept an apparent chaos which is a natural result of the different individual tendencies and aptitudes which the *gurus*, adepts of the " Short Path," refuse to crush. " Liberty " is the motto on the heights of the " Land of Snows," but strangely enough, the disciple starts on that road of utter freedom, by the strictest obedience to his spiritual guide. However, the required submission is confined to the spiritual and psychic exercises and the way of living prescribed by the master. No dogmas are ever imposed. The disciple may believe, deny or doubt anything according to his own feelings.

---

[1] Compare *Dhammapada* : " When the learned man drives away vanity by earnestness, he, the wise one, climbing the terraced heights of wisdom, looks down upon the fools. Free from sorrow, he looks upon the sorrowing crowd, as one that stands on a mountain looks down upon them that stand upon the plain." The *Dhammapada* is a work belonging to the Buddhist canonic Scriptures in Pali language.

[2] In a general way, one must understand here, the realization of the non-existence of a permanent *ego*, according to the Tibetan current formula : " *The person is devoid of self ; all things are devoid of self.*"

I have heard a lama say that the part of a master, adept of the " Short Path," is to superintend a " clearing." He must incite the novice to rid himself of the beliefs, ideas, acquired habits and innate tendencies, which are part of his present mind, and have been developed in the course of successive lives whose origin is lost in the night of time.

On the other hand, the master must warn his disciple to be on his guard against accepting new beliefs, ideas and habits as groundless and irrational as those which he shakes off.

The discipline on the " Short Path " is to avoid imagining things. When imagination is prescribed, in contemplative meditation, it is to demonstrate by that conscious creation of perceptions or sensations, the illusory nature of those perceptions and sensations which we accept as real though they too rest on imagination ; the only difference being that, in their case, the creation is unconsciously effected.

The Tibetan reformer, Tsong Khapa, defines meditation as " the means [1] of enabling oneself to reject all imaginative thoughts together with their seed."

It is this uprooting of the present " imaginative thoughts," and the burning of their " seed," so that no fanciful ideas may arise in the future, that constitutes the " clearing " which I have just mentioned.

Two exercises are especially prescribed by the adepts of the mystic path.

The first consists in observing with great attention the workings of the mind without attempting to stop it.

Seated in a quiet place, the disciple refrains as much as he can from consciously pointing his thoughts in

---

[1] The word used by the author is *khungs*, which means the " source," the " origin." The quotation is taken from the work called *The Lamp of the Way*. A similar definition is found in the Yoga sûtras of Patanjali.

a definite direction. He marks the spontaneous arising of ideas, memories, desires, etc., and considers how, superseded by new ones, they sink into the dark recesses of the mind.

He watches also the subjective image which, apparently unconnected with any thoughts or sensations, appears while his eyes are closed : men, animals, landscapes, moving crowds, etc.

During that exercise, he avoids making reflections about the spectacle which he beholds, looking passively at the continual, swift, flowing stream of thoughts and mental images that whirl, jostle, fight and pass away.

It is said that the disciple is about to gather the fruit of this practice when he loosens the firm footing he had kept, till then, in his quality of spectator. He too—so he must understand—is an actor on the tumultuous stage. His present introspection, all his acts and thoughts, and the very sum of them all which he calls his *self*, are but ephemeral bubbles in a whirlpool made of an infinite quantity of bubbles which congregate for a moment, separate, burst, and form again, following a giddy rhythm.

The second exercise is intended to stop the roaming of the mind in order that one may concentrate it on one single object.

Training which tends to develop a perfect concentration of mind is generally deemed necessary for all students without distinction. As to observing the mind's activity it is only recommended to the most intellectual disciples.

Training the mind to " one-pointedness " is practised in all Buddhist sects.

In Southern Buddhist countries—Ceylon, Siam, Burma—an apparatus called *kasinas*, which consists of clay discs variously coloured, or a round surface covered by water, or a fire at which one gazes through a screen in which a round hole is pierced—are used for this purpose.

Any of these circles is stared at until it is seen as clearly when the eyes are shut, as when they are open and actually looking at it.

The process does not aim at producing an hypnotic state, as some Western scholars have said, but it accustoms one to concentrating the mind. The fact that the subjective image has become as vivid as the objective, indicates—according to those who patronize that method —that " one-pointedness " has been reached.

Tibetans consider the object chosen to train oneself to be of no importance. Whatever attracts and retains most easily the thoughts of the disciple should be preferred.

There is a story well known in the Tibetan religious world which illustrates a successful result of this practice.

A young man begs the spiritual guidance of a mystic anchorite. The latter wishes him to begin by exercising himself in the concentration of mind.

" What kind of work do you usually do ? " he inquires of his new disciple.

" I keep the yaks [1] on the hills," answers the man.

" All right," says the gomchen. " Meditate on a yak."

The novice repairs to a cave roughly fitted up to serve as a habitation—a few such shelters can always be found in the regions inhabited by herdsmen—and settles down there.

After some time, the master goes to the place and calls to his pupil to come out of the cave.

The latter hears the gomchen's voice, gets up and wants to walk out through the entrance of his primitive dwelling. But his meditation has achieved its purpose. He has identified himself with the object on which all his thoughts have been concentrated, he has forgotten

[1] Yak, spelt gyag. The Tibetan wild hairy ox that has been domesticated.

his own personality, he feels himself a yak. Now, though the opening is large enough to allow the passage of a man, it is too narrow for a big bull, so, while struggling against an imaginary obstacle, the young man answers his *guru* : " I cannot get out, my *horns* prevent me."

Though deeply respectful of everything connected with religion, Tibetans always retain a keen sense of humour They do not fail to notice the comic effect that such practices produce when performed by simpleminded novices.

The following story was told me in the course of a tramp with a *naljorpa* from Gartog.

After having spent some time with his *guru* to receive his instruction, a zealous disciple was returning to his hermitage. While walking, he began to meditate and, according to a well-known reverential custom, he imagined his worshipful teacher was seated on his head. After a time, he entered a state of trance in which he felt perfectly sure that he was carrying his lama.

A stone or some other obstacle caused the man to fall, but so strong was his concentration of thought that the shock did not break it. He got up loudly apologizing :

" I beg your pardon, ' Precious One.' I am so sorry to have let you fall, I hope you have not hurt yourself. . . . Where are you, now ? . . ."

And the good disciple hurried away to examine a ravine near by in case his lama had rolled into it.

Another story about " the lama on the head " was told me by a Dugpa [1] lama. The joke is coarser than the former one and reflects the mind of the sturdy massive Dugpa hillmen.

A nun, it is said, was advised by her spiritual teacher to imagine him seated on her head when meditating.

[1] A native of Bhutan.

She did so accordingly and was so successful that the weight of the venerable lama who was a well-fed, tall and stout man, gave her great pain. Women of all countries, we must believe, are peculiarly clever at finding a way out of their troubles.

When paying another visit to her *guru* he asked if she had carried out his instruction and imagined that he was seated on her head.

" I did, 'Precious One,'" answered the nun, " and indeed, your weight became so painful, that I changed places with you and sat on your head myself."

One variety of exercises in concentration consists in choosing some kind of a landscape, a garden for instance, as a subject of meditation.

First, the student examines the garden, observing every detail. The flowers, their different species, the way in which they are grouped, the trees, their respective height, the shape of their branches, their different leaves and so on, noting all particulars that he can detect.

When he has formed a subjective image of the garden, that is to say when he sees it as distinctly when shutting his eyes as when looking at it, the disciple begins to eliminate one by one the various details which together constitute the garden.

Gradually, the flowers lose their colours and their forms, they crumble into tiny pieces which fall to dust and finally vanish. The trees, also, lose their leaves, their branches shorten, and seem to be withdrawn into the trunk. The latter grows thin, becomes a mere line, more and more flimsy till it ceases to be visible.

Now, the bare ground alone remains and from it the novice must subtract the stones and the earth. The ground in its turn vanishes. . . .

It is said that by the means of such exercises one succeeds in expelling from the mind all idea of form and matter and thus gradually reaches the various states of consciousness such as that of the "pure, boundless space," and that of the "boundless consciousness." Finally one attains to the "sphere of void," and then to the sphere where "neither consciousness nor unconsciousness" is present.[1]

These four contemplative meditations are often mentioned in early Buddhist Scriptures and are recognized by all sects as part of the spiritual training. They are called "formless contemplations."

Many methods have been devised which lead to these peculiar states of mind. Sometimes the later states are produced by a contemplation absolutely devoid of cogitations, while in other cases they follow a series of minute introspections or are the result of prolonged investigations and reflections regarding the external world. Lastly, it is said that there are people who suddenly reach one or another of these four states of mind without any preparation, in any place or during any kind of occupation.

The following exercise has already been briefly described in the story of the man who felt himself to be a yak. However, it includes developments that were unknown to the hero of that story.

For instance, the disciple has chosen a tree, as an object of meditation, and has identified himself with it. That is to say that he has lost the consciousness of his own personality and experiences the peculiar sensations that one may ascribe to a tree. He feels himself to be composed of a stiff trunk with branches, he perceives the sensation of the wind moving the leaves. He notes the activity of the roots feeding under the ground, the ascension of the sap which spreads all over the tree, and so on.

Then, having mentally become a tree (which has

[1] That is to say that it is an indescribable state to which the ordinary notions of consciousness and unconsciousness cannot be applied.

now become the subject) he must look at the man (who has now become the object) seated in front of him and must examine this man in detail.

This done, the disciple again places his consciousness in the man and contemplates the tree as before. Then, transferring his consciousness once more into the tree, he contemplates the man. This alternative trans-position of subject and object is effected a number of times.

This exercise is often practised indoors with a statue of a stick called *gom shing* (meditation wood).[1] A burning incense stick is also used in an obscure or completely darkened room to dispose the mind to meditation. But I must again lay stress upon the fact that it is not intended to produce an hynotic state.

Preparation for meditation is called *niampar jagpa*. It consists in bringing the mind into perfect stillness and the contemplation of the tiny dot of fire at the top of the stick helps in producing that state of calm.

People who habitually practise methodical contem-plation often experience, when sitting down for their appointed time of meditation, the sensation of putting down a load or taking off a heavy garment and entering a silent, delightfully calm, region. It is the impression of deliverance and serenity which Tibetan mystics call *niampar jagpa*, " to make equal," " to level " —meaning calming down all causes of agitation that roll their " waves " through the mind.

Another exercise which, however, seems to be seldom practised, consists in " displacing one's consciousness in one's own body." It is explained as follows.

We feel our consciousness in our " heart." Our arms seem to us to be " annexes " to our body, and our feet seem to be a distant part of our person. In fact,

---

[1] Properly speaking, the *gom shing* is merely a stick at which one gazes to obtain fixity of mind. The burning incense stick is a variety of *gom shing*.

arms, feet and other parts of the body are looked at as if they were *objects* for a *subject* dwelling elsewhere.

Now the student will endeavour to make the " consciousness " leave its habitual abode and transfer it, for instance, to his hand, then he must feel himself to have the shape of five fingers and a palm, situated at the extremity of a long attachment (the arm) which joins on to a big moving structure, the body.

That is to say, he must experience the sensation that we might have if, instead of having the eyes and the brain in the head, we had them in the hand and then the hand was able to examine the head and the body, reversing the normal process which is to look downwards in order to see the hands or the body.

What can be the aim of such strange exercises ? The most frequent answer given to my questions will probably seem unsatisfactory by many inquirers, yet it is probably quite correct.

Some lamas have told me that the aim of these practices can hardly be explained, because those who have not felt their effects could not understand the explanations.

One attains, by the means of these strange drills, psychic states entirely different from those habitual to us. They cause us to pass beyond the fictitious limits which we assign to the *self*. The result being that we grow to realize that the *self* is compound, impermanent ; and that the self, *as self*, does not exist.

One of these lamas seized upon a remark I had made as an argument in support of his theory.

When he spoke of the heart as the seat of thought and mind, I had said that Westerners would rather place thoughts and mind in the brain.

" You see," immediately replied my interlocutor, " that one may feel and recognize the mind in different places. Since these Philings [1] experience the sensation

[1] Foreigners.

of thinking in their *head*, and I experience it in my *heart*, one may believe that it is quite possible to feel it in the *foot*. But all these are only deceitful sensations, with no shadow of reality. The mind is neither *in the heart* nor *in the head*, nor somewhere outside of the body, apart, separated, alien to it. It is to help one realize this fact that these apparently strange practices have been devised."

Here again we meet with the " clearing " process. All these exercises aim at destroying habitual notions accepted by routine and without personal investigation. The object is to make one understand that other ideas can be put in their place. It is hoped that the disciple will conclude that there cannot be any absolute truth in ideas derived from sensations which can be discarded while others, even contradictory to them, take their place.

Kindred theories are professed by the followers of the Chinese Ts'an sect.[1] They express them in enigmatical sentences such as :

" Lo, a cloud of dust is rising from the ocean and the roaring of the waves is heard over the land."

" I walk on foot, and yet on the back of an ox I am riding."

" When I pass over the bridge, Lo ! the water floweth not, but the bridge floweth.

" Empty handed I go, and behold ! the spade's handle is in my hand."

And so on.

The doctrine of the Ts'an sect has been defined by one of its followers as " the art of perceiving the polar star in the Austral hemisphere." This paradoxical saying resembles that of the lama who said to me : " One must discover the white in the black and the black in the white."

I shall cite a question, current in Tibet, which mystic

[1] Called Zen sect, in Japan.

hermits, as well as philosophers living in monasteries, put to their pupils.

" A flag moves, What is that which moves ?—Is it the flag or the wind ? "

The answer is that neither the flag nor the wind moves. It is the mind that moves.

The followers of the Ts'an sect ascribe the origin of this question to the sixth Patriarch of their sect. Once, in the courtyard of the monastery, he saw two monks looking at a flag floating in the air. One of them declared : " It is the flag that moves." The other affirmed : " It is the wind that moves." Then the master explained to them that the perception of a motion which they experienced was not really due to the wind or to the flag, but to something existing in themselves.

We are in doubt as to whether such ways of thinking have been imported into Tibet from India or from China. I may, however, state the opinion expressed by a lama : " The *Bön pos*," he said, " taught such things long before Padmasambhava came to Tibet."[1]

Abandoning further investigations on the transcendental results of transferring one's mind to different parts of one's body, I may remark that during this exercise, a peculiar sensation of heat is felt at the spot where one has " transported his consciousness."

It is rather difficult to ascertain whether the phenomena consists in a real increase in heat or a subjective sensation only. The very idea of undertaking such investigation would break the concentration of mind and so destroy the cause that produced heat. As to making observation upon other people, it is almost impossible. Tibetan hermits and their disciples have nothing in common with Western professional mediums who work for money and allow us to examine the phenomena which they produce. The most insignifi-

[1] This means before Buddhism spread into Tibet.

cant pupil of a *gomchen* would feel astonished if such a proposal was made to him. I can hear him answer : " I do not care whether you believe or not in these phenomena, and I have no desire to convince you. I am not a juggler giving theatrical performances."

The fact is that Orientals, excepting vulgar charlatans, do not make a show of their mystic, philosophic or psychic knowledge. It is most difficult to win their confidence in these matters. A traveller in search of information may be the guest of a lama for several months, drink tea daily with him and go away thinking his host is an ignoramus, while on the contrary, the lama could have answered all his questions and told him more things than he has even thought of.

Whether the heat be actual or subjective the exercise has more than once warmed my feet, and given me a refreshing sleep while spending the night under a tent— or even without any tent—outdoors in the snow. But unless one has been trained for a long time in the practice, it requires strenuous efforts which make it extremely tiring.

To conclude, I will call attention to the fact that the terms which I have translated by " consciousness " and " mind " have not exactly the same signification in Tibetan as in English.

Tibetans distinguish as many as eleven kinds of " consciousness " and have three words in their language which we are compelled to translate by " mind," though each of them bears a special philosophic meaning.

A frequent way of ascertaining the degree of the concentration of mind is to place a small burning lamp on the head of the novice who is to remain in solitary meditation.

Tibetan lamps consist of a cup-like receptacle. made of metal or mud ; the base of the lamp enlarges at the bottom, which is shaped like a second cup turned upside down. These lamps are filled with melted butter ; a wick is thrust into a small cavity bored for that purpose at the bottom of the cup. When the butter cools it forms a cake and the lamp is ready to be lighted.

This apparatus easily rests on the crown of the head as long as one preserves absolute immobility, but it falls off at the slightest movement. Now as perfect concentration produces complete immobility, any failure is proved by the fall of the lamp.

It is said that a lama who had once placed a lamp on the head of a pupil found him the next day still seated in meditation, but with the lamp beside him on the ground without any butter in it. Answering his master's question, the novice who had not understood the aim of the exercise replied :

" The lamp did not fall down, I myself took it away when the butter was exhausted and it went out."— " How could you know that the lamp went out, or even that you had a lamp on your head, if you had reached true concentration of mind ? " retorted the teacher.

Sometimes a small bowl filled with water is used instead of a lamp.

Certain masters also command their disciples, either before the time of their meditation or immediately after it, to carry from one spot to another a bowl with water up to the brim. This exercise aims at testing the degree of tranquillity of the mind. The slightest agitation of the mind, whatever may be its cause—joy or sadness, memory, desire, etc.—is likely to produce a movement of the body. Now, the least quivering of the fingers is sufficient to shake the bowl and the quantity of water poured out, as well as the number of times the accident happens, discloses the more or less violent movement of the mind. Such at least is the theory on which the exercise is based.

This theory and the exercises which have been devised from it, are known all over the East. Indians tell pretty stories about them. Here is one.

A *rishi* [1] had a disciple whom he believed already far advanced in spiritual development. Wishing that he might receive supplementary teaching from Janaka, the kingly Sage of great repute, he sent the young man to him. At first Janaka left the new-comer for several days outside his palace gate without allowing him even to enter the courtyard. Nevertheless, the well-trained disciple, though he was of noble descent, did not show the least sign of being grieved, offended, or displeased by this humiliating treatment.

When he was finally admitted to the presence of the king, he was given at the door of the throne hall a bowl filled with water up to the brim and ordered to walk with it in his hand all round the hall.

Janaka, though his mind was utterly indifferent to all worldly things, was surrounded by true Oriental splendour. Gold and precious stones glittered on the walls of the great hall, the courtiers wearing costly jewels surrounded their sovereign, and the palace dancing girls, as beautiful as goddesses and scantily clad, smiled at the young stranger when he passed before them.

Nevertheless the disciple went through the prescribed ordeal without spilling a drop of water. Nothing offered to his eyes had been capable of producing the slightest movement in his mind.

Janaka sent him back to his *guru* saying that he did not need any lessons.

Tibetans are acquainted with the theory regarding the *khorlos* (wheels) which is classic among the followers of Hindu Tantrism. Most likely it has been imported into Tibet from India or Nepal, but the interpretation given by the lamas differs on a number of points from that which is current in Hindu circles.

[1] A Sage often possessed with supernormal powers.

The *khorlos* are said to be centres of energy that are situated in various parts of the body. They are often called "lotus." The practices connected with the *khorlos* belong to the esoteric teaching. The general aim of the training in which the *khorlos* play a part is to direct a stream of energy to the higher lotus : the *dabtong* (lotus with a thousand petals) which is situated at the top of the head. The different kinds of exercises in this training aim at utilizing the energy naturally expressed in animal manifestations connected with sex, for the development of intelligence and supernormal powers.

The lamas belonging to the Dzogschen sect are practically the only masters of this teaching.

Again, certain disciples are advised to contemplate the sky and sometimes to confine themselves to this practice only. Some lie flat on their back in the open, in order to look at the sky with no other object in sight. This contemplation, and the ideas which it excites, is said to lead to a peculiar trance in which the notion of personality is forgotten, and an undescribable union with the universe is experienced.

All lamas agree regarding the usefulness of most of these strangely artful training practices. Yet, when reading certain treatises about them or listening to oral explanations given by some mystic masters, one not unfrequently detects a restrained impatience. The teacher who instructs us seems to say : Yes, all that is necessary, perhaps, even indispensable to the majority of novices, but as a preparatory drill only, the goal is elsewhere. Let us make haste and finish with the preliminary process.

The following sober method keeps closer to this goal ; at any rate its working is more easily understood.

The master orders his disciple to shut himself in *tsams* and to meditate—taking his *Yidam* (tutelary deity) as object of his contemplation.

The novice dwelling in strict seclusion, concentrates his thoughts on the *Yidam*, imagining him in the shape and form ascribed to him in books and images. Repeating certain mystic formulas and constructing a *kyilkhor* are parts of the exercise of which the aim is to cause the *Yidam* to appear to his worshipper. At least, such is the aim that the master points out to the beginner.

The pupil breaks his contemplation during the time strictly necessary to eat [1] and the very short time allowed for sleep. Often the recluse does not lie down and only dozes in one of those *gomti* which have been described in a previous chapter.[2]

Months and even years may elapse in that way. Occasionally the master inquires about the progress of his pupil. At last a day comes when the novice informs him that he has reaped the fruit of his exertion : the *Yidam* has appeared. As a rule, the vision has been nebulous and lasted only a little while. The master declares that it is an encouraging success, but not as yet a definitive result. It is desirable that the recluse should longer enjoy the hallowed company of his protector.

The apprentice *naljorpa* cannot but agree, and continues his effort. A long time again elapses. Then, the *Yidam* is "fixed"—if I may use that term. He dwells in the *tsams khang* and the recluse sees him as always present in the middle of the *kyilkhor*.

"This is most excellent," answers the master when he is informed of the fact; "but you must seek a still greater favour. You must pursue your meditation until you are able to touch with your head the feet of the *Yidam*, until he blesses you and speaks to you."

Though the previous stages have taken long to be

---

[1] Generally the recluse has only one meal a day, but drinks buttered tea several times. However, during such periods of retreat some ascetics subsist on water and roast barley flour only.

[2] See the end of Chapter II.

effected they may be considered the easiest part of the process. The following are much more arduous to attain, and only a small minority of novices meet with success.

These successful disciples see the *Yidam* taking on life. They distinctly feel the touch of his feet when, prostrated, they lay their head on them. They feel the weight of his hands when he blesses them. They see his eyes moving, his lips parting, he speaks. . . . And lo ! he steps out of the *kyilkhor* and walks in the *tsams khang*.

It is a perilous moment. When wrathful demi-gods or demons have been called up in that way, they must never be allowed to escape from the *kyilkhor*, whose magic walls hold them prisoners. Set free out of due time, they would revenge themselves on the person who has compelled them to enter this prison-like consecrated circle. However, the *Yidam*, though his appearance may be dreadful and his power is to be feared, is not dangerous because the recluse has won his favour. Consequently, he may move about as he pleases in the hermitage. Even better, he may cross its threshold and stand in the open. Following his teacher's advice, the novice must find out if the deity is willing to accompany him when he walks out.

This task is harder than all previous ones. Visible and tangible in the obscure hermitage fragrant with incense, where the psychic influences born from a prolonged concentration of thought are working ; will the *Yidam's* form be able to subsist in quite different surroundings under the bright sunlight, exposed to influences which, instead of supporting it, will act as dissolving agents ?

A new elimination takes place amongst the disciples. Most *Yidam* refuse to follow their devotee into the open. They remain obstinately in some dark corner and sometimes grow angry and avenge themselves for the disrespectful experiments to which they have been submitted. Strange accidents occur to some anchorites, but others succeed in their undertaking and wherever they go enjoy the presence of their worshipful protector.

"You have reached the desired goal," says the *guru* to his exultant disciple. "I have nothing more to teach you. You have won the favours of a protector mightier than I."

Certain disciples thank the lama and, proud of their achievement, return to their monastery or establish themselves in a hermitage and spend the remainder of their life playing with their phantom.

On the contrary, others trembling in mental agony prostrate themselves at their *guru's* feet and confess some awful sin. . . . Doubts have arisen in their mind which, in spite of strenuous efforts, they have not been able to overcome. Before the *Yidam* himself, even when he spoke to them or when they touched him, the thought has arisen in them that they contemplated a mere phantasmagoria which they had themselves created.

The master appears afflicted by this confession. The unbeliever must return to his *tsams khang* and begin training all over again in order to conquer his incredulity, so ungrateful to the *Yidam* who has favoured him.

Once undermined, faith seldom regains a firm footing. If the great respect which Orientals feel for their religious teacher did not restrain them, these incredulous disciples would probably yield to the temptation of giving up the religious life, their long training having ended in materialism. But nearly all of them hold on to it, for if they doubt the reality of their *Yidam*, they never doubt their master's wisdom.

After a time the disciple repeats the same confession. It is even more positive than the first time. There is no longer any question of *doubt* ; he is thoroughly *convinced* that the *Yidam* is produced by his mind and has no other existence than that which he has lent him.

"That is exactly what it is necessary for you to realize," the master tells him. "Gods, demons, the whole universe, are but a mirage which exists in the mind, 'springs from it, and sinks into it.'"[1]

[1] A declaration continually repeated by Tibetan mystics.

CHAPTER VIII

PSYCHIC PHENOMENA IN TIBET—HOW TIBETANS
EXPLAIN THEM

IN the preceding chapter I have aready mentioned some incidents that may be classified as psychic phenomena. It may be useful to take up the subject again, for the fame which Tibet enjoys in foreign countries is largely due to the belief that prodigies happen there as plentifully as wild flowers grow in the fields.

Whatever certain people may think about the matter, strange events are far from being usual in Tibet, and it is good to bear in mind that the observations which I have condensed into a few pages are the result of researches which lasted more than ten years.

The fascination exercised by Tibet as an abode of sages and magicians dates from a time long back. Even before the Buddha, Indians turned with devout awe to the Himalayas, and many were the extraordinary stories about the mysterious, cloud-enshrouded northern country extending beyond their mighty snowy peaks.

The Chinese also seem to have been impressed by the strangeness of Tibetan wilds. Amongst others, the legend of her great mystic philosopher Laotze relates that, at the end of his long career, the master riding an ox started for the mysterious land, crossed its border, and never returned. The same thing is sometimes told about Boddhidharma and some of his Chinese disciples, followers of the Buddhist sect of meditation (Ts'an sect).

Even nowadays one may often meet Indian pilgrims on the paths that climb towards the passes through which one enters Tibet, dragging themselves along as in a dream ; hypnotized, it seems, by an overpowering vision. When asked the motive of their journey most of them can only answer that they wish to die on Tibetan ground. And too often the cold climate, the high altitude, fatigue and starvation help them to realize their wish.

How can we explain this magnetic power in Tibet ?

There is no doubt that the reputation enjoyed by the " Land of Snow " for being a country of wizards and magicians, a ground on which miracles daily occur, is the main cause of its attraction over the majority of its worshippers. But now one may ask for what reason Tibet has been credited with being the chosen land of occult lore and supernormal phenomena.

Perhaps the most obvious cause is that already mentioned, the extreme remoteness of the country, enclosed between formidable mountain ranges and immense deserts.

Men compelled to abandon cherished ideals incompatible with their stern, prosaic surroundings, are eager to transplant them to a more favourable fairyland. As a last resource they build gardens in the heaven and superterrestrial paradises to shelter their day dreams, but how much more readily will they seize upon the opportunity of lodging them in an earthly country. Tibet offers that opportunity. It has all the physical features of a true wonderland. I do not think it is exaggerated to say that its landscapes surpass, in all respects, those imagined by the fanciful architects of gods' and demons' worlds.

No description can convey the least idea of the solemn majesty, the serene beauty, the awe-inspiring wildness, the entrancing charm of the finest Tibetan scenes.

Often, when tramping across these solitary heights, one feels like an intruder. Unconsciously one slackens pace, lowers one's voice, and words of apology for one's unwarranted boldness come to the lips, ready to be uttered at the first sight of a legitimate superhuman master on whose ground one has trespassed.

Common Tibetan villagers and herdsmen, though born amidst such surroundings, are strongly influenced by them. Translated by their primitive mind, their impressions take the form of these fantastic demigods and spirits of a hundred kinds with whom they have densely populated the solitudes of Tibet, and whose whimsical demeanour is the inexhaustible theme of a rich folk-lore.

On the other hand, just as the Chaldean shepherds of yore observing the starry sky, on the shore of Euphrates, laid the foundation of astronomy, so Tibetan anchorites and itinerant *shamans* have long pondered over the mysteries of their bewitching country and noted the phenomena which there found a favourable ground. A strange art had its origin in their contemplations and, many centuries ago, the magicians from the northern Transhimalayan land were already known and held in high repute in India.

Now, in spite of its remoteness, Tibet is not altogether inaccessible. This, I can well testify. I have several times reached its southern tableland through different Himalayan passes, travelled for years in its eastern provinces and the northern Changthang,[1] and, during my last journey, I crossed the whole country from its south-eastern border to Lhasa. Any robust man or woman who does not fear hardships, might do the same but for the policy which closes Tibet.

It is certain that, especially since the introduction of Buddhism, numbers of Indians, Nepalese, Chinese and other travellers have visited Tibet, seen its bewildering sites and heard about the supernormal powers with

---

[1] *Chang*, " north " ; *thang*, a large track of more or less level ground. The Changthang is the vast grassy desert which extends between Tibet and the Chinese Turkestan.

which its *dubtobs* are credited. Amongst them, a few have probably approached the lamas or Bönpos magicians and listened to the mystic doctrines of contemplative hermits. Their travellers' tales, which inevitably grew and amplified as they were circulated, must have greatly contributed, together with the causes I have mentioned and other less apparent ones, to create around Tibet the glamorous atmosphere it now enjoys.

Must we conclude that the renown of Tibet as the land in which prodigies flourish, is entirely based on delusion? This would be as great an error as the uncritical acceptance of all the native tales, or of those lately conceived by the fertile brains of some facetious Westerners.

The best way is to be guided by the rather surprising opinion of the Tibetans themselves regarding miraculous events. None in Tibet deny that such events may take place, but no one regards them as miracles, according to the meaning of that term in the West, that is to say as *supernatural* events.

Indeed, Tibetans do not recognize any supernatural agent. The so-called wonders, they think, are as natural as common daily events and depend on the clever handling of little-known laws and forces.

All facts which, in other countries, are considered miraculous or, in any other way, ascribed to the arbitrary interference of beings belonging to other worlds, are considered by Tibetan adepts of the secret lore [1] as psychic phenomena.

In a general way, Tibetans distinguish two categories of psychic phenomena.

1. The phenomena which are *unconsciously* produced either by one or by several individuals.

---

[1] May it be said, once more, that " secret lore " is not to be understood as an esoteric Buddhist doctrine, but as traditional erudition and methods of realizing aims that are not necessarily spiritual.

In that case, the author—or authors—of the phenomenon acting unconsciously, it is obvious that he does
not aim at a fixed result.

2. The phenomena produced *consciously*, with a view
of bringing about a prescribed result. These are
generally—but not always—the work of a single person.

That " person" may be a man or may belong to
any one of the six classes of sentient beings which
lamaists acknowledge as existing in our world.[1] Whoso-
ever be its author, the phenomenon is produced by the
same process, in accordance with some natural laws :
there is no *miracle*.

It may be of interest to remark here that Tibetans
are staunch determinists. Each volition, they believe,
is brought about by a number of causes, of which some
are near and others extremely remote.

I shall not lay stress on that point which is outside
the present subject. However, the reader must bear in
mind that, according to Tibetans, each phenomenon,
consciously or unconsciously generated, as well as each
of our bodily or mental actions, is the fruit of manifold
combined causes.

Amongst these causes, the first and more easily dis-
cernible ones are those which have arisen, in the mind
of the doer of the action, the conscious will of doing it.
To these causes Tibetans assimilate those which, even
unknown to the doer, have put into motion some forces
which have led him to perform the action. Both kinds
are styled *gyu*, " immediate or principal cause " Then,
come the outside causes, not originating with the doer,
which may have helped the accomplishment of the
action. These are called *kyen*.[2]

---

[1] See page 260.
[2] As an instance, the seed is the *rgyu* of the plant. The soil and
the various substances which exist in it, the water, air, sun, the
gardener who has sown the seed, etc., etc., are *rkyen* (pronounced
gyu and *kyen*).

The remote causes are often represented by their
" descendants." [1] These " descendants " are the present conditions which exist as the effects of bodily or
mental actions which have been done in the past, but
not, necessarily, done by the doer of the present act
himself.

So, when concentration of thoughts is mentioned
here below as the direct cause of a phenomenon, one
must remember : first that, according to Tibetan mystics,
this concentration is iot spontaneous, but determined ;
and secondly, that beside this direct apparent cause,
there exist, in the background, a number of secondary
causes which are equally necessary to bring about the
phenomenon.

The secret of the psychic training, as Tibetans conceive
it, consists in developing a power of concentration of
mind greatly surpassing even that of men who are, by
nature, the most gifted in this respect.

Mystic masters affirm that by the means of such
concentration of mind, waves of energy are produced
which can be used in different ways. The term " wave "
is mine. I use it for clearness sake and also because,
as the reader will see, Tibetan mystics really *mean* some
" currents " or " waves " of force. However, they
merely say *shugs* or *tsal* ; [2] that is to say, " energy."
That energy, they believe, is produced every time that
a physical or mental action takes place.—Action of the
mind, of the speech and of the body, according to the
Buddhist classification.—The production of psychic
phenomena depends upon the strength of that energy
and the direction in which it is pointed.

1. An object can be *charged* by these waves. It then
becomes something resembling our electric accumulators

---

[1] ln Tibetan *rigs*. As an instance : the milk is present in the
butter or cheese ; the seed is present in the tree born from it.
Tibetans freely use these illustrations

[2] Written *rtsal*.

and may give back, in one way or another, the energy stored in it. For instance, it will increase the vitality of one who touches it, infuse him with courage, etc.

Practices grounded on this theory and aiming at beneficial results are current in Tibet. Numbers of lamas prepare pills, holy water, knotted scarves, charms printed on paper or cloth, which are supposed to impart strength and health, or to keep away accidents, evil spirits, robbers, bullets and so on.

The lama must first purify himself by a proper diet and then concentrate his thoughts on the object which he means to empower, in order to load it with wholesome influences. Several weeks or months are sometimes deemed necessary for that preparation. However, when it is only a question of charmed scarves, these are often knotted and consecrated in a few minutes.

2. The energy which is communicated to an object, pours into it a kind of life. That inanimate object becomes able to move and can perform certain actions at the command of its maker.

The *ngagspas* are said to resort to these practices, to hurt or kill without arousing any suspicion that they are responsible for the casualty.

Here is an instance of the way in which the sorcerer proceeds.

Taking with him the object which is to be animated— let us say a knife destined to kill someone—the *ngagspa* shuts himself in seclusion for a period that may last over several months. During that time he sits, concentrating his thoughts on the knife in front of him and endeavouring to transfer to the inanimated object, his will to kill the particular individual whose death has been planned.

Various rites are often performed in connection with the *ngagspa's* concentration of mind. These aim at adding to the energy which the latter is capable of generating and transfusing into the knife. Beings deemed more powerful than the sorcerer are either besought to co-operate willingly with him or coerced and compelled to let their energy flow into the weapon.

These " beings " are often of a demoniacal kind, but in the case when the murder is deemed a righteous action,[1] useful to the welfare of many, lofty benevolent entities may be called in as helpers. These are always respectfully implored and no one attempts to coerce them. Some *ngagspas* think it useful to bring the weapon into touch with the man whom it is meant to kill or with objects habitually used by him.

Other adepts of the black art scoff at such a childish practice and declare that it discloses utter ignorance regarding the causes which may bring about the killing or hurting that is to appear accidental.

When the sorcerer supposes that the knife is ready to perform its work, it is placed near the man who is to become its victim so that, almost always, he may be led to use it. Then, as soon as he seizes it, the knife moves, gives a sudden impulse to the hand which holds it, and the man against whom it has been prepared stabs himself.

It is said that when once the weapon has been animated in that way, it becomes dangerous for the *ngagspa* who, if he lacks the knowledge and cleverness required to guard himself, may fall its victim.

Auto-suggestion is likely to result from the protracted meditation and the elaborate rites performed by the sorcerer while dwelling in seclusion, and it would not be surprising if some accident occurred to him. Nevertheless, apart from the stories of demons and spirits there may be a phenomenon similar to that which is

---

[1] As were the murders of harmful beings by King Gesar of Ling or the murder of the King Langdharma, who meant to re-establish the pre-buddhistic shamanism in Tibet. Lamaists differ on that point from orthodox Buddhism which expressly forbids killing.

said to occur when the phantom created by a magician breaks away from its maker's control.

Certain lamas and a few Bönpos have told me that it is a mistake to believe, in such cases as I have just mentioned, that the knife becomes animated and kills the man. It is the man, they said, who acts on auto-suggestion as a result of the sorcerer's concentration of thought.

Though the *ngagspa* only aims at animating the knife, the man against whom the rites are performed is closely associated in his mind with the idea of the weapon. And so, as that man may be a fit receiver of the occult " waves " generated by the sorcerer—(while the knife is not) he falls unconsciously under their influence. Then, when touching the prepared knife, the view and touch of the latter put into motion the suggestion existing, unknown to him, in the man's mind, and he stabs himself.

Moreover, it is strongly believed that without any material object for transmission, proficient adepts of the secret lore can suggest, even from afar, to men or other beings, the idea of killing themselves in one way or another.

All agree in saying that any such attempt cannot be successful against an adept in psychic training because such a one detects the " waves " of forces pointed at him and is able to discriminate their nature and thrust back those which he deems harmful.

3. Without the help of any material object, the energy generated by the concentration of thoughts can be carried to more or less distant points. There this energy may manifest itself in various manners. For instance :

It can bring about psychic phenomena.

It can penetrate the goal ascribed to it and thus transfer the power generated elsewhere.

Mystic masters are said to use this process during the *angkur* rites.

Much could be said about these rites and the spirit which pervades them. The limited space allowed in an average size volume forbids an exhaustive account of all theories and practices of mystic Lamaism and I have reluctantly had to omit for the present a number of interesting subjects. I shall confine myself to a few words.

Lamaist *angkur*, literally " empowerment," is not an " initiation," though, for lack of other words, I have sometimes used that term in the course of the present book. The various *angkurs* are not meant to reveal esoteric doctrines, as initiations were, among the Greeks and other peoples. They have a decidedly psychic character. The theory about them is that " energy " may be transmitted from the master—or from some more occult store of forces—to the disciple who is able to " tap " the psychic waves in transmission.

According to lamaist mystics, during the performance of the *angkur* rite a force is placed within the disciple's reach. The seizing and assimilating of that force is left to his ability.

In the course of talks I had on this subject with mystic initiates, they have defined *angkur* as " a special opportunity " offered to a disciple of " empowering himself."

By the same method, mystic masters are said to be able to dispatch waves of energy which, in case of need, cheer, refresh and invigorate, physically and mentally, their distant disciples.

The process is not always meant to enrich the goal to which the waves are directed. On the contrary, sometimes when reaching that goal, these waves absorb a portion of its energy. Then, returning with this subtly stolen spoil, they pour it into the " post " from which they have been sent forth, and in which they are reabsorbed.

Some magicians, it is said, gain great strength or

prolong their lives by incorporating this stolen energy.

4. Tibetan mystics also affirm that adepts well trained in concentration are capable of visualizing the forms imagined by them and can thus create any kind of phantom : men, deities, animals, inanimate objects, landscapes, and so forth.

The reader must recall what has been said on this subject in reference to the *tulkus* [1] and the innumerable phantoms which, according to the Dalai Lama, a *Changchub semspa* [2] has the power to generate.

These phantoms do not always appear as impalpable mirages, they are tangible and endowed with all the faculties and qualities naturally pertaining to the beings or things of which they have the appearance.

For instance, a phantom horse trots and neighs. The phantom rider who rides it can get off his beast, speak with a traveller on the road and behave in every way like a real person. A phantom house will shelter real travellers, and so on.

Such happenings abound in Tibetan stories and especially in the famous epic of King Gesar of Ling. The great hero multiplies himself. He produces phantom caravans with tents, hundreds of horses, lamas, merchants, servants and each of them plays his part. In battles he creates phantom armies which kill their enemies just as well as if they were authentic warriors.

All this appears to belong to the realm of fairy tales and one may wisely assume that ninety-nine out of a hundred of these stories are purely mythical. Yet disconcerting incidents occur, phenomena are witnessed which it is impossible to deny. Explanations of them are to be found by the observer himself, if he refuses

[1] See Chapter III.
[2] In Sanskrit a Bodhisatva. A highly spiritually developed being nearing the perfection of a Buddha.

to accept those offered by Tibetans. But often these Tibetan explanations, on account of their vaguely scientific form, attract the inquirer and become themselves a field of investigation.

Western travellers who have approached the Tibetan border and formed a superficial idea of the common folk's superstitions will be most surprised to hear of the strangely rationalistic and sceptical opinion of prodigies which these apparently credulous simpletons harbour in the depth of their minds.

Two stories, which are known and famous all over Tibet, will serve to illustrate the matter. Whether the facts related be authentic or not is of no importance to us. Our interest hangs on the explanation given of the cause of the miracle and the spirit which pervades the whole story.

Once upon a time, a trader was travelling with his caravan on a stormy day, and his hat was carried away by the wind.

Tibetans believe that to pick up a hat which has fallen down in such circumstances in the course of a journey will bring bad luck. So yielding to that superstition, the merchant abandoned his hat.

It was a soft felt hat, with fur laps that can be worn turned up or covering the ears, as the weather requires. Buried between the thorny shrubs where it had been violently tossed by the wind, its shape was hardly recognizable.

A few weeks later a man passing by that place at dusk noticed an undistinguishable form which seemed to be crouched among the thickets. He was not too brave and hurriedly passed his way. On the morrow he told some villagers that he had seen " something strange " at a short distance from the path. Other travellers also remarked at that very spot, a peculiar object whose nature they could not ascertain, and spoke of it to the villagers. Then, others again and again had a look at the innocent hat and called the attention of the country people to it.

Now sun, rain and dust helped to make the hat a still more mysterious-looking object. The felt had taken on a dirty yellowish-brown colour and the fur laps looked vaguely like an animal's ears.

Traders and pilgrims stopping in the village were warned that, at the skirt of the forest, a "thing," neither man nor beast, remained in ambush and it was necessary to be on the watch. Someone suggested that the "thing" must be a demon and soon the object, anonymous till then, was promoted to the rank of a devil.

As months went by, more people cast a fearful glance at the old hat, more people spoke about it and the whole country came to talk of the "demon" hidden at the border of the wood.

Then one day it happened that some passers-by saw the rag moving. Another day it tried to extricate itself from the thorns that had grown around it, and finally it followed a party of wayfarers who ran, panic-stricken, for their lives.

The hat had been animated by the many thoughts concentrated on it.

That story, which Tibetans affirm to be authentic, is given as an instance of the power of concentration of mind, even when unconsciously effected, and not aiming at a prescribed result.

The second story has all the appearances of having been invented by a miscreant joker to ridicule the devotees, but it is not so. No one in Tibet finds it laughable or irreverent. The fact related is accepted as revealing a strict truth about all cults. Whatever it may be, the worshipped object is only possessed with the power, which is supplied to it by the collective concentration of thoughts and the faith of its worshippers.

The aged mother of a trader who went each year to

India, asked her son to bring her a relic from the Holy Land.[1] The trader promised to do so, but his mind being much occupied with the cares of his business, he forgot his promise.

The old woman felt very sad, and the next year, when her son's caravan started again, she renewed her request for the holy relic.

Again the trader promised to bring one, and again he forgot it. The same thing happened for the third time the following year. However, this time the merchant remembered his promise before reaching his home and was much troubled at the idea of once more disappointing his aged mother's eager expectation.

As he pondered over the matter, seeking a way to mend his neglect, he caught sight of a piece of a dog's jaw lying near the road.

A sudden inspiration came to him. He broke off a tooth of the bleached jaw-bone, wiped away the earth which covered it and wrapped it in a piece of silk. Then, having reached his house, he offered the old bone to his mother, declaring that it was a most precious relic, a tooth of the great Sariputra.[2]

Overjoyed, her heart filled with veneration, the good woman placed the tooth in a casket on the altar of the family shrine. Each day she worshipped before it, lighting lamps and burning incense. Other devotees joined in the worship and after a time rays of light shone from the dog's tooth, promoted holy relic.

A popular Tibetan saying is born from that story :

> " *Mös gus yöd na*
> *Khyi so öd tung.*" [3]

Which means " If there is veneration even a dog's tooth emits light."

[1] India, the cradle of Buddhism, is the " Holy Land " of Tibetans.

[2] A prominent personal disciple of the Buddha.

[3] Spelt *mos gus yod na, khyi so hod hphrung.*

Once more we see that Tibetan theories about all phenomena are always the same at heart. All are grounded on the power of the mind and this is only logical for people who consider the world, as we see it, to be but a subjective vision.

The power of becoming invisible at will, exhibited by numbers of magicians in the tales of all nations, is finally ascribed, by Tibetan occultists, to the cessation of mental activity.

Truly, Tibetan legends tell us about material contrivances for causing invisibility. Among them is the *dip shing* which appears in so many stories. It is the fabulous wood which a strange crow hides in its nest. The smallest fragment of it ensures complete invisibility to the man, beast or object which holds it or near which it is placed. But great *naljorpas* and *dubchens* need not possess any magic material implement to make themselves invisible.

From what I have been able to understand, adepts in psychic training do not see this prodigy in the same way as the profane. According to them, it is not a question of juggling oneself away, but of taking care not to arouse any feeling in the sentient beings by whom one is surrounded. By that means one's presence is not detected or, at a lesser degree, one is scarcely noticed by those before whose eyes one passes ; one does not excite any reflection in their mind and does not leave any impression in their memory.

The explanations which have been given to me of this matter may be roughly summarized as follows.

When one walks, making a loud noise and many gestures, jostling against men and things, one arouses many sensations in many people. Attention is roused in those who feel these sensations and that attention is directed to the one who causes them. If, on the contrary, one steals along noiselessly without touching anybody, one arouses few sensations ; these are not vivid, they awaken only slight attention in those who experience them and, consequently, one is but little noticed.

Yet, however motionless and silent one may be, the work of the mind generates an energy which spreads all around the one who produces it, and this energy is felt in various ways by those who come into touch with it. But if one succeeds in stopping *all* activity of the mind, one arouses no sensations in others and so one is not seen.

As I thought this theory too fantastic, I objected that in any case, the material body must remain visible. The reply was as follows : At each moment, a large number of objects are within our view, yet we only notice a few of them. The others do not make any impression on us. No " knowledge—consciousness " (*nampar shespa*) [1] follows the visual contact (*mig gi regpa*), we do not remember that this contact has taken place. Practically, these objects have remained *invisible* to us.

However interested we may feel in the other strange accomplishments with which Tibetan adepts of the secret lore are credited, the creation of thought forms seems by far the most puzzling.

We have already seen in the preceding chapter how the novice is trained to build up the form of his tutelary deity, but in that case the aim is a kind of philosophical enlightenment. The goal is different in other cases.

In order to avoid confusion, we will first consider another kind of phenomena which is often discussed, not only in Tibet, but in various other Eastern countries and even in the West. Some profess to see a certain analogy between these and the creation of thought-forms, but, in fact, the process is not at all the same.

In nearly all countries there are people who believe in a subtle soul or spirit which, while the body lies asleep or in a cataleptic trance, can roam about in

[1] Spelt *rnam par shespa.*

various places [1] and perform different deeds, sometimes associating for that purpose with a material body other than that with which it is habitually united.

Tales of witches going to the sabbat were common during the Dark Ages and investigations proved that, generally, the witch was lying unconscious in a trance all the time. Nevertheless, when coming to her senses again, she described at length the wonders of the infernal orgy at which she believed she had been a guest. Numbers of hysterical women have been burnt at the stake for having such delusions.

In India, countless legends relate the strange adventures of men, demi-gods, or demons who enter dead bodies, act in guise of the dead man and then revert to their own frame which had meanwhile remained unconscious.

The most famous of these stories is that of Shri Sankarâcharya, the celebrated Vedantin philosopher to whom Indian Brahmins are indebted for having re-established them in the privileged position that had been severely shaken by the rationalist Buddhist doctrine. His personality as it appears to us through half-legendary biographies must have been most remarkable. Unfortunately a sort of political caste interest seems to have dimmed his otherwise bright intelligence. It made him a champion of baneful social theories which were in complete contradiction to the lofty pantheism which he preached.

Sankarâcharya—so runs the story—had challenged a rival philosopher named Mandana, who was a supporter of the ritualistic creed of *Karma-mimansa*,[2] and it had

---

[1] About this subject see also what is said about the " *delogs* " in Chapter I : " Death and Hereafter."

[2] The doctrine that salvation can only be attained through sacrifices to the deities, worship, sacraments and ritualistic performances. Sankara held the opposite view, that is to say, salvation is the fruit of knowledge.

been settled that whoever was defeated in the discussion should become his opponent's disciple and embrace the same condition of life as his master.

Consequently—Mandana being a householder and Sankaracharya a *sannyāsin* [1]—if Mandana's arguments triumphed, Sankara would have to give up his religious garb and marry, while in the event Mandana would be compelled to renounce his wife and home and to don the orange robe—the badge of ultimate renunciation.

It happened that Mandana was losing the controversy and Sankara was about to claim him as a disciple, when Mandana's wife Bharati, who was a learned lady, interfered.

The holy Scriptures, she said, declare that wife and husband are one. So, having defeated my husband you have only defeated one-half of our being. Your victory cannot be admitted until you defeat me also.

Sankara had no reply ; the objection was grounded on orthodox beliefs. He began another philosophic tournament. The lady, understanding that her knowledge and controversial ability could not vie with those of her opponent, saved herself by a clever stratagem.

Indian sacred Scriptures classify among the orthodox sciences, the art of sensual love. Bharati put certain questions on that peculiar subject to Sankara which confounded the ascetic.

He excused himself for his ignorance by saying that he had been absorbed since his youth in philosophic meditations, and, as *sannyāsin*, being a strict celibate, women and all things connected with them were utterly unknown to him. However, he deemed himself quite capable of acquiring the knowledge which he lacked. Would not his charming adversary grant him about a month's leave to seek enlightenment ? He was willing to resume the controversy at the end of the fixed time.

[1] An ascetic who has entirely renounced the world.

Here Bharati must have imprudently undervalued the capacity of her opponent, or thought that such a short time would not be enough for him to master the required science. She acquiesced and Sankara started in quest of teachers.

Now it happened that, at about that time, a rajah named Amaruka died. Sankara, who could not have undertaken his study in the person of an already famous ascetic, here saw a convenient opportunity. He ordered his disciples to guard his body in a remote spot while he transmitted his " subtle self " into the body of the prince which was being carried to the funeral pyre. The resuscitated Amaruka was taken back to his palace to the great joy of his several Ranees, legitimate wives and a good number of pretty concubines.

Sankara showed himself a zealous scholar, pleasantly astonishing his spouses who had been somewhat neglected by the late elderly rajah. The ministers and councillors noticed, also, that since his resurrection their lord's intelligence had astonishingly increased. This clever ruler appeared altogether most unlike the dull rajah whom they had known for years.

And so the women of the palace and members of the State council began to suspect that the spirit of some powerful *siddha* [1] was using the body of the late Amaruka. Fearing that he might leave it and return to his own proper abode, they ordered a search to be made for an abandoned body in some remote spot and decreed that if any were found, it should be burnt immediately.

As for Sankara, he had become so wholly engrossed in his study, that he had entirely forgotten his personality and had no desire to reintegrate the ascetic philosopher's body that he had left in charge of a few disciples.

When their *guru* did not return at the appointed

[1] A man who possesses supernormal powers.

time, the disciples felt rather uneasy, and on hearing of the search they were thoroughly terrified. They ran quickly to the rajah's residency, gained admittance before him and sang a philosophic song which Sankara had composed. This aroused the *guru's* memory. His spirit sprang out of the rajah's body and swiftly entered his own, which had just been discovered and was already placed on a pyre to be burned.

Having thus completely mastered his subject, he confronted Bharati once more and astonished her by his superior knowledge. The lady had to admit she was defeated.

This tale could easily take its place among those of Boccacio. Yet, for hundreds of years, it has been popular amongst Sankara's followers without their seeing anything silly or shocking in it. However, they are apparently beginning to realize that the story is not very creditable to the memory of their teacher, and some of them have declared that it was invented by certain simple-minded zealots.

For us the story is valuable as a piece of information. It shows that the belief in the passing of some subtle *self* from one body to another, and even in its roaming about disembodied, was current in India. Such belief was not infrequent in Tibet, where the " translation " of the *self* from one body to another one is called *trong jug*.[1] Possibly the theories regarding *trong jug* have been imported from India. Milarespa, in his autobiography, relates that his *guru* Marpa was not taught the secret of *trong jug* by his own teacher Narota, but when already old, made a journey to India to learn it.

It is to be noted that believers in the " translation " of an ethereal *self* or " double," generally depict the body from which it withdraws, as remaining inanimate. Here lies the essential difference between that supposed

[1] Spelt *grong hjug*.

phenomenon and the apparitions, voluntary or unconsciously created, of a *tulpa*,[1] either alike or different
from its creator.

In fact, while the translation, as related in Indian
or Tibetan stories, may well be regarded as a fable,
the creation of *tulpas* seems worthy of investigation.

Phantoms, as Tibetans describe them, and those that
I have myself seen do not resemble the apparitions
which are said to occur during spiritualist seances.

In Tibet, the witnesses of these phenomena have not
been especially invited to endeavour to produce them,
or to meet a *medium* known for producing them.   Consequently, their minds are not prepared and intent on
seeing apparitions.   There is no table upon which the
company lay their hands nor any *medium* in trance,
nor a dark closet in which the latter is shut up.   Darkness is not required, sun and open air do not keep away
the phantoms.

As I have said, some apparitions are created on
purpose either by a lengthy process resembling that
described in the former chapter on the visualization of
Yidam or, in the case of proficient adepts, instantaneously
or almost instantaneously.

In other cases, apparently the author of the phenomenon generates it unconsciously, and is not even in
the least aware of the apparition being seen by others.

In connection with these kind of visualization or
thought-form creation, I may relate a few phenomena
which I have witnessed myself.

1. A young Tibetan who was in my service went to
see his family.   I had granted him three weeks' leave,
after which he was to purchase a food supply, engage
porters to carry the loads across the hills, and come
back with the caravan.

Most likely the fellow had a good time with his

[1] *Tulpa*, spelt *sprulpa*, " magic, illusory creations."

people. Two months elapsed and still he did not return I thought he had definitely left me.

Then I saw him one night in a dream. He arrived at my place clad in a somewhat unusual fashion, wearing a sun hat of foreign shape. He had never worn such a hat.

The next morning, one of my servants came to me in haste. " Wangdu has come back," he told me. " I have just seen him down the hill."

The coincidence was strange. I went out of my room to look at the traveller.

The place where I stood dominated a valley. I distinctly saw Wangdu. He was dressed exactly as I had seen him in my dream. He was alone and walking slowly up the path that wound up the hill slope.

I remarked that he had no luggage with him and the servant who was next me answered : " Wangdu has walked ahead, the load-carriers must be following."

We both continued to observe the man. He reached a small *chörten*, walked behind it and did not reappear.

The base of this *chörten* was a cube built in stone, less than three feet high, and from its needle-shaped top to the ground, the small monument was no more than seven feet high. There was no cavity in it. Moreover, the *chörten* was completely isolated : there were neither houses, nor trees, nor undulations, nor anything that could provide a hiding in the vicinity.

My servant and I believed that Wangdu was resting for a while under the shade of the *chörten*. But as time went by without his reappearing, I inspected the ground round the monument with my field-glasses, but discovered nobody.

Very much puzzled I sent two of my servants to search for the boy. I followed their movements with the glasses but no trace was to be found of Wangdu nor of anybody else.

That same day a little before dusk the young man

appeared in the valley with his caravan. He wore
the very same dress and the foreign sun hat which I
had seen in my dream, and in the morning vision.

Without giving him or the load-carriers, time to
speak with my servants and hear about the phenomenon,
I immediately questioned them. From their answers
I learned that all of them had spent the previous night
in a place too far distant from my dwelling for anyone
to reach the latter in the morning. It was also clearly
stated that Wangdu had continually walked with the
party.

During the following weeks I was able to verify
the accuracy of the men's declarations by inquiring
about the time of the caravan's departure, at the
few last stages where the porters were changed. It
was proved that they had all spoken the truth and
had left the last stage together with Wangdu, as they
said.

2. A Tibetan painter, a fervent worshipper of the
wrathful deities, who took a peculiar delight in drawing
their terrible forms, came one afternoon to pay me a
visit.

I noticed behind him the somewhat nebulous shape
of one of the fantastic beings which often appeared in
his paintings.

I made a startled gesture and the astonished artist
took a few steps towards me, asking what was the
matter.

I noticed that the phantom did not follow him, and
quickly thrusting my visitor aside, I walked to the
apparition with one arm stretched in front of me. My
hand reached the foggy form. I felt as if touching a
soft object whose substance gave way under the slight
push, and the vision vanished.

The painter confessed in answer to my questions
that he had been performing a *dubthab* rite during the
last few weeks, calling on the deity whose form I had

dimly perceived, and that very day he had worked the whole morning on a painting of the same deity.

In fact, the Tibetan's thoughts were entirely concentrated on the deity whose help he wished to secure for a rather mischievous undertaking.

He himself had not seen the phantom.

In these two cases, the phenomenon was produced without the conscious's co-operation of its author. Or, as a mystic lama remarked, Wangdu and the painter could hardly be termed the *authors* of the phenomena. They were but one cause—may be the principal one—amongst the various causes which had brought them about.

3. The third strange occurrence I have to relate belongs to the category of phenomena which are voluntarily produced. The fact that the apparition appeared in the likeness of the lama who caused it, must not lead us to think that he projected a subtle *double* of himself. This is not the opinion of advanced adepts in Tibetan secret lore.

According to them such phantoms are *tulpas*, magic formations generated by a powerful concentration of thought. As it had been repeatedly stated in the preceding chapters *any* forms may be vizualized through that process.

At that time I was camping near Punag ritöd in Kham. One afternoon, I was with my cook in a hut which we used as a kitchen. The boy asked me for some provisions. I answered, " Come with me to my tent, you can take what you need out of the boxes."

We walked out and when nearing my tent, we *both* saw the hermit lama seated on a folding chair next my camp table. This did not surprise us because the lama often came to talk with me. The cook only said " Rimpoche is there, I must go and make tea for him at once, I will take the provisions later on."

I replied : " All right. Make tea and bring it to us."

The man turned back and I continued to walk straight toward the lama, looking at him all the time while he remained seated motionless.

When I was only a few steps from the tent, a flimsy veil of mist seemed to open before it, like a curtain that is slowly pulled aside. And suddenly I did not see the lama any more. He had vanished.

A little later, the cook came, bringing tea. He was surprised to see me alone. As I did not like to frighten him I said : " Rimpoche only wanted to give me a message. He had no time to stay to tea."

I related the vision to the lama, but he only laughed at me without answering my questions. Yet, upon another occasion he repeated the phenomenon. He utterly disappeared as I was speaking with him in the middle of a wide bare track of land, without tent or houses or any kind of shelter in the vicinity.

The creation of a phantom *Yidam* as we have seen it described in the previous chapter, has two different objects. The higher one consists in teaching the disciple that there are no gods or demons other than those which his mind creates. The second aim, less enlightened, is to provide oneself with a powerful means of protection.

How does the phantom of the deity protect its creator ? By appearing instead of the latter.

It is the custom in Tibet that the lamas who are initiated to that peculiar practice " put on " each morning the personality of their *Yidam*. This being done, the evil spirits who happen to meet these lamas do not see them as men, but under the frightful shape of the terrible deities ; a sight which of course prevents them from attempting any mischief.

Expert magicians in this art can, it is said, hide their own real appearance under any illusory form they choose.

Among the many who, each morning, gravely take on the shape of their *Yidam*, probably very few are really capable of showing themselves as such. I do not know if they succeed in duping the demons, but they certainly do not create any illusion to human eyes. Yet I have heard that some lamas have been seen in the appearance of certain deities of the lamaist pantheon.

Incited by many wonderful legends regarding the power of ancient *tubthobs* to create *tulpas*, a small number of *ngagspas* and lamas endeavour, in great secrecy, to succeed in that peculiar branch of esoteric lore.

However, the practice is considered as fraught with danger for every one who has not reached a high mental and spiritual degree of enlightenment and is not fully aware of the nature of the psychic forces at work in the process.

Once the *tulpa* is endowed with enough vitality to be capable of playing the part of a real being, it tends to free itself from its maker's control. This, say Tibetan occultists, happens nearly mechanically, just as the child, when his body is completed and able to live apart, leaves its mother's womb. Sometimes the phantom becomes a rebellious son and one hears of uncanny struggles that have taken place between magicians and their creatures, the former being severely hurt or even killed by the latter.

Tibetan magicians also relate cases in which the *tulpa* is sent to fulfil a mission, but does not come back and pursues its peregrinations as a half-conscious, dangerously mischievous puppet. The same thing, it is said, may happen when the maker of the *tulpa* dies before having dissolved it. Yet, as a rule, the phantom either disappears suddenly at the death of the magician or gradually vanishes like a body that perishes for want of food. On the other hand, some *tulpas* are expressly intended to survive their creator and are specially formed for that purpose. These may be considered as veritable *tulkus* [1] and, in fact, the demarcation between *tulpas* and *tulkus* is far from being clearly drawn. The existence of both is grounded on the same theories.

Must we credit these strange accounts of rebellious " materializations," phantoms which have become real beings, or must we reject them all as mere fantastic tales and wild products of imagination ?—Perhaps the latter course is the wisest. I affirm nothing. I only relate what I have heard from people whom, in other circumstances, I had found trustworthy, but they may have deluded themselves in all sincerity.

Nevertheless, allowing for a great deal of exaggeration and sensational addition, I could hardly deny the possibility of vizualizing and animating a *tulpa*. Besides having had few opportunities of seeing thought-forms, my habitual incredulity led me to make experiments for myself, and my efforts were attended with some success. In order to avoid being influenced by the forms of the lamaist deities, which I saw daily around me in paintings and images, I chose for my experiment a most insignificant character : a monk, short and fat, of an innocent and jolly type.

I shut myself in *tsams* and proceeded to perform the prescribed concentration of thought and other rites. After a few months the phantom monk was formed. His form grew gradually *fixed* and life-like looking. He became a kind of guest, living in my apartment. I then broke my seclusion and started for a tour, with my servants and tents.

The monk included himself in the party. Though I lived in the open, riding on horseback for miles each day, the illusion persisted. I saw the fat *trapa*, now and then it was not necessary for me to think of him to make him appear. The phantom performed various actions of the kind that are natural to travellers and that I had not commanded. For instance, he walked,

[1] See Chapter III.

stopped, looked around him. The illusion was mostly visual, but sometimes I felt as if a robe was lightly rubbing against me and once a hand seemed to touch my shoulder.

The features which I had imagined, when building my phantom, gradually underwent a change. The fat, chubby-cheeked fellow grew leaner, his face assumed a vaguely mocking, sly, malignant look. He became more troublesome and bold. In brief, he escaped my control.

Once, a herdsman who brought me a present of butter saw the *tulpa* in my tent and took it for a live lama.

I ought to have let the phenomenon follow its course, but the presence of that unwanted companion began to prove trying to my nerves ; it turned into a " day-nightmare." Moreover, I was beginning to plan my journey to Lhasa and needed a quiet brain devoid of other preoccupations, so I decided to dissolve the phantom. I succeeded, but only after six months of hard struggle. My mind-creature was tenacious of life.

There is nothing strange in the fact that I may have created my own hallucination. The interesting point is that in these cases of materialization, others see the thought-forms that have been created.

Tibetans disagree in their explanations of such phenomena ; some think a material form is really brought into being, others consider the apparition as a mere case of suggestion, the creator's thought impressing others and causing them to see what he himself sees.

In spite of the clever efforts made by the Tibetans to find rational explanations for all prodigies, a number remain unexplained, perhaps because they are pure inventions, or perhaps for other reasons.

A Tibetan generally admits that highly advanced

mystics need not die in the usual way, but may dissolve
their bodies when and where they like and leave no
traces.

It is said that Reschungpa disappeared in this way
and that during a special contemplative meditation
Dagmedma the wife of Lama Marpa ended her life by
incorporating herself in her husband.

But these are all personalities of long-past centuries :
it is more interesting to hear about an occurrence of
recent date. And the interest still increases when the
prodigy, instead of taking place in some lonely hermitage, happened before hundreds of witnesses.

I may say at once that I was not amongst the latter
and that my information is derived from the account
of men who affirmed that they saw the wonder. My
only connection with the miraculous event is that I
personally knew the lama who is believed to have
vanished in a mysterious way.

The latter, styled Kyongbu rimpoche, was one of
the spiritual teachers and religious advisers of the
Tashi Lama. When I visited Shigatze in 1916 he was
already an old man and lived as a hermit, some miles
away from that town, near the bank of the Yesru
Tsangpo (Brahmaputra). The mother of the Tashi
Lama held him in high reverence and when I was her
guest I heard several extraordinary stories about that
venerable lama.

It was reported that as years went by, the size of the
learned ascetic gradually decreased. This, according
to Tibetans, is a sign of great spiritual achievement and
legends relate how the bodies of some *dubtobs* who had
been tall men, became reduced to minute proportions
and finally disappeared.

At that time, the new temple sheltering the huge
image of the coming Buddha Maitreya was near completion and a consecration ceremony was being talked
of. The Tashi Lama wished his old spiritual adviser

to perform the consecration rite, but the latter declined, saying that he would have passed away before the temple could be finished.

To this the Tashi Lama replied—it is said—by beseeching the hermit to delay his death till he had blessed the new building.

Though such a request may astonish the reader, it is in accord with Tibetan ideas regarding the power which high mystics possess, of choosing the time of their death.

The hermit promised to perform the consecration.

Then, about one year after my visit to Shigatze, the temple being ready and a day appointed for the *rabnes* [1] solemnity, the Tashi Lama sent a beautiful sedan-chair and an escort to Kyongbu rimpoche to bring him to Tashilumpo's gompa.

The men of the escort saw the lama sitting in the chair. The latter was closed and the porters started.

Now, thousands of people had gathered at Tashilumpo [2] for the religious festival of inauguration. To their utmost astonishment they saw the lama coming alone and on foot. Silently he crossed the temple threshold, walked straight towards the giant image of Maitreya until his body touched it, and then gradually became incorporated with it.

Some time later the sedan-chair with the escort arrived. Attendants opened its door . . . the chair was empty.

Many believe that the lama has never been seen again.

The occurrence was odd enough to hold my attention, but my interest was deepened by the fact that I had been acquainted with its hero and the initial circumstances that led up to the prodigy, that is to say with

[1] Abbreviation of *rabtu nespa,* spelt *rabtu gnaspa.* To consecrate new buildings, images, etc.
[2] The large monastery next Shigatze.

the request of the Tashi Lama regarding the consecration of the temple ; and further because the place
where the wonder is said to have happened, was
familiar to me.

I burned with the desire of going to Shigatze, to
inquire about the lama's last days, and discover his
tomb, if he was really dead. But when I heard of the
bizarre miracle I was at Lhasa in disguise, and neither
Yongden nor I could have kept up our *incognito* in
Shigatze, where we both had a number of acquaintances. To be unmasked meant to be immediately
escorted over the border and I intended, after my stay
at Lhasa, to visit Samye monastery, and several others,
in Southern Tibet. Also to tour the historical ground
of the Yarlung province. This compelled me to renounce any attempt at investigation.

Yet, before we left Tibet, Yongden managed to put
some discreet questions about the Shigatze wonder to
a few men who seemed capable of holding somewhat
enlightened views on the subject.

Unfortunately, the event was already several years old.
Great changes had taken place in Tsang [1] since that time
and more than one prodigy had been related in connection with the Tashi Lama's flight to China. [2] Moreover,
the political atmosphere was not favourable to Tsang.
Men of rank had become exaggeratedly reserved about
the least thing which could be interpreted as exalting
the exiled Tashi Lama and those who were near to
him. Nor did they dare increase the prestige of the
Maitreya temple whose erection—according to the
public rumour—had aroused unfriendly and jealous
feelings at the Lhasa Court.

We gathered the following opinions :

1. The lama had created a phantom of himself
which appeared to have entered the sedan-chair, and

---

[1] *Tsang*, the vast territory of which Shigatze is the capital.
[2] See *My Journey to Lhasa*.

then acted as has been told in the temple of Maitreya. This phantom had vanished, as its master wished, when touching the image, while the lama may have all the time remained in his hermitage.

2. Or Kyongbu rimpoche had been able to produce, from afar, a collective hallucination.

3. Some suggested that the lama was already dead when the miracle took place, but had left behind him a kind of phantom of his creation, which he sent to Tashilumpo.

4. I also remembered that a disciple of Kyongbu rimpoche had told me that, by the means of certain kinds of concentration of mind, a phenomenon may be prepared in connection with a peculiar event which is to take place in the future. Once success is obtained with the concentration, the process goes on mechanically, without further co-operation of the man who has projected the energy required to bring about the phenomenon. It was even said that this man is, in most cases, completely incapable of preventing the phenomenon which he had planned to take place at the appointed time. The energy generated, which has shaped itself in a certain way, is now beyond his control.

Much more could be said regarding psychic phenomena in Tibet, but the account of a single inquirer cannot be very complete, especially under the difficult conditions in which researches must be pursued in that country.

I earnestly wish that my account may awaken in some scientists, more qualified than myself for such work, the desire to undertake serious investigations of the phenomena which I have briefly mentioned in the present book.

Psychic research may be guided by the same spirit as any scientific study. The discoveries which can be made in that field have nothing of supernatural, nothing which may justify the superstitious beliefs and ramblings in which some have indulged regarding the matter. On the contrary, such research may help to elucidate the mechanism of so-called miracles, and once explained, the miracle is no more a miracle.

THE MASKS OF GOD: ORIENTAL MYTHOLOGY

Joseph Campbell

The author explores Eastern mythology as it developed into the distinctive religions of Egypt, India, China, and Japan.

HINDU MYTHS

Translated by Wendy O'Flaherty

Here is a new selection and translation of seventy-five seminal myths of Hindu gods and demons, expressing in vivid symbols the metaphysical insights of ancient Indian priests and poets.

BUDDHISM

Christmas Humphreys

The religion-philosophy known as Buddhism includes a vast range of thought: the most exalted philosophy, a psychology from which the West is slowly beginning to learn, a religion, a way of self-development to self-enlightenment, spiritual science, mysticism, and religious art. This volume covers not only the history and evolvement of Buddhism and its various schools but also its condition in the world today.

BUDDHIST SCRIPTURES

Translated by Edward Conze

These writings were recorded between A.D. 100 and 400, the Golden Age of Buddhist literature. Edward Conze has concentrated on texts intended for the layman and on texts exhibiting more of the humanity than the profundity of the scriptures.

RELIGIONS, VALUES, AND PEAK EXPERIENCES
Abraham H. Maslow

Abraham H. Maslow here articulates one of his prominent theses: The "religious" experience is a rightful subject for scientific exploration and speculation, and, conversely, the "scientific community" will see its work enhanced by acknowledging and studying the species-wide need for spiritual expression.

ON THE PSYCHOLOGY OF MEDITATION
Claudio Naranjo and Robert E. Ornstein

Two innovative psychologists here unite their work in an examination of both the spiritual ground of all forms of meditation and the implications for modern psychology of the manifold approaches to meditation.

MYSTICISM: A STUDY AND AN ANTHOLOGY
F. C. Happold

Mysticism is concerned with spiritual knowledge—knowledge of truths we cannot understand with our minds. In this book the author combines both a study of mysticism and an anthology of mystical writings.

DEPRESSION AND THE BODY
Alexander Lowen, M.D.

Here is an eminent psychiatrist's revolutionary plan for conquering depression, involving a return to the body—a reestablishment with our one instrument of self-expression—through a series of simple but remarkably effective exercises that can reawaken the depressed person to his own inherent energies.